North Korea
On the Inside, Looking In

by Dualta Roughneen

BENNION
KEARNY

Published in 2014 by Bennion Kearny Limited.

Copyright © Bennion Kearny Ltd 2014

Dualta Roughneen has asserted his right under the Copyright, Designs and Patents Act, 1988 to be identified as the author of this book.

ISBN: 978-1-909125-61-2

All Rights Reserved. No part of this publication may be reproduced, stored in a retrieval system, or transmitted in any form or by any means, electronic, mechanical, photocopying, recording or otherwise, without the prior permission of the publisher.

This book is sold subject to the condition that it shall not, by way of trade or otherwise, be lent, re-sold, hired out or otherwise circulated without the publisher's prior consent in any form of binding or cover other than that it which it is published and without a similar condition including this condition being imposed on the subsequent purchaser.

Bennion Kearny has endeavoured to provide trademark information about all the companies and products mentioned in this book by the appropriate use of capitals. However, Bennion Kearny cannot guarantee the accuracy of this information.

Published by Bennion Kearny Limited
6 Woodside, Churnet View Road, Oakamoor, ST10 3AE

www.BennionKearny.com

Acknowledgements

Credit is due to Kongdan Oh and Ralph C Hassig, authors of *North Korea Through the Looking Glass*, and Marcus Noland, author of *Avoiding the Apocalypse: The Future of the Two Koreas*. The insights in those two books form the basis of background information to a number of these chapters. Also, Robert Willoughby deserves credit for his research into the *North Korea Bradt Travel Guide*, which helped me find my way around.

About the Author

Dualta Roughneen is a Chartered Civil Engineer who has spent 10 years working in humanitarian contexts across the globe. He has worked in Ethiopia, Afghanistan, North Korea, Sudan, Liberia, Cameroon, Niger, and most recently in the Philippines, in conflict, post-conflict, and man-made or natural disasters. With a MSc in Human Rights from University College Dublin, Dualta has been published previously by CSP (2010) 'The Right to Roam: Travellers and Human Rights in the Modern Nation State'.

Table of Contents

Introduction		1
Chapter 1	The First Few Days	7
Chapter 2	It's Not Like Afghanistan	19
Chapter 3	Getting Acquainted With The Countryside	31
Chapter 4	Getting To Know The Place	45
Chapter 5	Yes, This Is Christmas	59
Chapter 6	The Big Freeze: 2005	73
Chapter 7	Day After Day – Getting Into A Routine	85
Chapter 8	The Man Behind The Stories	97
Chapter 9	Inspiration For The Masses	113
Chapter 10	The North, The South And The Economy	125
Chapter 11	The Nuclear Issue, Kidnappings And The Pyongyang Times	137
Chapter 12	The Pen Is Mightier Than The Sword	149
Chapter 13	Building Toilets And Diplomacy	155
Chapter 14	Prayers, Rugby And The Cold	165
Chapter 15	The Demilitarized Zone And A Particular State Of Mind	175
Chapter 16	A Dagger Aimed At The Heart Of Japan	183
Chapter 17	To China By Roads And Bridges	189
Chapter 18	Springtime, Bird 'Flu And Defeat	201
Chapter 19	Mass Games Training, Surveying And One Lost Puppy	209

Chapter 20	The Manifesto And The Invisible Hand	221
Chapter 21	The Rattlin' Bog	231
Chapter 22	The Looking Glass	241
Chapter 23	Summertime And The Living Is Not Easy	251
Chapter 24	A Bit More Of The Countryside	263
Chapter 25	At Breaking Point	275
Chapter 26	Six-Party Talking Shops	283
Chapter 27	Group Think. Tank	293
Chapter 28	Last Orders?	301
Epilogue		307
Postscript		311

Introduction

*The proletarians have nothing to lose but their chains.
They have a world to win.*

The Manifesto of the Communist Party

It was the era of the Celtic Tiger in Ireland and Irish people were no longer travelling only to the United Kingdom and the United States to emigrate. Tiger travel was very much a rite of passage. Students were getting J-1 visas to the US to party for the three months of their first university summer; others were taking a year out and heading to Australia to do fruit picking and bar work, and go surfing; holidays in Asia were increasingly popular, with the beaches of Thailand the main attraction. North Korea, however, was not a place that ever featured in anyone's travel plans. The Far East was never really on my radar either, until one summer, just after I had returned to Ireland from a tough but very exciting year in Afghanistan. It was 2004. I was at a loose end, and keen to spread my wings in another direction. Sierra

Introduction

Leone and the Democratic Republic of the Congo were possibilities, until the offer of a job in North Korea came along.

To start off, you should be aware of my circumstances. I am a civil engineer by trade – unfortunate in certain respects, I used to think. However, this short career, with the limited technical expertise gained working as an engineer on roads and landfills in Ireland, with a construction company for nine months, and for local government on a landfill for a similar length of time, has afforded me opportunities to travel to some odd little corners of the world. Both jobs ended to enable me to go travelling. Whether the travelling is a product of my desire to be an aid worker, or my job as an aid worker is a front to my desire to travel, I am not sure. I would like to think that the good in me is driving the selfish, but who can tell? Either way, I get to see some weird and wonderful places for nice lengths of time, and get paid for it.

This isn't the heart-rending tale that you might expect from an aid worker's diary. It isn't a story about hungry children in dustbowl Darfur, or tears and suffering in Tibet, or one of putting smiles on hungry faces. This is much less than that, much more mundane. But once in a while, I am in the privileged position of being able to peer into the home of a North Korean rural dweller. I get to see the simple delight one little tap and one metre of galvanised-iron pipe can make to the life of a little old woman who has been getting water from the river for the last twenty years since the big pump-house down the river breathed its last breath. No life saved, but a very simple, yet important, difference in the woman's life. No more washing clothes in the ice-cold river in winter, no more carrying buckets from the stream for drinking and for cooking. Hopefully no more sick children; a clean, warm house and a back that doesn't ache as much when the cock crows. That's the theory. The limited access we have as foreigners to follow up and monitor projects means that we can't be sure.

Introduction

Like most people, I knew very little about North Korea before I went, except the few excerpts and snippets that made it into the Irish news. I knew it was somewhere very different, a reclusive state with some variant of communism. I began to read a bit more, and then there was no option but to grab my golden ticket and board the plane. There were personal considerations – committing to a year alone in a strange new world wasn't easy but the DPRK had grabbed my attention. The last bastion of Communism in the Stalinist–Leninist mould, it may not be around much longer. I knew that it was a strange sort of privilege to get paid to visit the place. Few ever get to go there.

I managed to squeeze more than the year out of my contract, and ended up in the place for more than two. There was something addictive about the country, about the people and about the way of life. It is a strange bubble for expatriates to live in. I met people who had been there much longer than I had been and a few acquaintances remain.

What is strange and exotic about the country gradually becomes ultra-routine. The country is oddly banal; the circle of people an expat can mix with socially is incredibly small, and over time the lifestyle kills softly. Living in a closed community, with limited travel, the feeling of not being sure if you are being watched and monitored, doing pretty much the same things day in, day out, creates a bubble that shields you from the harsh realities of life in the country. You never get to really know an average Korean, or really understand their life, however long you stay. You never get to see the worst aspects of life there. Expatriate life in developing countries, in particular working with the UN and NGOs, tends to be a life bubble-wrapped. In North Korea, however, it is not the NGOs that provide the wrapping, but the Korean government.

When I knew I was going to Korea, and had learned that Internet and email were almost impossible at the time, telephone calls ridiculously expensive, and international post extremely

Introduction

slow, I decided to keep an electronic diary of my time there, in an effort to stay in touch with people. I had never even heard of a blog, though the authorities would not have welcomed such a thing if I had attempted it. In the end, the e-diary lasted only a few emails, as I realised that people were not going to keep reading it. However, maintaining a record of my time became a bit of a mania with me. For about the first six months, I kept an intense record of my stay before gradually weaning myself off long before I left the country.

What follows is a record of my thoughts from my time there, as they happened. I have avoided going back to correct any of my thoughts that may have evolved or been proven wrong over the duration, in order to maintain a fair representation of my state of mind while I was there. I never expected to be in the country as long as I was – upon my arrival I was already planning my departure. Gradually, though, I forgot to get around to leaving, until I was almost forced out by the Government. It was a good job that they did push me. Though I would never be an apologist for the State, I was gradually becoming ambivalent to the regime there; I was not really seeing things for what they actually were, and I was getting my feet under the table. My affections for individuals, and for Korean people in general, were becoming a sedative, and getting mixed up with my views toward the regime. Much reporting in the media assumes, because the system is grey and stifling, that the people are somehow the same. This is not the case at all, and I hope my scribbles manage to convey some of the colour I saw.

Since my first exodus from the country, I have been back there to work for a few more months, helping to re-establish some water programmes that I had designed, and then for one more week, a year later, made possible thanks to some friends. A few people who I consider friends I was not able to meet again. They had moved on in life; it is almost impossible for an outsider to penetrate the boundaries of Korean society. I hope that someday I will get to travel back to say hello and find out how the people

Introduction

I cannot contact at the moment are doing. I hope that this will be under the shadow of the invisible hand rather than the iron fist.

1

The First Few Days

Communism doesn't work because people like to own stuff.
Frank Zappa

Where does anyone start when talking about this place? I am barely in the country, so I should probably hold off on making any sweeping statements. My first few days here were taken up with simply getting oriented between my new office and my new apartment. In between getting lost on a fairly straightforward fifteen-minute walk on each of my first two mornings, my days have been spent wondering to myself at various idiosyncrasies of the Democratic People's Republic of Korea, the DPRK – North Korea to most people.

I don't know if anyone will ever read my thoughts on North Korea, but I have a feeling I should write them down anyway. As I don't have any real access to email, these scribblings will probably form a large part of my correspondence with the outside world – the real world, outside of the bubble that is the

Chapter 1

DPRK. I expect that most of my observations will be wrong, or will change and adapt over time, but I intend to write down what I see as I see it, and any errors will have to be forgiven as the product of a newcomer's naivety and wide-eyed wonder. Perhaps I will give up after a few days, when my back gets sore from typing, and the arthritis in the knuckles starts to kick in, but in the meantime I will continue typing.

I don't think this diary will be a political profile of the country. Neither will it be a profile based on in-depth conversations with Korean people, because I am simply not allowed to talk to them. The select few who can talk to me know not to say much anyhow. Nor can I talk to the beneficiaries of any of the projects I take part in. This will be very much an outsider's view – something like watching television with the sound off, where you have to make your own interpretation of the storyline.

I am an engineering project officer in Pyongyang, the capital of North Korea, working with an international non-governmental organisation (NGO). It is 2004. I am twenty-six years old. When I interviewed for the job, they were quick to figure out that I am technically inept engineering-wise. I didn't get the post I originally applied for, slightly more senior than this, in Sierra Leone. I held my hands up to admit that I know very little about water and sanitation. So, knowing I was a bit of a bluffer but hopefully seeing potential in me, I was offered this job in Korea. Could I really say no? It's one of the last communist strongholds in the world, and is increasingly isolated by its own policies, since various other communist bastions have begun to open up. The economic situation here, without the support of former allies such as Russia and China who have liberalised economically, has deteriorated drastically. The country is in serious decline, without money, without energy and without resources. It has dropped from being one of the most developed countries in the region, admittedly aided by generous Russian support, to being one of the poorest, stymied by the stubbornness of Kim Il Sung and Kim Jong Il *[and, as of 2011, Kim Jong Un]*.

The First Few Days

The high levels of paranoia here, I think, stem from the desire of those in power to keep regular people in the country ignorant of the outside world. They are afraid to let foreigners in, or give them any access to the people, so the general populace has no idea about any alternate life outside of North Korea. Thanks to incessant propaganda and information control, the people are in a constant state of readiness to fight their capitalist enemy, who they believe they gloriously defeated back in the 1950s.

Neither North nor South Korea recognises the Korean peninsula as being two countries. They are both technically still at war. There has been a lot of concern recently (and rightly so) about the DPRK developing nuclear armaments, but it turns out that the South has been busily doing the same thing. The difference is, the South is cooperating with independent inspectors.

However, it's a little early for me to be formulating theories or trying to sort this place out. I have only been here a few days. All of this information is coming from listening to other people, particularly my slightly eccentric and much travelled flatmate. He talks a lot, and has been around the world and back. Afghanistan, Tajikistan, forty-eight of the fifty US states ... Born in South Africa, he worked on a coffee farm in Zimbabwe, in a time when it was safe to be a white man running a big farm in Zimbabwe. He has seen and done a lot.

I've been to some interesting places too, albeit under the protective umbrella of the NGO world, where everything is well organised and generally secure and comfortable – except when you break security protocol and carry $20,000 in Afghan money in a rucksack and sleep in villages four hours' walk from anywhere with your arms hugging the bag of cash for dear life ... But that's another story.

When I got home from Afghanistan, I took a while to decide what to do next. If someone asked what I was doing, I would merely say I was between jobs. People would think I was unemployed, get embarrassed and quickly slink off, feeling really

Chapter 1

bad about asking such an innocent question. I never much wanted to talk about my time there, though I am not sure why.

*　*　*

I went to play football today with a few lads I don't know. Some of them work for other NGOs in the area, some of them are from the UN or various embassies, and there were a few Vietnamese playing too – I initially assumed they were Korean. One of the Vietnamese stood on my toe in his football boots and it hurts. There were a few good players, a few bad ones and a few in between. One of the good ones is a young Libyan, the son of the ambassador here. Then there is a guy from an Italian NGO who is fairly handy, and an old man called Mullah who, if he was a lot younger, would be pretty good. It turns out that there are games organised, when we get permission from the Government, in some of the other counties, against county teams. This bunch play regularly, in the shadow of the great big stadium, which, with a capacity of 140,000, is purportedly the second biggest in the world – second only to the Maracana in Brazil I believe. It's called the MayDay Stadium. May Day, Labour Day, is a holiday celebrated here with picnics and partying by the river. We are called the Pyongyang International Soccer Selection. It's always nice to find a regular game of 'ball.

*　*　*

The place I am staying is at the top of a six-storey apartment block made out of concrete. It looks dull and it is dull, though practical. The apartment is in a small area of Pyongyang called the Diplomatic Compound, where most of the NGO/UN workers, and a lot of the foreign diplomatic representatives, live and work. The Diplomatic Compound. It really tells the story of what it is not. Our local bar in the Compound is called the *Pyongyang Friendship Health Service Centre*. There are lots of 'Pyongyang Friendship ...' places in the Diplomatic Compound. All of the guards, at the various embassies, wave and say hello as you walk along, while in the rest of the city the people move

The First Few Days

around like ants – very grey, depressed ants, in their dull clothes and old-style haircuts. These are my first impressions anyhow.

Let me tell you about my flatmates and co-workers, and some of the people around the place.

I live with two people at the moment, both of whom will soon be leaving to pursue different ventures. Actually, I don't think either of them is too sure where exactly they are going to end up, or how they will get there. One, who I have mentioned previously, is a bit of an eccentric agronomist. Aged thirty-four, he has been around the world and back, undertaking all sorts of daring deeds. He has sort of taken me under his wing, as you should, showing me the ropes while I am living with him. He brings me to play golf, to football and to the shops. He is married, with a baby boy of sixteen months. He has lived in South Africa as a child and in England as a teenager. Then Zimbabwe, Tajikistan, Burundi and Afghanistan, and now the DPRK. He is off to Khartoum shortly.

The second is a Water and Sanitation engineer, whose boots I will be filling. I have just spent the last hour washing up after her as she prepares food for her going-away brunch in the apartment. Every utensil I washed she would gleefully pick up again, and use for some other oil-based foodstuff. Water and Sanitation will be referred to throughout the rest of this as *WatSan*, and WatSan is one of those little popular expressions that are particular to the aid world. Everyone, especially in this place, seems to use it as a means of identifying a person. You are either WatSan or not. I find it a bit strange. I am a civil engineer, I suppose, by trade. I don't know a whole lot about WatSan, but am getting to grips with it. She has been here for just over a year, after spending a few months in Darfur. I didn't take to her too quickly, but over the course of a few drinks and chatting to her, she has grown on me. She is going home to take a few months' break.

Chapter 1

The other important people in the picture are my co-workers. There is the Country Director, who seems like a really nice woman, though I don't mix with her too much at work as she is in the upstairs office. A Kiwi I believe, she seems really easy going, and there are no problems talking to her. She seems to like to party a lot, and everyone in the place seems have a good word for her. She has crazy, curly red hair, and stands out a mile from the crowd.

Then there is an administrator from South East Asia somewhere (I have been told, but can't remember), and a forestry person from somewhere in the Balkans. I have yet to meet the administrator and the forestry person. He is huge and she is tiny, apparently. They are just back from R&R somewhere. R&R – Rest and Relaxation, not Recuperation – is another aid-work term. It means extra time aid workers in difficult countries take off, on top of holidays, to recharge batteries or simply get back in touch with reality. Here I have five weeks' holidays in the year, similar to any job, but I also get an extra week after three months and another after nine months, which is the R&R. There is debate over whether R&R is necessary in the DPRK, as it is not exactly hardship. But the place is not easy to live in, what with all the restrictions, the paranoia, the uncertainty and the lack of contact with the outside world. So the argument goes. I will find out.

Back to my workmates. There are also Koreans that work with us. This bit is complicated, so bear with me. They work for the Korean government, either the Ministry of Foreign Affairs (MFA) or the FDRC (Flood Damage Rehabilitation Committee), a government department set up in 1997 to deal with the damage caused by floods and drought and subsequent famine in the country. These are the people we work through. But our office pays the ones that work in the office, through the FDRC or MFA. There are *Kim*s, *Sin*s, *Ri*s and *Mun*s. A lot of names, and I tend to mix them up.

The First Few Days

We also have what is called a Liaison Officer for our office. He deals with any issues we have that involve us wanting to do anything at all, or get anything, or go anywhere. He gets us clearance through the Government, and everything needs prior planning and permission. The Liaison Officer would be the man to sort out visas and the like. He is our link to the Korean hierarchy.

Then there are the translators. That would be the rest of them. One is bigger than your average Korean woman. She is very chatty, has a good sense of humour and seems to know her job. I have not really dealt with any of the others, though I expect once I start travelling and working in the field outside Pyongyang this will change. 'The field' is an aid-worker term for where we actually do work, as opposed to being stuck in the office. One of the Koreans has just returned from a trip to Cambodia. It was his first time out of the country, seeing anywhere other than the DPRK. I think he was particularly taken by the impromptu nature of life outside the DPRK – being able to take trips down rivers and into the countryside without having to ask permission.

A lot of time in the aid world is spent watching cheap rip-off DVDs bought in China or such places, because often there isn't access to decent television. I was pleasantly surprised to find that we have BBC World and ABC here in the DPRK. I was under the impression before coming here that I would be totally out of the current affairs loop. Last night we watched, for reasons unknown, a film called 'Thirteen Going on Thirty'. It got frisbeed off the balcony as soon as it was over.

I think I have already mentioned paranoia in this text. There is an element of paranoia that runs through the expatriate community here. Maybe it is justified – I am not quite sure yet. The government rules with an iron grip. There is talk of agents keeping detailed files on each expat, monitoring our movements, listening to phone calls, bugging, and discreetly following us around the city. The people saying this could just be having a

Chapter 1

laugh at the expense of a naïve newcomer to the country. I am not sure if I believe it all, but the truth is that nobody really knows. I would like some concrete proof.

I have a really strange feeling of not knowing where I stand in this place. People say it is the safest place in the world to do aid work, because crime is almost nil. Foreigners, especially low-level minions like me, can never really see the internal mechanisms of the country, because we are shielded from so much, and there are so many places we cannot go to, even in Pyongyang. When I go out running, people don't stare at me like they do in Ethiopia or Afghanistan; they make an effort not to look, diverting their eyes. No one except the Diplomatic Compound people makes eye contact with you. It is unnerving. Running past a military group yesterday around the corner from the Diplomatic Compound, the marching soldiers had a good laugh at this strange foreigner lumbering past them. Laughter was duly returned. I don't know why I was laughing, and I suspect neither did they. But I can choose to run. I don't think they have so many options. Mind you, the cyclists here don't extend much courtesy, and are quick to cycle in your way on the footpath. I get the impression that, in Pyongyang especially, foreigners are basically disliked, and only barely tolerated. I am determined to find out for myself.

* * *

One of the first little nuances of the place that made me smile were the traffic ladies. These are not traffic wardens, but full-time traffic-directing girls. Wearing pristine bright-blue military-esque uniforms, they mechanically direct traffic at junctions, spinning first left, then right, up street and down street, sticking out their flashing red batons with rehearsed precision, every movement carefully choreographed. This is not anything like a policeman back in Ireland when traffic lights break down. To be uncharitable, I would say that they remind me a little of Data from 'Star Trek: The Next Generation'. I entertain myself by

The First Few Days

extending them a big wave and smile, watching as they try not to grin back. I imagine every wave will go into my file.

Apparently, the traffic ladies are all hand-picked by the Dear Leader, Kim Jong Il. There is one junction where a roundabout has been constructed, unfortunately rendering the traffic lady redundant, and now she stands at the side of the roundabout looking a little lost. Poor girl. The traffic ladies also whistle at anyone who crosses the road at the wrong place, and apparently give warnings and tickets to people. It seems that expatriates take a little pleasure in getting across the road just in time to be seen by the lady, but too late for her to do anything but blow her whistle. The traffic ladies are a constant source of fascination for foreigners, and from what I can gather, desire as well.

* * *

Things are definitely not as I expected here. Looking out the window of the jeep, at arm's length from the people our projects are supposed to benefit (beneficiaries: another aid-worker term), everything just seems different from anywhere else I have been. I know it is the last bastion of communism, and things are going to be odd, but it's hard to pinpoint precisely what some of the differences are. Part of it is that everything seems so regimented, and public displays of emotion are invisible to me so far. When I see groups of people with the ridiculous task of sweeping dust from dirt roads and other group tasks, I seriously wonder what goes through the heads of those in charge.

North Korea is divided up into provinces and then counties. We live in South Pyongan Province, where Pyongyang is, and work in North Pyongan. The provinces are split into counties, and we work in Songchon, Namchong and Rongchon, each of which has a principle large town of the same name. Each county is divided into areas called a 'ri' (or 'li', depending on how you pronounce the interchangeable Rs and Ls). These areas each have a central village and a number of 'work teams'. What a nice term that is: work team. A work team is really a small village that works

Chapter 1

together and has to produce a certain quota of whatever they are growing. A work team is effectively a farm, and each farm has a farm manager.

The outputs of these collective farms are collected and sent to warehouses, and then distributed around the county or region. People in the countryside also have a small area around their basic houses, with which to make their own little bit extra. There are a lot of peppers ripening on the slate roofs of these houses.

The country seems to be administered from a national level down to a farm level. Each central village has a school, clinic, kindergarten and garage that serves the ri. It seems a fairly streamlined and idealised system – if the Government only had the resources to maintain it. Since the collapse of communism throughout Russia and the opening up of China, North Korea is effectively on its own, without any real trading partners or allies. Despite the insistence on continuing with 'socialism in our own style', and the philosophy of *Juche*, which is some sort of self-sustaining numerology developed by the Great Leader [more on this later], the country cannot maintain itself. This has become

The First Few Days

clear in recent years, as floods and drought have led to famine and a reluctant appeal to the outside world for assistance. This is how a number of non-governmental organisations, and people like me, have come to be operating here.

2
It's Not Like Afghanistan

*Communism is the death of the soul. It is the organization
of total conformity – in short, of tyranny – and it
is committed to making tyranny universal.*
Adlai E Stevenson

I am sure I will be commenting very soon on the more serious matters that are supposed to occupy the minds of self-styled do-good aid workers like myself. But I can't at the moment, because I have just been brushing my teeth in the hotel I am staying in (I am out in the field, monitoring some projects), and after spitting into the sink, I was surprised to find it dripping onto my big toe. No drainpipe. No electricity. Battery power that is rapidly dying.

* * *

One of my new colleagues was telling me that there are three types of people you will meet in places like this. The first is the type based on the missionary – the good person that feels it is a calling to be in a place like this, doing the ground work, putting

Chapter 2

in the hard yards, sacrificing time to make a difference to the underprivileged and oppressed. Then there is the other extreme – the mercenary, the person here on business, trying to take advantage of situations or living off the regime and the system. Equally mercenary are those just coasting in middle-management, well paid, with hardship and travel allowances, going through the motions. In between, there are people who are trying to find their place in society, not necessarily sure where they belong and sometimes unable to settle in their own surroundings. He reckons that most of us, at different times, drift between the three personas, and at some stages in our lives settle temporarily at different corners of the triangle. You might start off looking to save the world, then get disillusioned, drift by, meet a girl, have children. Then you are looking at aid work as a means to get by and support your family. Soon you see a business opportunity when the aid work dries up, and this then becomes profitable. Or you might stay doing aid work, though the drive is gone, enjoying the salary and the low costs of living. Maybe later in life, when the kids are gone, the missionary drive returns.

I must say that life as an aid worker – roughing it in Ethiopia and Afghanistan – has not been that tough so far. Sure, it has moments of difficulty, days of relative hardship, sleeping rough, lack of remuneration and all that, but even in the toughest places, it is all right. So far, it has been an adventure. North Korea, with all its peculiarities, is not the end of the world, or the last outpost of hardship. I have been told it does get to you psychologically after a while and you need your R&R. That could be true. I will find out later.

*　*　*

On Saturday I woke up very early, after drinking beers in the Random Access Club (RAC), the bar in the Diplomatic Compound, until the early morning. I went out for a quick run around the block, as much to kill off the latent energy and sweat out the beer as to see the town a bit closer. When I got back, I cooked a fry and then went to the fifty-metre swimming pool in the centre of Pyongyang, which is only open on Saturdays for foreigners, and swam a few lengths with the seven other people in the pool. I climbed the ten-metre diving board, looked down, and climbed back down again. I climbed the five-metre board with the same result, cursing my cowardice. Next I went for my first ever sauna, and was amazed by how much I sweated. I shouldn't have been too surprised – I tend to break into a sweat in an Afghan winter walking up ten steps. The sauna was followed by a trip to the driving range, one of three in Pyongyang. Here, alongside one other, I attempted to smack balls at our leisure as far as we could. I could not manage to make a decent connection, despite the best efforts of a female Korean coach to perfect my grip, my stance and my swing. I just didn't feel comfortable with my head down and my backside out. It wasn't quite as therapeutic as I had imagined. Following that was a tough game of three-a-side volleyball at the World Food Program office. The day was rounded off with a few cheap beers in the Friendship Health Service Centre until about one in the morning. It's a hard life.

* * *

… the power keeps going off. I am typing in the dark with a dwindling battery …

* * *

Afghanistan was much more basic. The highlight was a substandard game of volleyball at the UN compound or five-a-side at the Turkish embassy if I managed to make it to Mazar-I-Sharif once a week. Football at the embassy sounds quite glamorous, but if you saw the place, you'd quickly see that it was the opposite. There are a lot of similarities between here and Afghanistan, such as the climate and the terrain. North Korea, though far wetter, also suffers from freezing winters and very hot summers, and like Afghanistan, has an unfortunate number of

Chapter 2

mountains and very little arable land. I wonder would things be better here had the DPRK been in the flatter, more opulent South, and would the South be faring as well if it occupied the less fertile, mountainous North?

The first difference for me between here and Afghanistan is the level of hardship. I am referring to hardship for the aid worker, not for the people, because I think well-being is a very personal thing, and I couldn't make a judgment on the levels of hardship people who live all their lives in these places really suffer. A lot of it is relative. If you opened the eyes of the average Korean to life outside the DPRK, to the affluence and comfort of some other places, would it really help them? Or would they then be worse off, knowing there was so much they could never attain? In Afghanistan, people in the countryside noticeably lack a lot more than their DPRK counterparts. The standard of housing, the clothing, the variety of crops, and the infrastructure, are far worse than in the DPRK. You could also add that the women in Afghanistan have it far worse than the men, by virtue of the religious restrictions imposed on them. A woman is subservient to her husband there, to the extent that women's lives are totally dictated by men, whether fathers, brothers or husbands. In the DPRK, people have better access to education – literacy is at almost 100% – and the infrastructure is better. State-sanctioned restrictions on personal freedoms in the DPRK makes life harder than it should be, though, not to mention shortages that are exacerbated by a moribund State system.

The nature of this system could be illustrated slightly with an extract or two from the Pyongyang Times, the DPRK English-language newspaper. The front-page headline is, 'Kim Jong Il Inspects Army Units'. The text beneath the photo reads, 'He gave them a pair of binoculars, a machine gun and an automatic rifle as gifts before having a photo session.' Below that is, 'Greetings to Cambodian King, Tunisian President', congratulating the two of them on their recent appointments; followed by, 'DPRK Leader's Works Published Abroad'. They were published in Venezuela and Haiti. Also in the paper is the sarcastic headline, 'Thanks to Pro-American Stooges'. This refers to the South Korean political leaders, stating '… they argued that South Korea should serve the U.S. as master and maintain the U.S. colonial system'.

For me, the work here will be completely different from what I was doing in Afghanistan. Here I am very much in a technical role, answerable to a more senior engineer. I don't have as much control or autonomy over what I am doing, but that's a good thing, as I have a lot to learn in terms of engineering in a development context. I don't think I will get quite the satisfaction, or the adrenalin rush that went with it, as I got from being in charge of my own projects in Afghanistan – however self-indulgent that might sound. Let me explain.

In Afghanistan, I was on my first 'mission'. I was enthused to the full, working ridiculous hours and spending most of my time at the optimum stress level to get the work done, without actually getting burned out. That's my view anyway – those who had to deal with me might think otherwise. I had a lot of control, from a project-management point of view. In terms of construction projects, and to an extent designing, I was left with the final say, with my boss effectively rubber-stamping my decisions. That is quite a risk for an organisation to take, and a lot of responsibility to lay on someone who is relatively inexperienced.

I was involved, for example, in a bridge project from start to finish, which was ultimately my responsibility. I had not worked on a bridge before, but I had to make sure it was right, both in design and implementation. There was a high safety factor included, just to be sure – which had the knock-on effect of not producing the most efficient or cost-effective design. Money perhaps not so well spent. I have also supervised a few dams, numerous piped-water systems, however basic, and innumerable well-digging projects, without ever really being cognisant, or

Chapter 2

considerate, of the impact on water-table levels, or sustainability issues that I am just starting to understand now.

The work is slightly different here, limited to more technical piped-water systems and latrines. It is less exciting and varied, but it is giving me a chance to develop my skills and get educated in a particular area. I am torn between specialising to an extent, or, like in Afghanistan, working on the management side of projects. I would like to be able to combine both, but realise that I need to be patient. To be honest, I hate detail, and I am not as patient as I should be. It's like when I was standing on the top of the high diving board in the fifty-metre pool. I didn't want to jump, but I wanted to have jumped.

* * *

My beard is growing again. It is too cold to shave my head, and I can't shave my face without shaving my head or I look a bit deranged. Last year in Afghanistan, I was out in a place called Pushti Ban, surveying a potential road to link five villages. I was walking ahead of our Afghan engineer and my translator in an isolated area, pretty far from anywhere. I walked over the brow of a hill, and met an Afghan farmer coming along the track in the opposite direction. I stopped. He stopped. As I had only been in Afghanistan for a few weeks, I couldn't really say much, and we both went our respective ways. When he met the other two about ten minutes later, he was excited to tell them about a westerner who was wandering the hills just ahead of them. My colleagues were amused. A few months later, with the effects of the sun, my sallow skin and a good beard, along the same road, I was mistaken for the translator, and the translator was assumed to be the uppity foreign engineer.

One distinction that North Korea has, among aid-receiving countries, is that of security. It has been said that the DPRK is the safest place for an aid worker to live, and I would be inclined to agree with that. The only worry is the fear of a nuclear disaster, or a rapid deterioration in relations between the North

It's Not Like Afghanistan

and South, or George Bush or someone like him putting his foot in it and saying something stupid about an axis of evil and getting all the various warmongers riled up. Personal safety is not really an issue here. For various reasons, crime in the country is very low.

It is the norm for NGOs in developing countries to take security seriously – or at least to try to create that impression. Obviously NGOs are seen as having money, and in some countries a high percentage of foreign investment is in the form of aid and handled by the United Nations and NGOs. In developing countries, foreign aid workers have much more money than their potential beneficiaries. Local staff are also often much better paid than their contemporaries, and will thus become targets for petty criminals. They can also be targeted by more serious criminals, and kidnapping is always a real threat, as evidenced recently in Iraq and Afghanistan among other places. Aid workers can be seen as political bargaining currency.

There are other threats that have to be taken seriously – for example, mines and other pieces of unexploded ordinance (UXOs), which are manifest in many developing countries, as well as less than stringent controls on firearms. I have gotten very used to seeing guns around the place since I started working outside Ireland. The only previous recollection of a gun I have, before my exotic travels, is my uncle shooting rabbits up the hill behind the house. And I might have imagined that. Guns and bombs and mines are all very real issues in Afghanistan, impacting seriously on how NGOs do their work, not to mention how they affect the lives of the people who eke out a living in their midst. Aid workers are therefore overloaded with communications equipment, and numerous guidelines have to be followed to reduce risk and avoid hazards. Any time I was out in the field in Afghanistan, I carried a VHF (very high frequency) radio everywhere I went, and we had CODAN (I think that's a brand name) UHF (ultra, instead of very) in all the cars.

Chapter 2

In the DPRK, we are not allowed to have any of those things. The state's own security precludes having these usual aid-worker essentials. I found this a little disorienting at first. No bleating out, 'Sierra foxtrot kilo alpha two four, do you read? Roger, out,' anymore. No global positioning system equipment or mobile phones. Forays in the field, visiting projects, involve absolutely no communication with the office. This has its own freedoms, but totally goes against protocol for any other country aid organisations work in.

Similarly, because it is much more difficult to meet and talk with your 'average Joe', it is harder to appreciate what the real issues are for Joe and Jodie, when designing projects or programmes. On top of this, access to the actual places where the money is spent is contingent on approval by central government. This means being accompanied wherever we go by local government officials. Normal ways of working on development or aid programmes go out the window, and all those guidelines on best practice in monitoring and assessment are redundant.

Normally, for any decent NGO, having local partners to implement projects, being able to carry out needs assessments and baseline studies, and monitoring projects as they progress in order to ensure they reach required international emergency standards (see theSPHEREproject.org), or national acceptable construction standards where they exist, are fundamentals. But if you want to work in the DPRK, you have to ditch protocol and do what you are told, while fighting to earn that bit of space (or so I am told – I have not been here long enough to know) to work according to accepted norms for aid work. As mentioned in Chapter 1, our projects are implemented through the FDRC (Flood Development Rehabilitation Committee), who accompany us when we want to monitor project progress. Though the people we work with try to help, they have to put up barriers where we don't want barriers. I would like to be able to talk to the people that need water, to see exactly what they need and what works best for them. I would like to see whether the project actually works effectively in the end, without wondering whether the feedback I get is coerced or managed. I would like to know that the right types of projects are being done, that the needs are being addressed, but it is hard to really know for sure. The first principle of any NGO is supposed to be to do no harm, but with so little access, it is hard to know whether even this minimum is being achieved.

In Aybak in Samangan Province, Northern Afghanistan, where I worked, we had a team of three Afghan engineers, five site supervisors, two translators and myself, all to supervise rehabilitation work in the area. In the DPRK, we have no Korean engineers to work with, which makes it more difficult again to monitor and implement work. It would be very useful to work with a Korean engineer or construction technician of some sort, someone who knows the methods of local construction far better than a twenty-six-year-old Irish engineer, and probably knows far more about engineering in general.

* * *

We were driving into Songchon around lunchtime today, and there was a kid on the street kicking stones in the air, innocently entertaining himself as we drove past. I saw his face pale as he realised one of the stones was about to hit the car, about two seconds before it actually hit, and could see him dreading the inevitable as the stone dropped, almost in slow motion. It reminded me of a time when I was about four years old, and myself and my brothers and sisters were outside on the back lawn with Da. I had a piece of three-quarter-inch copper pipe in my hand, about six inches long. I threw it up into the air and across the lawn, and quickly realised it was heading in the direction of Da's head. It just seemed to hang there, suspended in space, delaying the inevitable. I could do nothing but watch or look away (but you always watch). The stone didn't damage the car, though the kid had gone through hell for a few seconds. The

Chapter 2

pipe did hit Da's head, though, and I spent two hours hiding behind a wall.

* * *

I watched James Bond: Die Another Day last night. It is set partly in DPRK and in the Demilitarised Zone (DMZ) between the North and South. I never checked exactly where it was filmed, but it is interesting to compare what I have seen to what is portrayed in the movie. I really don't think the North Koreans are as advanced or technologically innovative as they are portrayed in that film.

I have noticed, as I am driven around to these small towns, that there are these peculiar structures, about four or five on each side, at various points along most roads. They are made of concrete, and consist of a bottom and a top piece. The two pieces are cuboids, truncated, with sides two feet in length. A wedge shape is taken out of both, and one is sat atop the other. A small concrete brick where the two wedges were taken out holds the top piece in place. From what I can guess, though no Korean will tell me, the concrete brick is designed to be knocked away, allowing the top block to fall off and block the road, stopping enemy advances along these narrow mountain roads. The country is in a state of readiness for war.

I wonder if I will start to get paranoid while I am here.

* * *

On Tuesday, I noticed a few soldiers walking up a narrow path with guns on their back; nice shiny new guns, not the rusty ones that most soldiers seem to carry. Then I saw a few more going up a different path, but up the same hill, and a couple more further on. They were trekking up narrow paths that seemed to lead to nowhere except a hill you can't see around or over. Apparently they were returning to a camouflaged military base over the brow of the hill. It was well camouflaged.

* * *

It's Not Like Afghanistan

There is a brass band that practises right beside the Diplomatic Compound. Brass bands are ten-a-penny here. It is all you hear. This one is unusually bad. They never play in sync with each other, and they all seem to be playing random songs, or random notes, out of tune. This is right beside our apartment block. Some of the trumpets play directly out the windows – badly – in our direction, usually early on a Saturday morning. Make what you want of that. I am not paranoid yet. Am I?

* * *

I am still smoking and it's November 23rd. I have been here almost three weeks and I haven't managed to quit yet, despite a few aborted attempts. I have publicly declared twice, in the RAC, that I am quitting for good. An hour or two later and all I could think about was cigarettes. I couldn't concentrate on having a conversation with anyone. Everyone smokes, and all I could see was cigarettes. I reckon that if I can give up in the afternoon and get through the next day, then I should be all right. I won't give up over a weekend when I am out for drinks with a lot of smokers.

3

Getting Acquainted With The Countryside

*The day of the combination is here to stay.
Individualism has gone, never to return.*

John D Rockefeller

Today, we had a really nice picnic lunch in a place called Changsong, despite the fact that it was raining most of the day. We were surveying in a river valley for rural water schemes that will be funded under new ECHO (EU 'emergency') funding. We are getting the surveying and design out of the way now, in anticipation that the proposal will be approved. Though the DPRK is not necessarily an emergency country in the eyes of most people, it receives funds from the EU as an emergency country, and has done so since around 1997 when it had floods, droughts and famine in fairly quick succession. That was when

Chapter 3

the DPRK was forced to swallow its pride and ask for international assistance. The UN's World Food Programme started what was at times their biggest operation, mainly funded by Japan, the US and South Korea – the sworn enemies of the DPRK.

Now the DPRK has made it clear that it wants bilateral aid, which means funding directly country to country, instead of multilateral aid, which comes through NGOs like Concern, Save the Children, and the like. I think that they find us an inconvenience, as they have to accommodate us in order to get the money into the country. They would rather be getting non-emergency aid, longer-term bilateral development assistance, and skip the hassle of having nagging, intrusive foreigners giving them grief and wanting to see this, that, and the other. Foreigners always want to monitor programs and carry out needs assessments, and this means talking to regular folk.

Our picnic today was under a concrete bridge in this valley. We had lots of little fish, and egg soup. Normally when we are in the field, we have lunch at one of the villages we are working in, wherever we happen to be around half-past twelve. This is usually organised through the Farm Manager (the person in charge of all the various work teams on a farm) or the Team Leader (the person in charge of an individual work team). This is normally in a village-centre house, but today it was organised under a bridge, which was novel and very nice. There are days when these long lunches are a nuisance and can be frustrating, especially with the short winter days. It can also be a nuisance as people tend to want to wash down the meal with the local rice wine. Sometimes, we are given so much food that I feel awkward eating it, because I know these people don't have a lot themselves, and lunch is seemingly arranged at the instruction of the FDRC, who facilitate our work here. The food usually comes from the village communal stores, and not from individuals, but it eats into what is a very limited supply. Today, we were given a bottle of local honey as a thank-you when the locals heard we

Getting Acquainted With The Countryside

were intending to build a piped-water system to reach every house in the village. The gesture was impromptu and felt very genuine

* * *

Yesterday morning was a good example of how life can be made difficult for NGOs. On Monday, two days ago, we needed to borrow a theodolite (electronic surveying equipment) from the Red Cross. This was easily arranged, and the machine was dropped over to our office. Then in the evening I was told we could no longer carry out any surveying. Now it all has to be done by Koreans, as they don't want any foreigners looking through anything with a telescopic lens while in the countryside.

My feet are wet from being out in the hills surveying today, I feel horrible and I think I am getting a cold.

* * *

One thing I always get asked, by school-kids especially, after coming back from wherever I have been working, is 'What do they eat in ...?' Well, tonight for dinner I had some meat (cold), with very fatty bits dominating the tiny meaty bits, some spinach (cold) and some *kim-chi*, which is pickled cabbage and the country's national dish (cold). *Kim-chi* is particular to Korea. Along with (cold) noodle soup and rice, it forms the staple diet of most people. Cold noodle soup is just as it sounds, cold noodles in a watery soup with a few bits added. It is also about as appetising as it sounds. I had it once, and never again I say. I don't like the feeling of grainy bits in my soup or my noodles, and I thought I was going to have to make a run to the toilet when I ate them. The *kim-chi* is not too bad, and is becoming more appealing with time, but it can be harsh on an empty stomach, and yet it is always served first. Then they have lots of eggs: egg soup, fried eggs, boiled eggs, omelettes, egg with this, egg with that ...

Chapter 3

There tends to be meat in some form for breakfast, lunch and dinner, and the favourite seems to be *bul-goggi*. I think the name refers to the way they cook the various types of meat – on a hot plate over a gas or charcoal flame. It is eaten straight away, dipping the meat in something like soy sauce and vinegar. It is super. All meals come with lots of different bits and pieces, put out in front of you on small plates. It creates an awful lot of washing up, and there are no dishwashers here. The bits and pieces can range from mussels to small fish, smaller than sardines even, to random bits of roots! I haven't had caffeine in three days, which is the longest I have abstained in years. These are the foods I see when I am in the countryside. I am under no illusion that the average farmer would eat nearly so well.

* * *

I was talking this evening with one of my Korean colleagues while we were having dinner in the hotel in Songchon. The subject turned to jokes, and a few were shared. Sometimes jokes just don't translate. I went first, with a fairly standard 'Paddy Irishman' joke:

During the war, an Englishman, a Scot and Paddy Irishman were in German-occupied France. They were hiding out in a shed when they heard footsteps and German voices. They quickly hid. When the Germans entered, there was no sign of anyone, just three sacks on the ground. A soldier kicked one sack. The Englishman said 'miaow'. The soldier kicked the next sack, and the Scotsman went 'woof, woof'. The soldier gave the third sack a good kick with his steel-toed boots, and Paddy Irishman shouted 'potatoes, potatoes'.

There was silence from the Koreans. Okay, your turn. One of the local FDRC officials stepped up to the mark. His favourite Korean joke I think got completely lost in translation:

A woman was cycling on her bike, but she didn't know how to cycle. She called out in front of her to an old woman, 'Please help me, I don't know how to cycle.' The old woman turned around, and the cyclist careered straight

Getting Acquainted With The Countryside

into her. The old woman said, 'You only called out to me so you could hit me.'

There was no laughter from the Koreans when it was told, and none from me when it was translated. But it still remains his favourite joke. Maybe they are told it has to be their favourite and that's that, or maybe it has a deeper meaning. I tried again:

Two peanuts were walking down the road and one of them was assaulted.

Silence. Then a joke about a snail was told, and the lads were falling over themselves. It was retold again and again. Even the waitress thought it was hilarious:

A snail comes up to the door of a house and knocks. A man opens the door and the snail looks up. The man looks down and boots him out onto the driveway. Six months later, there is a knock at the man's door. He opens it and looks down, and the snail says, 'Why did you do that?'

From my perspective, though, the funniest was the one I told about the duck. A classic case of a joke going wrong:

A duck goes into a bar and says to the barman, 'Do you have any bread?' and the barman says, 'No.' The duck says to the barman, 'Do you have any bread?' and the barman repeats, 'No, we don't sell bread.' The duck says, 'Have you any bread?' The barman says no. Duck says, 'Have you any bread?' The barman says no. Duck says, 'Have you any bread?' The barman says no. The duck says, 'Have you any bread?' The barman says no. The duck says, 'Have you any bread?' The barman says no. Duck says, 'Have you any bread?' The barman says, 'No ... and if you ask again I will nail your beak to the bar.' The duck says, 'Have you got any nails?' The barman says, 'No.' And then the duck says, 'Have you got any bread?'

It's a pretty good one, but it turns out that the translator changed the story slightly. In the last few lines it was the barman asking the duck for nails, and the duck holding up his wings and saying, 'No, I have no nails on my wings.' Obviously a pun on the two uses for the word 'nail'.

Chapter 3

Whatever the internal systems in the country, people here, like everywhere else, drink and smoke and tell bad jokes over dinner, have affairs, and do the same things as most people around the world. There are inter-office liaisons that have been hinted at – I will not slander those involved or risk spreading scurrilous rumours, but the intrigues are much the same as at home. No Christmas parties here though.

* * *

A note for today: I am talking from an engineering perspective now, so maybe you want to skip on to the next paragraph. Work today consisted of surveying two work teams in the farm of Chomsang: Work Team 5 and Work Team 6. (The moratorium on surveying had lasted about two days.) When I say we were surveying work teams, we were not surveying people, but rather the small villages that are peripheral to the central villages on a Farm. Villages of approximately fifty houses. The plan will be to protect their spring, up above the village, so that it is not open to pollution, and then pipe the water to the village, having a tap in each house. We will probably use low-cost polyethylene pipe, from 20mm to about 75mm in diameter, for the system. The area needs to be surveyed to see if the spring is high enough above the village to get water, in a pipe, to all houses in the village. Based on the survey measurements, the amount of water available, and the amount of water required (150 litres per person per day, according to the Korean National Guidelines), the pipe sizes and any tanks necessary to allow this delivery, are selected using fairly complex equations, very much simplified by computer software: simple spreadsheets in my case with embedded formulae. The main technical issue is that there is a loss of energy as water flows through a pipe. The smaller the pipe, the greater the energy loss; and the bigger the pipe, the more expensive to buy from one of our cheap suppliers in the DPRK or China.

Getting Acquainted With The Countryside

The weather today is dank and miserable, typical on a day when I want sunny weather. The plan is to get a lot of surveying done today. This involves running up hills in the rain, slipping on muck and standing in the cold looking through a fogged-up theodolite. Two days until the weekend, when I am back in the bright lights of Pyongyang, and we still won't have all the villages surveyed. I will have to arrange another trip out of Pyongyang, which is hassle enough.

Now the electricity has gone in my room and I haven't brushed my teeth yet. I can't find my toothbrush. I don't like going to bed without brushing my teeth. I will taste the raw *kim-chi* mixed with the local acorn wine, *sul,* or *soju*, all night. Tomorrow night, incidentally, we are having a *soju* drinking contest. My boss has gathered seven different types of *soju*, from seven counties. They are all made locally and taste different, and the objective is to drink samples of the *soju* from unmarked bottles, choose the best

Chapter 3

tasting *soju*, and identify as many as possible. We could all get rather tipsy.

* * *

One day later. I am writing one line, to say that we are very drunk.

* * *

Seven samples of *soju* drank three times. That's 21 shots. Only 25% proof, so it's really only about ten units of alcohol. I think. My head hurts. I can't remember which *soju* was the best. I think it was from a workteam in Rongchon. The local council officials had a good time sampling. They were pretty flaked. Singing lots of rousing Korean songs about Kim Il Sung and the Motherland and reunification. Some of them a bit sad. No smokes today.

* * *

No, I stand corrected. I am gaining some recollection as the fog lifts. Let me tell you a bit about the *soju* contest. This information comes courtesy of my colleagues. In first place, unsurprisingly, was Songchon *soju*, as it is the *soju* of the hosting location, and easily recognisable by three of the adjudicators. In second – and by default the real winner, as it hadn't the benefit of any hometown votes – was a Namchong *soju*. The idea of the competition was that seven of us would drink a sample of each before, during and after dinner, and rate each one after tasting. However, according to the FDRC boss in Songchon, each had to be sampled before dinner, during meat, after meat, before soup and after soup. Who were we to argue? Thirty-five samples. That explains the horrors today. In the end, our driver got sick after five rounds, and the local boys, having recognised their home brew, voted it through in a narrow victory. Personally, I preferred the much maligned Ryongchon *soju*, though after a few rounds I no longer cared.

* * *

Getting Acquainted With The Countryside

Another day later, and I am twenty-four hours through my third attempt to stop smoking. It has been an extremely difficult few days. The hangover from the *soju* has not cleared up just yet. I don't really know if I want to quit cigarettes – they are a comforter when I have no one to talk to in a bar; they are an excuse for a break from the monotony of work; and they warm me up on a cold day. They are wonderful, but they make me cough a lot, and I know once I have got through the next few days without them I will wonder what the fuss was about. Until then though, I will get a bit sad at the thought of not having a cigarette tomorrow night in the RAC, when all around me are smoking and I am looking at them thinking about how much more comfortable I would feel in the crowd if I had a cigarette. Then I will have one, and then two, because one always leads to two. Then I will be back off the wagon, back to smoking about twenty a day. Maybe. But I got through tonight.

* * *

I think it is time to start talking a little about the politics and external relations of the DPRK. My impression from the few conversations I have had so far is that most people here are absolutely ready and willing to take up arms and fight off foreign invaders. Any attempt from outside at 'regime change' would be viewed not as liberation but as aggression in the eyes of almost every farmer or school-kid in the country. Until a more open type of government can be achieved here, an intervention of any kind would likely increase the hatred, and give more fuel to the propaganda machine.

Kim Il Sung is the Eternal President of the Democratic People's Republic of Korea. Kim Jong Il is his son. Kim Il Sung led the North Korean people to an apparent victory in the Korean War (1950–53). He declared himself leader of the army and the country once an armistice with the South, and the United Nations, had been signed at the demilitarised zone, the strip of land that presently divides the Korean peninsula. The first Kim

Chapter 3

was, in a manner of speaking, an exceptional leader. He might not have been a nice leader, in the liberal democratic, protecting and respecting human rights mould, but he took over a fledgling country, consolidated power and gradually eliminated any rivals and threats he felt were around him. In 1994, Kim Il Sung died, and was given the title of Eternal President. Kim Jong Il will only ever be known as the Dear Leader. He can't be the Great Leader. Though he has done very little, apart from watch the country he inherited slide into disrepair, he has had a persona built for him, pretty much at his own making and initially under his father's watch.

One legacy of the regime of Kim Il Sung is *Juche*. This is a principle or philosophy, based on numeracy and self-sufficiency. I don't know the ins and outs of it at all, and am waiting to find out more. There is a big tower in the centre of Pyongyang, a 170-metre-high, square-based tapering spire, called the *Juche* tower. It has 25,550 blocks, one for each day of Kim Il Sung's life, and is capped with a 20-metre-high, 45-ton, illuminated metal torch. It is presumed to have been based on the Washington Monument, but is taller for the sake of being taller. It is said that the big red illuminated flame at its top uses more electricity than the rest of the power-starved city put together.

Everywhere, all over the country, there are giant portraits and murals of Kim Il Sung, or his son, or the pair of them together, looking like stately gentlemen. They stand over great sweeping valleys or ride big white horses, with great big smiles on their great big faces. In every town, village or work team, there is at least one monument to the Great Leader. When passing through the countryside, you see huge white letters on the sides of hills, similar to the Hollywood sign in Los Angeles, proclaiming something in Korean script. These messages eulogise the Great Leader's exploits, or encourage farmers to work hard for the sake of the glorious socialist motherland's future. They always end in an exclamation mark!

Getting Acquainted With The Countryside

* * *

I am typing here in the dark, by the light of the computer screen, and I know it will soon die. More than a month in Korea, and I have just finished one of my most frustrating days here so far. Everything got delayed or managed to go wrong somehow. Out here in Namchong, I am supposed to be surveying four water systems in two days; it is now eight in the evening, and I have not even finished one. That means spending another night out here. The hotel is nice, if only it had power. I am thinking I am going to be very cold in a few hours, as there is only one blanket on the bed, and no underfloor heating. Underfloor heating is common here – usually fuelled by wood burned in a space beside the house, with hot air travelling through channels under the floor, heating the space above them. It can be too hot to sit on sometimes, which can make mealtimes uncomfortable. Sometimes the heating comes from electric cables under the floor, but I have heard this tends to be unreliable and dangerous.

The surveying today looked doomed from the start, once I saw the village location and then the spring location – way up a tree-

Chapter 3

lined mountain with interlocking spurs, out of view of anywhere where you could carry out a speedy survey with one set-up. Backsights and foresights were going to be needed, with a lot of comical coordination across a wide valley. I did eventually find a spot, a kilometre-and-a-half away from the spring, where I could see the spring and one half of the village. I thought I was on to a winner, but I did not count on the poor eyesight of the Korean carrying the staff. Though I could get readings from the staff, he could not read my hand movements, or even see the red flag flying indicating that it was time to move to the next spot. Thus, over an hour was wasted on the first two sightings and a number of one-mile jogs across the valley and back for myself.

While I was trying to survey, I did get to have a very close look at a mine in operation. This was a shaft going down into the earth, with train tracks for hauling coal and that dirty dust that has every tree in the county filmed with a black layer of scum. Looking down the shaft, all I could see was darkness. I tried to take a photo of it – pretending to take a picture of a few curious kids, covered in coal dust and snot, checking out the foreigner with the strange yellow machine frantically waving a red flag across a valley and cursing in frustration. But I was rushing and nervous, knowing that photos of anything to do with mines are frowned upon, so I didn't quite capture it.

I would not fancy having to spend my working day down those tunnels. It is bad enough driving through the low tunnels they have here on many of the roads. They can be pretty dangerous, especially when there are drunk Koreans wobbling on their bikes coming at you after a healthy serving of *soju* for lunch. It is not uncommon to meet a few drunken cyclists in the countryside in the early afternoon. I don't really blame them for getting drunk.

The country is, I think, about eighty percent mountainous, so there is quite a lot of tunnelling through hills in order to save going around or over them. The tunnels are impressive, though none of them can compete with the Salang Tunnel in

Getting Acquainted With The Countryside

Afghanistan, on the road linking Mazar to Kabul. The highest trafficable tunnel in the world, apparently, it is covered in snow for most of the winter. I was lucky enough to drive it on my only proper road trip in Afghanistan. I think it was the only day I got to drive, due to security restrictions. Here, I can drive around Pyongyang once I have my license and pass the test.

Those mine shafts are pretty intimidating, especially when you see hundreds of people making their way home at six in the evening, covered in coal dust, wearing yellow hats with little lights on them. It would put you in mind of Wales in the days of Arthur Scargill. In these mining areas, the communities are split between mining villages and farming ones – one village will be totally dedicated to mining, and the next one over is devoted to farming. Seemingly they don't get on too well across the divide. Resources such as water are not supposed to be shared between villages, according to the *Juche* principle of self-sufficiency. Each little village is supposed to have its own supply, while the State provides certain common goods, such as food and heating for example. Whatever is farmed or mined goes straight to the State warehouses, and is then redistributed to farmers and miners alike. Farmers get smaller rations though, as mining is considered to be the more demanding work.

The bottoms of my trousers are covered with black coal dust from a few hours of being near a mine. I can't imagine what the miners' lungs must be like. Mine are not feeling too good today, after reneging on my vow to quit smoking as soon as I got to the RAC on Friday night. I fought the urge for a while, but gave up after about two beers. I did, after all, bring a pack of cigarettes as backup in case I couldn't hack it, which means I was only fooling myself. Tomorrow is another day I suppose. I like cigarettes.

4
Getting To Know The Place

Civil government, so far as it is instituted for the security of property, is in reality instituted for the defense of the rich against the poor, or of those who have some property against those who have none at all.

Adam Smith

I watched a brief documentary DVD on Darfur last night, and felt a sort of perverse envy of some old workmates from Afghanistan, who are working there now in what seem like really, really difficult conditions. I think working in places like that is what this work is really about. Though this is such an interesting place to be, the situation here, now, is not comparable to anything like Darfur. Don't get me wrong, there are needs, and there are a lot of people that have those needs. I don't think there is the same level of material poverty here. But people are

Chapter 4

lacking something different, something that probably only system change can bring.

There are few NGOs working here, and not too many foreigners of any sort, most of them mashed into Pyongyang's Diplomatic Compound most of the time. The Russians and Chinese have their own enormous embassies, like mini-towns, in the centre of Pyongyang. Some of the NGOs here include:

Triangle: French, pronounced Tree-angle. I don't know what to make of them yet, but they seem good fun.

CESVI: Italian, nice crowd, seem friendly and interesting and interested.

GAA: German. Very serious.

Save the Children: I haven't got to know them yet.

PMU: They seem to be Nordic, but that's all I know at this stage.

Handicap International: Generally anti-landmine, but dealing with medical and amputation stuff and prosthetics.

Premiere Urgence: French, I think, small, don't say much. Don't know what they do. First-aid?

Concern Worldwide: a mixed bunch. Varied.

There are a number of United Nations agencies, notably UNICEF, WFP, WHO and UNDP. Then there are the embassy people – the ambassadors, their spouses and kids, and a few other attachés. The majority of the embassies seem fairly obscure through my biased, Eurocentric glasses – places such as Mongolia, Iran, Cambodia, Indonesia and Pakistan – along with a few less obscure countries, like Romania, India and Russia. Great Britain, Sweden and Germany are all lumped into one building together. Finally, there are some corporate entrepreneurs. I have only met a few, such as a man running a pharmaceutical business, trying to introduce fast-dissolving aspirin to the Korean economy.

Getting To Know The Place

* * *

Another frustrating day's surveying has been had by all. I think myself and my Korean colleague have to work on our communication skills. My patience is wearing thin. Why does everything take so long? He is quite a nice guy, but just misses the concept of being timebound. Because he has done surveying before, and knows the basics of it, I try to give him some slack to work away by himself, stepping in when I need a certain point surveyed. But he turns everything into a discussion, and it's terribly annoying when twilight is approaching and shadows are passing over the hills. A communication failure nearly cost us the whole afternoon's work. I had a few FDRC officials with me to hold the target (the thing the engineer points the telescope thing at – the light rebounds off it, and the telescope thing calculates angles and distances), and away we went. Well, away I went, while the surveyor spent half an hour getting to where he was going. By that time, the man at the spring had stuck the target in the ground facing the wrong way, and had sat down out of sight and lit a fire to keep himself warm. I spent the next twenty minutes shouting and cursing. Quietly, to myself.

This evening I enjoyed a nice quiet chat with my colleague over dinner. It is an eye-opener, listening to him and his views on the outside world, especially as he has had more access than most Koreans to foreigners, and to literature, outside of what you can get in the university libraries. He wondered why Guinness would have a factory in Nigeria, as Nigeria is in Africa, and they have no money there. He couldn't comprehend how an African could afford Guinness.

* * *

This diary has become part of my ritual now – writing a few pages into it whenever I am out in the field, with no electricity, waiting for the battery on the laptop to run out, as it invariably does each night.

Chapter 4

This week should be interesting. The Irish ambassador to South Korea will be visiting for a few days, and I will be out in the field showing him what good work we are doing. Keeping the good foot forward. I wonder whether he will remember a friend of mine who is teaching down South, from the time he misplaced his passport in Busan, South Korea? Other than that, I am in Songchon for a few days, looking at a project site to see if there is any work getting done. Last week there was very little progress and I had to put on my annoyed face and say I would be back again next week. I think I will make a big effort to get a picture of the billowing clouds coming from the thermal power station, if I can escape from company for a minute – or stop for a toilet break nearby.

The weekend was a tough one with two late nights, both unplanned. I didn't mean to stay out late either night, but it just happened that I was a little inebriated and didn't want to go home. This was not aided by the fact that I don't seem to be able to sleep in Pyongyang, and am now very tired. Add to this the running, cycling, swimming, volleyball and football that I tried to cram into about thirty hours, and I am a bit wrecked. I cycled out to football on my little bicycle, freshly pumped with air, and froze on the way there, froze more while playing football, and was like an icicle on the way back. I was so cold, I was unable to use the brakes on my bike, lock my bike, or use the keys to get into my apartment. I had to knock on the door with my elbows to get let in by my British colleague.

* * *

Wherever you go, I think, no matter the country or the system, kids are the same. I thought initially when I got here that the kids were different to those in Afghanistan or Ethiopia, but they're not at all. They are all intrigued by foreigners, more so here, I guess, than in other places, as there are so few of us around. Once you break the ice with them, merely by a nod or a wave, they burst into smiles, and then either shy away behind one of

Getting To Know The Place

their mates or simply stare at you, wondering. In Ethiopia, and from what I hear of Africa generally, kids are far more vocal about their fascination with white people, with shouts of 'ferenji', which a lot of people find annoying or even disconcerting. In Afghanistan the kids are not so 'in your face'; they keep their distance more than in Africa. In Korea it seems quite similar.

Here, notably in the schools where we are building latrines, kids crowd around, but at a distance, just watching and whispering. But as soon as eye contact is made, and you give the thumbs up or a wave, there is a change in tone. Whispering becomes more audible, and soon there are peals of laughter. Then they wave back, trying to incite another reaction. There was one young lad outside the hotel today, as I was finishing my cigarette. When I saw him looking at me, I bowed, as Korean kids seem to do as a mark of respect to their elders. He bowed back and then, seeing that I was smiling, bowed again, and I bowed, and we had a great game of bowing.

When travelling in the countryside by car, it is a little strange to see how children greet oncoming vehicles. There could be a line of eight or nine kids walking on the road, and as a vehicle passes, hats are quickly whipped off their heads and a Mexican wave-type bow happens. This is not just to foreigners' cars, but to any car passing. It reminds me of when I was a school kid, and we would have a visitor to the classroom. The whole class had to stand up to say, 'Fáilte romhat, a dhuine uasail' (Irish for, 'Welcome, important person'). The way the kids give the greeting, with big smiley heads, bowing in sequence, one after the other, makes it look like they are having a laugh at our expense. It is almost mocking, but it isn't.

I had a nice chat with one of my female Korean colleagues today in the jeep, as we snaked along mountain roads, through deforested valleys, rising and then falling, with a sheer drop on my side of the car. About seven of us were squeezed into a five-seater, and the two of us were squashed into the front passenger

Chapter 4

seat – quite a change from Afghanistan, where I was not even able to travel in the same car as an Afghan woman. I tentatively broached the subject of the Korean War. This is the story in her mind:

It is the fault of the Americans that the peninsula is divided in two. After the Second World War, when the country was liberated from Japan, the USSR and the USA agreed to occupy half of the peninsula each, until a working government could be set up. The Russians left the North, but the States decided to stay and occupy the South, attempting to take over the North in the Korean War, which the US initiated. The day that the ceasefire was signed is celebrated in the DPRK as the day the North Korean army defeated the great American army. The reason the peninsula is not now united is because the United States continues to occupy the South, under the guise of a *stooge* South Korean government.

I tried to understand what she thought would happen if the US occupying forces left. How would the peninsula be governed, and the two sides united? She was adamant that it would be one state, with two different governments and regimes, and that everyone would be willing to go along with this. Then she changed the subject.

* * *

Another technical brief: I wish the lads doing the building here would go to the trouble of putting cement in the mortar when they are building latrines. We buy more than enough cement for each latrine, knowing that some of it will be put to *other* use, but each time there seems to be less and less available for what the cement is intended. At times like that I have to go into bad-cop mode. Sometimes I genuinely am annoyed, especially when I have to leave the comfort of Pyongyang and come out here to see rubbish work, or no work at all. That's half the job I suppose, but sometimes my time is just wasted. If the work is of good quality, there is no need to go see it and make sure. But I don't

Getting To Know The Place

want a heavy concrete roof falling on the head of some poor kid in a toilet. With some of the work that I have seen in the last few days, it is a distinct possibility.

* * *

It is quiet in the office this week. My two flatmates have now left for good. Both have gone to Sudan – one to Khartoum and the other to Darfur. All of the Koreans are at Project Cycle Management training in Koppensang House – one of the fancy places just outside Pyongyang – learning how to manage project cycles. Project cycle management and logical frameworks are the current mania in development work. Under the present regime, I am not sure the training will get put to much use. It is a bit of quiet time for me, punching numbers into my computer to come out with some nice little water-system designs for the villages we have been surveying in the last week. After that, I have to do the really dull stuff – converting the designs into bills of materials and tender documents. Life as a humanitarian aid worker is not all glamour and pizzazz.

My Croatian colleague has been having a really bad time over the last few weeks. He is a really nice lad, who has been through a lot already. His father died suddenly a few weeks back, just after I got here, and he went home in a hurry, just in time to make the funeral. On his way back to the airport again, a bus smashed into the back of the car. He had to climb out the window of the car, check whether his stepsister was okay, pull his luggage out through the window, and then walk to the airport in the lashing rain, with a few weeping cuts to his face. When he got to the airport, he had the wrong ticket, looked a complete state, and had much trouble convincing the airline to let him get his flight. Cutting to the chase, he now has concussion. He was getting sick a lot, and had to fly back to hospital in Beijing to get seen to. The medical facilities are not the best here, though Pyongyang does have one huge maternity hospital, just down the road from our office.

Chapter 4

* * *

I am all alone in the flat now, and it is quite lonely. It is a big flat, with three bedrooms, a kitchen and a sitting room. Room for a pony, and only me to fill it. I will miss my flatmates, who were a bundle of energy, enthusiasm, stories and encouragement. One did try to annoy me regularly by mocking my religiosity, but I think he was doing it to get a rise out of me more than anything else. He wasn't irreligious, though from what I have seen in my short career so far, there does seem to be a generally anti-religious tone in NGO circles. Maybe it is just the people I tend to drift toward, but it is a little unsettling. There is definitely a certain snobbery or a snide attitude that suggests there is something wrong with religious motives playing a role in one's reasons for doing this work. I would not be a supporter of evangelisation masquerading as humanitarianism, but somehow a secular humanism is deemed to be the only viable humanism in some circles. It is not something I have got my head around yet. There are a lot of people working in this world, where tolerance is one of the core issues at all policy levels, yet in trying to be so tolerant, there is a danger of becoming intolerant of many things. It is one of those irreconcilable paradoxes.

Religious freedom was one of the most basic and clear-cut of human rights when the United Nations established the Charter of Fundamental Rights in 1948. In this country, there is no religious freedom, yet I never hear a mention of that very clear and definite denial of a human right. I think that the Western world considers the right to religious freedom as one of those rights that is only incidentally important. It is only important if people are willing to fight for it. If they accept the denial quietly, it is not such a big deal. If it does not lead to large scale religious wars, then it is not to be worried about too much. If it leads to violence and torture, it is the violence and torture that are to be responded to, not the denial of religious freedom. In the western, 'free' world, the religion of the public space is secular. And it dominates it. It doesn't share.

Getting To Know The Place

There is no religious freedom in this country. Religions are considered anti-nationalistic; they go against the spirit of self-sufficiency and industrialisation that the *Juche* idea is based around. Religion is outlawed in practice, if not in the word of the law. There are estimated to be about 4,000 Catholics and 12,000 Protestants in the country, but there are no priests and there is no Mass. As far as I can gather, anyone openly practising a religion here is liable to be jailed and punished. That is conjecture at this stage and based on nothing I have explicitly seen or heard here. I was supposed to go to the Mausoleum of the Great Leader Kim Il Sung today, where he rests in state. It is supposed to be an emotionally charged place, with queues of bereft Koreans keening and lamenting, and very sombre music in the background. Though I would have been fascinated to see the place, and to observe the people, I couldn't go and give credence to the system and its lies in that manner. I couldn't go into the place and then refuse to bow to Kim Il Sung, as that would put the Koreans I work with in a very difficult situation. It would be disrespectful to the people that are obviously in awe of this man. It would be an insult to them personally, so best to stay at home.

* * *

I am having a lot of trouble with the Internet. There is a landline here that connects the Diplomatic Compound to the outside world. International calls are very expensive, so I don't make them too often. There are no mobile phones at all at the moment. This will change over time, but mobile communication is more difficult to monitor and control than landlines. Connectivity here is very tightly controlled. Only certain people are connected to certain systems. In the countryside, there are no phones in houses, only in offices, and that is how communication is maintained at a local level. Offices at a particular level can only phone certain other offices – only central offices can also contact provincial-level offices. If Koreans in our office wish to contact county officials, they cannot call from the phone in our office in the Diplomatic

Chapter 4

Compound, but have to go to their ministry office to make contact. In the county towns, there are only a few phones that would be able to contact Pyongyang. I gather some people in Pyongyang have phones in their homes, but I am not sure how widespread this is.

There is limited Internet connectivity in the country as a whole. I have seen no internet access outside of Pyongyang, and even in Pyongyang it is very restricted. Students in the universities have access to chatrooms, but only internally controlled ones. There is no access to social-media information-sharing sites that could corrupt the minds of the Koreans. There is no access to external news websites. In the Diplomatic Compound, we access the Internet through a dial-up connection. We have only one computer connected to the Internet, so we download emails in the morning, and then again in the evening. There used to be a charge per byte or per email, but now there is a monthly flat rate. Two East Germans, who have been living here since before the collapse of the Berlin Wall, manage the service. The Koreans are generally not allowed to use the Internet in our office. That restriction is put in not by us, but by the Government. Only the Liaison Officer really has any access, and I think that is limited too. I am trying to order Christmas presents for the family, to go with the great Christmas cards that left the country yesterday. I apologise in advance to all if the presents are poor, but I am limited in what I can get here and my credit card limit is also fairly low. Self-imposed restraint.

* * *

Today I went on a mini-tour of the city. It wasn't on a tour bus or anything like that; no masses of Japanese and Chinese tourists with their cameras and flags, following the leader. It was just me and my Liaison Officer being brought to the *Juche* Tower, the Metro and to Kim Il Sung Square. It wasn't quite the official grand tour that I was expecting, but it was better for it. I was a little weary from the night before, having drank a glass of gone-

Getting To Know The Place

off Kahlua. We didn't get to go see the statue of the Great Leader, or lay a bouquet of flowers at his feet or anything like that, which is good, as I am still debating whether I would have or not. The *Juche* Tower is very impressive in its enormity, though I had to wonder at the little display at the bottom, which holds lots of plaques acclaiming the *Juche* idea and Korean reunification, sent by various random organisations in countries like the Gambia and Ghana, with lots from groups in India and Venezuela.

The view from the top of the tower is incredible. You can pretty much see across the city, down the Tedonggang (*gang* means river in Korean) to the big Chinese-run hotel on the island on the river. Turning your head thirty degrees, you can see the Koryo Hotel, where many foreign visitors and dignitaries stay. A bit more to the east is the statue of Kim Il Sung, and further on is a cast-iron mounted statue of the mythical horse Chollima [more on this soon]. You can't quite see the Arch of Triumph, hidden by a small hill, but there is the *MayDay* Stadium and the impressive suspension bridge that spans the river beside it. You can just barely see into the forbidden city – the area of Pyongyang that is restricted to the very few important members of the elite. I drove up towards one of the fenced-off entrances to the area by mistake one time, and was quickly ushered back down the street by a nervous-looking guard.

Chapter 4

The Pyongyang Metro is quite impressive. It is still in good shape, working well compared to many of the other redundant elephants around the place. The best bit is the escalator, which goes down, in one single staircase, to a depth of about sixty metres. Kim Jong Il, like his father before him, has a penchant for giving on-the-spot guidance on almost any subject at any time, and many of his words of wisdom have been given in and around the Metro. His advice is always heeded – I don't think anyone would question him. He tells farmers they should grow more, and tells truck manufacturers it would be better if they made more. I think one of his best was one day when he was travelling on the Metro, as he 'wanted to sit among the people'.

Getting To Know The Place

He decreed that there should be punctual running of the Metro at all times. Simple, sound advice. If only we had him working for Dublin Bus.

The stations of the Metro are fantastically decorated with murals, feel-good nationalistic propaganda designed to inspire the populace to great things. One is the 'Rebuilding of the City', depicting muscle-bound Superman-esque figures with sledgehammers, strong square jaws and chiselled forearms, smiling to themselves as they work. Another depicts country workers – peasants – all smiling gleefully, standing behind the Great Leader as he gazes across a golden field of wheat. Another mural, 'A Day of Innovation', features a group of people moving en masse in one direction to the mines, clean and coiffured and wearing shiny yellow helmets, while another group moves off in the opposite direction to the fields, carrying sickles and spades, accompanied by a *Chollima* tractor. Chollima is the brand of tractor made in North Korea, but production has slowed almost to standstill. The tractors in the murals are the same as the ones they have today, but shinier. Most Korean tractors are old and decrepit, kept in service by the innovations of the farm mechanic, using whatever diminishing means are at his disposal.

The ceilings of the stations are extremely high and very ornate, festooned with dramatic chandeliers, with each station having its own theme. The most popular are variations on attempts at representing grapes at harvest time. My local guidebook contains a strange little story about a boy who thought the chandeliers were really grapes. When he said this to his mother, everyone looked skywards – or roofwards – and his mother said, 'No, why they are chandeliers.' Everyone laughed, for the Metro is a place of laughter, and it is air conditioned to refresh the workers.

Then we went to Kim Il Sung Square, a typical, spacious Russian/communist-type square – no trees or grass. It is similar in atmosphere to Tian'men, though not nearly as big and without the forbidding entrance to the Forbidden City. It has quite nice

Chapter 4

buildings around it, especially the Kim Il Sung Library. This is an old-style Korean building, very oriental looking, and one of very few in the country that retains that style. The other two buildings circumscribing the square (can you circumscribe a square?) are like old institutions, one with a big picture of the face of the old man, and the other with pictures of Lenin and Marx. Korean socialism is said to be a mix of Leninism and Marxism. It would take a better man than me to tell you what that means. Incidentally, there is no reference to, or acknowledgement of, Chairman Mao.

5
Yes, This Is Christmas

In short, people decided that it was impossible to achieve any of the good of Socialism, but they comforted themselves by achieving all the bad.

GK Chesterton

Characteristic of the situation regarding technology in the country is the thermal power station in Rongchon. It billows out clouds of black, black smoke whenever it is actually working. It has gaping holes in the roof, seems to run at low output and constantly breaks down, providing an erratic electricity supply at a very low frequency that burns out motors. It is supplied with fuel dug out using very outdated mining methods. The country struggles to maintain the supply that is essential to keep it on an even keel. I know people believe the DPRK pumps huge amounts of money into defence and nuclear testing, but I would be surprised if this is done at the expense of energy and communications. I have just heard another horror story of a mine collapse in China – something that happens with alarming

Chapter 5

regularity. Given that technology and standards would be higher in China than here, I would not be surprised if that sort of thing was commonplace here. No one would ever hear about it if it happened.

* * *

Last Wednesday I had my North Korean driving test. From what I had been told prior to the test, no foreign aid worker has ever failed. This did not put me at ease. I was even a little nervous – I didn't want to be the first failure. I turned up at the test centre, and sat down in the tester's room for the theory element. For the first question, I was shown a picture of one of the traffic ladies standing face-on, with her right arm vertical in the air. I was asked what the signal meant. I answered that it meant 'stop', despite having been told before the test that this is an obligatory question and that it means the President is coming, and you have to pull in off the road immediately. Then the tester had a cigarette and offered me one. I accepted. He proceeded to explain that the sign means a VIP is coming (this was all through a translator, who has never driven and has no idea about driving, and isn't a very good translator). Then I was shown a picture of a traffic lady demonstrating the stop signal. Theory test over.

On to the practical test. This lasted just about as long as the theory exam. Turn right here, turn right here, turn right here, turn right here, and pull in outside the test centre. My translator turned around to me and said, 'Great, you did it.' I felt relieved. I think I was more nervous about failing something that is notoriously easy than I would have been if it was extremely onerous. There is no embarrassment in failing difficult things.

* * *

Today I received my license in the post.

* * *

I was being driven back to Pyongyang from Rongchon a few days ago. I am not allowed to drive outside the perimeters of

Yes, This Is Christmas

Pyongyang. There is about a twenty-kilometre radius within which foreigners can drive, as well as being allowed to take the main road from the capital to Nampo on the coast. Russian embassy people can also go to Hamhung on the east coast, where the nice beaches are. Anyhow, I have noticed that the road from Rongchon seems to have a more military flavour than other roads I tend to travel. That evening, I saw a group of children out running, in an orderly, regimented manner. Then another group of boys and girls, who looked very young to be doing serious running, came trotting along in the opposite direction. These were followed by another group, no older than ten or eleven, running in formation, carrying wooden pretend rifles and moving at a good pace. Then came another group, and another a bit further down the road. Further along, a woman with a loudspeaker was barking at groups of people, who seemed to be digging trenches a lot bigger than those you would use for potatoes. They seemed to be engaged in a trench-digging race; whether for the sake of the trenches or for the sake of the race, I am not sure.

* * *

I think I will be having my first white Christmas in a long, long time. It is supposed to be guaranteed white here, but I can't see any sign of it yet. Though it snows lightly every so often, it isn't nearly as cold as I was led to believe it would be. There is plenty of time yet. Apparently January is the month to dread as it gets really cold and the winter can feel interminable when it is still sub-zero well into March. I tried throwing snowballs at a few kids here in Songchon, but they just looked at me, a bit puzzled. My loud and very outgoing female translator, however, didn't need a second invite.

* * *

She was a lot quieter on Thursday night. We had dinner with the Korean Vice-foreign Minister and the newly appointed Irish Ambassador to the Korean peninsula. Unusually for her, she

Chapter 5

seemed highly deferential and a little out of her depth. I guess these ministers are held in high regard here. She hardly spoke, except to me. The Irish Ambassador to Korea is based in Seoul, but has diplomatic responsibilities for the DPRK as well. He used to be Ambassador to Saudi Arabia, and spent five years in Riyadh. Dinner was held at a very ornate country hotel, the Koppensang guesthouse. This, apparently, was the only place foreigners were allowed to stay in 1997, when the country first started receiving humanitarian food aid. It was also said to be deathly cold, because at that time there was no heating. Bleak days in Korea.

The food was not too good – cold noodles and pickled cabbage. I am still struggling to get to grips with the local cuisine. The waitresses spilled lots of wine on their odd-looking native Korean dress, which resembles very colourful maternity wear. Halfway through the dinner, the Korean Vice-minister got up from the table and left without a word. He didn't come back. The story was that he was rushed to hospital with a very bad stomach pain. The next day, I heard he had his appendix taken out. I reckon he was just bored, which I can understand.

The Irish Ambassador and his wife were lucky enough to be brought on a trip to the countryside, to get a view of the DPRK and the work we are doing. Considering they have not been outside of Seoul in their time in the South, it was a real experience for them to see the reality of life in the North, away from the propaganda of the South. Many of the diplomatic staff based in Pyongyang have never gone outside the capital or seen beyond the façade of the official city tours.

* * *

We were supposed to have an informal formal dinner for all NGO and UN workers and foreign embassy people, hosted by the Swedish embassy in the RAC, with a Nobel-prize theme. It ended up being cancelled, as two Korean WFP employees were killed in a car accident on the road to Pyongyang from

Yes, This Is Christmas

Hamhung. No one seems to know what happened, as it was the lead car in a convoy of six. The Koreans who died were a driver and the WFP Liaison Officer. The Liaison Officer role with the WFP would be considered a very senior job, given the amount of food aid that is coming into Korea through the WFP. It would almost be bordering on a diplomatic position. Both of the men who died had young families.

In the DPRK, as part of the pseudo-communist regime, there is what is called a public distribution system, or PDS. It is hard to understand exactly how the PDS works. Farming communities, on the communal land, get paid a certain amount each year, and it varies from year to year, based on what they grow. The produce goes to a county warehouse. There can be great variance in the amount of crops in the warehouses in each county, not to mention variance in what is produced on each farm, depending on the crop and the quality of land. Thus, the people in the better agricultural areas receive more pay than those in other areas. So there is more money in those communities, to purchase more of the more easily available food. In low-yield areas in poor counties, where there is limited produce, there is also limited money/credit to buy this more limited supply. So, in essence there is an imbalance across the country. A supply-and-demand market of sorts exists, which seems contrary to the communist/socialist ethos. Though the DPRK claims not to be a communist country – *Juche* is the philosophy that guides it – the fundamentals of the country are communist. Produce is harvested and brought to central warehouses. Then it is distributed to the non-farming communities – the office people, mining communities, and so on – at a heavily subsidised price. Market prices (some small markets have begun to appear) are eleven times the subsidised prices.

The farming communities have small plots to grow their own personal produce, which they apparently use far more efficiently than the communal land, so in reality farmers are far more food-secure than non-farmers, especially in times of hardship. They

Chapter 5

tend to be able to access a more nutritionally balanced and varied diet, which I was surprised at until I learned more about the system. The small private plots are typically used to grow vegetables rather than grain crops. In bad years, produce is less subsidised by the State, and thus costs more to the workers. They are probably also getting paid (credit) less in those hard years, which doubles the hardship in a way.

As I mentioned, markets have only recently begun to be established. They are operating not so much with Government approval, but with a grudging acceptance that they are to be tolerated, temporarily at least. There seem to be localised crackdowns on markets every so often – I get the impression that this is mostly for show, and to keep the scale of the markets within a certain limit. The markets here operate like alleyway markets in olden-day Ireland, or Afghanistan or Africa, though there aren't quite as many people buying and selling. There is little of the hustle and bustle that you would see in thriving urban markets, and the market areas are not overcrowded. At the same time, they do seem to provide some form of *life* to the towns around the market. It seems more natural. There is a throng of people, a bit of a buzz, with *individuals* milling around. People can be seen carrying bundles or dragging carts up hills, or cycling along with a huge pig tied to the carrier of a bicycle, foaming at the mouth. It is all so different to regular, orderly Korean street life, in which people move to work in their throngs, usually all mono-directional and not too happy-looking. Or come home in the opposite direction, far more animated.

So far, foreigners like me are not really allowed around the market areas. The markets may look impromptu, but they are allowed only in designated areas – areas that I am not supposed to be hanging around. People who want to sell at a market need to have a special permit. They can only sell what they have a permit to sell, and only a certain amount of it. The system is opening up, but very slowly. It is often a case of two very small steps forward and then another step right back again.

Yes, This Is Christmas

In Pyongyang, there are a few formal markets that I can go to. I will discuss these later. They are much more tightly controlled. When I am feeling particularly brave, in Rongchon for example, I try to wander off at lunchtime to have a quick look around, but this does not go down too well with my colleagues. I don't want to push my luck, or create problems for the Koreans I work with either.

Apparently the faces of the large towns have changed quite rapidly, and have brightened up considerably compared with a few years ago. There are far more shopfronts in the cities, and people selling increasingly varied items. There are definitely days, especially Fridays, when the towns are extremely busy, with many more people milling about than usual. These crowds can be very dangerous when it's icy. Cyclists and pedestrians tend to overreact to oncoming cars and panic. This leads to cyclists falling over or pedestrians slipping onto their backsides, with a car coming in the opposite direction struggling to get a grip on the ice. The cyclists' panic is not helped by the drivers' excessive use of car horns.

* * *

The difference in the countenance of people once the working day is done is really noticeable. Smiles and laughter are all around in the evenings when I am late heading back to Pyongyang, in stark contrast to the dreariness when I am leaving in the morning. I know it is the same in most places, but it really can affect your view of a place when you see smiling, laughing people as opposed to lines of grey, downtrodden faces. On winter mornings, when the trees are bare and the buildings in the background are all a washed-out monotone, bleak faces exacerbate the sadness, but on the same evening, beaming smiles and laughter stand out like bright splashes of colour on a grey canvas.

* * *

Chapter 5

When I go to the countryside, the people are constantly working – always carrying something, or digging something or pulling something. There are few people idling, and it strikes me that there must be hardly any leisure time for the people working in the communal farms, trying to make the quota for the county warehouse, and a bit more for themselves on their own little private patch. What really strikes me about the place is that there is no sense of fun. I don't want to perpetuate the idea that Korea is an entirely grey, dull and bleak place. In many respects, of course, it is. I don't say that the people don't enjoy themselves – I am not in a position to make such a judgment – but it isn't like Africa or other places in Asia, where monetarily and nutritionally people can be as poor or poorer. There are few public expressions of joy; rarely do I hear roars of laughter, or see groups of more than two, or at most three, chatting.

There is religious freedom in most African countries, less government control and intervention and much more personal freedom to live your life. Though people are more limited by nature and finances in some other countries, here the restrictions are all imposed by government. Enormous murals of Kim Il Sung and his son Kim Jong Il stand out everywhere, along with the huge signs emblazoned across hill and hollow telling the peasants to 'Aim High!' and 'Do It For Your Country', or wishing 'Long Life to the Dear Leader'. People don't complain publicly – perhaps this is because they don't know or haven't experienced anything else, but more likely it is because they cannot.

* * *

The organisation I work with has projects on water and sanitation, which is what occupies my time; also primary health care, particularly midwifery; and *livelihoods*. This is another buzzword in the aid world. What we are mainly doing here at the moment is building latrines for schools and hospitals, because children and sick people need somewhere half decent to do their

Yes, This Is Christmas

business. We are also designing piped-water systems that are safe for people to drink from, and buying the materials needed to build them, because many of the work farms do not have these and others have rusted away years ago.

We are also assisting in the repair of some massive pump stations and urban water systems. This is quite high-tech in some ways, but quite Neolithic in others. We are importing massive motors that are not really used anywhere outside of the DPRK and China. I know nothing about them, but the technicians here have been using them for years, and they work fairly well with the decrepit electrical supply system in many of these county towns. We are attempting some health and hygiene-awareness programmes for children in schools, but this is not easy – we don't know what the children know and what they don't know or need to know, and we don't get to talk to them or their teachers.

* * *

It is almost Christmas. It is only six days away, but I have never felt so little festive spirit or enthusiasm anywhere. Even in Afghanistan, Christmas was regarded as some sort of holiday, or it had some association with festivities and goodwill. But for the Koreans it means absolutely nothing. Even among the expatriates here, there doesn't seem to be much of a sense of Christmas joy, which is a little depressing. It seems that the holiday season will pass pretty much unnoticed. I have, I think, located a Catholic church, very near to here. The next question is how to find out what might be happening there for Christmas, if anything at all. Some people apparently approached the Koreans there last year about some sort of midnight Mass or gathering, as there aren't any priests in the country. This was met with a shrug and a non-committal 'we will see what we can do' answer. Nothing happened. But it could be interesting to go to the church and scope out the situation. I don't know how many among the foreigners here would be interested, as I get the feeling that there is a very high level of religious intolerance here.

Chapter 5

I got the same feeling in Afghanistan, where faith-based organisations were scorned or belittled, looked on as extremists or evangelicals, which the vast majority aren't at all. Most simply use their faith, and adherence to it, as guiding moral principles in their work. Many of them also adhere to the Humanitarian Charter, and other codes of international best practice. Yet, for many, this is not good enough, and I am not sure why. The discourse in this regard reflects the narrative that pervades the public square in liberal democracies around the world. Many NGO workers, who claim to be impartial in every respect, have a tendency to overswing and become somewhat religiously intolerant.

* * *

So, yes, this is Christmas (eve). Almost everyone has gone home. Well, most of the people I hang out with seem to have gone back to their nearest and dearest, or to somewhere warm. All the French left yesterday, as well as all of my colleagues, which means probably a quite depressing Christmas ahead. There is an invitation to the German embassy on Christmas Day – classical music and carol singing at two in the afternoon, and then hang around for a few drinks and dinner at five. I can see that being a long day, as I don't know too many people. I still hope I can get some form of Mass or church ceremony tomorrow, but I can see it being difficult. Last year in Afghanistan there was no Mass either, unsurprisingly, but about ten of us from the team got together in Mazar-I-Sharif for a super Christmas dinner and nice hot whiskies.

* * *

Christmas Day was interesting, if quiet. I went looking for the church that is supposed to be nearby, but I could not find it. Then there was the dinner in the German Embassy. Lots and lots of people turned up, many of whom I had never seen before. There was supposed to be a Korean orchestra playing, but they were not given permission by the powers that be, as it

Yes, This Is Christmas

talented children is to play for the great leader at some stage in their lives. Then there is the *Juche* tower, which I have described, and Kim Il Sung Square, which I drove by but didn't stop at. I drove under the Arc de Triomphe: Pyongyang Style, which is about three metres taller than the Paris original. I drove by the 140,000-seat *MayDay* Stadium, but I already play football in its shadow every Sunday, so it was no big deal. I know how to get home from there. I drove under the big thing that was erected on the tenth anniversary of Kim Il Sung's death – a vertical structure with something written on it. I don't know what it is.

The main landmarks that I use for getting around the city are the hotels. There is a big Chinese hotel, the Yang-gak-doh, on one side of the city, and there is the Koryo Hotel, a set of twin towers with a rotating restaurant on top, on the other. At least one of these is visible from pretty much anywhere in the metropolis. The *Juche* Tower stands out when it is lit up at night, and acts as a homing beacon for me. The best landmark, however, is a huge pyramidal building, about seventy-five stories high and about ninety percent finished. Most of the concrete work looks to be complete, and there is a rusted crane sitting at the very top of the building that hasn't moved in over a decade. The project was abandoned due to lack of funds apparently. It seems it is doomed to remain standing as a very visible reminder of the decline of the State, and of communism as a global power, until someone takes the decision to call in the bomb squad.

6
The Big Freeze: 2005

The Revolution will be complete when the language is perfect.
George Orwell

Wahey! 2005. *Juche* 94. This has probably been the strangest New Year's I have experienced. Not strange in an exciting, great-story-to-be-told kind of way, but unusual in that it was so sedate. There was dinner in the *Friendship* Health Service Centre – twenty euro a head, with food and drinks all in. I thought they were on to a loser with that, and that people would happily drink greater than their fill. It didn't happen that way though, and I would say that only a few of us got our money's worth. There was no countdown and, as people were in different rooms, it was New Year in one room and not in the other. The Korean TV channel was on, showing pictures of the Great Leader, and there was the sound of a gong in the background. Everything felt like it was in slow motion. At three minutes past midnight, people were waiting for someone to tell them it was the New Year.

Chapter 6

Myself and a Croatian fella had some fire crackers, so we lit them and said, 'Yaaay, Happy New Year,' and tried to get celebrations of some sort going. We failed. Pretty soon most people had gone home.

What was my New Year's resolution? It has been almost two days, and I have not had a cigarette. It is the weekend, the *Friendship* is closed, and I have hardly left the house except to go to the shop to buy some bread and go for a run. There are no smokes in the house. It is a lot warmer today than the last few weeks – I reckon it is almost touching zero today, which is about ten degrees more than usual, but it is just a lull and it will be a lot colder once the warm front has passed. I went for a nice run in shorts and T-shirt, as it is not as cold as usual. I actually broke a sweat, and was warm when I finished. It is nice to go for a run and not have to worry about losing the feeling in my fingers for a change. No one turned up for football, because there is a layer of snow on the ground, which makes it look deceptively cold. If only they would step outside.

* * *

I am passing a week out here, in and around a small village called Sinjidong. It is absolutely freezing. Over the last few days, it has gotten progressively colder, and these nights it is not easy to get to sleep. It is more difficult to get myself out from under my blanket in the morning. I can hardly feel my fingers when I am out surveying. I have to take off my gloves to press the button and turn the little wheels on the theodolite. In foggy weather, it can take more than a few minutes to get a sighting on the target, adjusting the knobs ever so slightly. I have never felt cold like this in Ireland. Add some wind chill to it, and you can really feel the cold through to your knuckles. I have a few surveys of rural water-supply systems to finish before the real hard winter sets in up here in the hills – it is better to be doing them at fifteen under than at twenty five under. They say it hasn't reached minus

The Big Freeze: 2005

twenty-five in the last few years in this place. I have heard it said that the last few winters have been mild. I hope this one is too.

* * *

On a lighter note, I went bowling last night in the big Chinese hotel before heading up here. I was with a few folks from Triangle and Concern. I actually won one game after a dismal showing in the first. I am fairly brutal at bowling. In the second-last game, I landed four strikes in a row and a spare, and the points just racked up. 165. I was impressed. I have never hit anything near that score before. In the next game though, I was back to my usual terrible level.

* * *

Back to the present: same old story – the electricity has just decided to get up and go again. I still have some work to do,

Chapter 6

putting data from today's survey into my computer, and am deciding whether to work or continue on with this. I think I will have a cigarette and think about it.

* * *

I got a really nice photo today, of a few kids having a snowball fight outside my hotel. They were on their way to school, in their boyscout-type uniforms with their little red scarves around their necks. They had built walls of snow facing each other, and were lying down behind their respective walls, as if in military bunker. Every so often, one would jump out and peg a few snowballs at, or over, the other wall. It was quite entertaining, until one of them spotted me with my camera. Then they just got up and walked off. There are hundreds of kids out in the snow here in Songchon, compared to very few in Pyongyang. Many of them seem to have improvised skis and sledges of sorts. I haven't seen any of them taking advantage of the hills and going tobogganing – mostly they just amble about on the road, pulling each other down the street. The kids are still saluting whenever we drive by on the country roads, taking their hats off and giving a courtesy bow. They should keep their hats on and stay warm. They do seem to be having a laugh though, hopefully at our expense.

Every kid in the country seems to have the same school uniform. A dark blue, but not quite navy, jumper, shirt and trousers and a red cravat. They all look the same and there are so many of them. There doesn't seem to be any sign of Chinese-style population control policies, though I have heard that more than two is frowned upon.

* * *

It is still cold in here. I have just had dinner, and am very full. Partly because I just kept eating to keep warm. We had *bul-goggi* again – meat, of various sorts, kind of fried or barbecued on a hot plate as you are eating. The soy, wasabi and vinegar dip that goes with it is tasty. Although 'dip' makes it sound a bit grand. Korean food generally is starting to grow on me. Having said that, I was silently happy to get some cold chips today for dinner. It is great to get some spuds once in a while. You can take the man from the bog, as they say, but not the bog from the man. I even drank some *soju*, just to try to stay warm, and it helped. I ate some *kim-chi*, as the vinegar seems to make the cold cabbage into an internal heater. I learned a lesson today though – if I finish my *kim-chi* in one sitting, another plate of it will arrive. I won't be doing that again. My translator had to go to bed, because he was too cold. And these Koreans are supposed to be tough?

* * *

There are a number of non-Korean people making their way into the corporate side of things here in the DPRK. There is one Chinese man who has found a niche in the market for sanitary towels. How he managed to find that niche I don't know, but I am sure it was not through regular market research. There are no telephone polls or Korea-barometer surveys here. Then there is a German man, who loves his whiskey neat and is not afraid to buy a round, who is in the pharmaceutical business. He is trying to break the aspirin market, as well as dealing in a few other drugs that are not readily available in Pyongyang. There is no real corporate market here, though the Koreans I work with are constantly buying aspirin or antibiotics for some illness or other. Those are the relatively well-to-do Koreans.

In Afghanistan, there was a big divide in the humanitarian sector as to whether corporate-sector people should come to the NGO social nights. A bit of a strange stand-off, but I think it was more related to security for the workers in the sector rather than ideological questions. There is a socialistic element to development that is anathema to entrepreneurship. There is not that sort of divide here though, as the expatriates are so few and far between. Whether they are mercenaries, good-for-naughts or the uber-altruistic, everyone tends to get on and mix well. You have much more access and interaction on a human level with

Chapter 6

the diplomatic corps here than anywhere else. Even a relative nobody like me gets to mix it up at embassy events.

The division between the corporate and the aid worker is not the only divide in the aid world. Though I don't know how pervasive it is, there tends to be a clear divide between the international (expatriate) and local staff. It is normal to see a party in a small town, full of foreigners, the majority of them white, and without a single local around. Justifications are often given for this – some of them stand up; some of them don't; and often they could be overcome. Security issues in Afghanistan tended to create a division, or apartheid, when it came to socialising. The religious divide in Islamic states, of course, plays a role. Foreigners drinking and partying, often very blatantly, is only barely tolerated by such states and cultures. When particular groups don't tolerate it, it can lead, and has led, to disastrous consequences.

The whole system in North Korea makes it difficult to have real social interaction. Often there is dinner and drinking, but this is usually work-related with colleagues, and semi-official. You cannot head to downtown Pyongyang on a Friday or Saturday night and meet up with your North Korean buddies. I have ventured downtown, to restaurants where I know I should not really go, and beyond serving me food, there has been no interaction. Language is a problem too, I guess, as only a few get to go to English-language universities and not many get taught English in school. Only once has a student been ballsy enough to come and ask me where I am from. I think that was mostly to impress his friends.

In Afghanistan, certain NGOs were reluctant to socialise with corporate-sector people, or to facilitate the intermingling of 'not-for-profit' and 'for-profit' people. Organisations have to be careful in places like Afghanistan about blurring the line between humanitarian organisations and others who they could be mistaken for. You also have to be careful about contact with the

The Big Freeze: 2005

military. Even if the soldiers are young lads, good fun and only out for some social interaction outside their barracks, there are risks involved. The perception of foreign forces in a country can vary. If the perception is bad, then being associated and creating an impression of being in cahoots is a serious no-no. Even if the military are liked and welcomed, they are still the people with guns. They have to keep the peace, make the peace, or sometimes enforce it, and often fight a war. Local feeling can quickly change with one stray bullet or that awful term 'collateral damage'.

Foreigners, whether aid workers or soldiers, rarely understand the dynamics of local politics. It was only toward the end of my stint in Afghanistan that I started to get a grip on the situation there. Once security threats become imminent and real, your perception changes. A trip I was expected to make one time from Samangan was abruptly cancelled because of some bad vibes coming from a blind local commander – we had refused to dig a well beside his house rather than in the centre of the village. The next day the partners, a local NGO/construction company, drove over a landmine on the road we probably would have driven down. One person died. There, but for the grace of God.

In Afghanistan, there was a big problem with people, including local and provincial government, not understanding the role an NGO played. This created a lot of tension. Profit-making businesses from Afghanistan were able to claim NGO status due to poorly defined legislation, which created bad feeling toward all NGOs. Provincial governors themselves could not tell the difference, and were convinced that international NGOs were taking donor money that should have been going toward rehabilitation of the country. Of course, the governors would rather the funds went through their departments, for good reasons or bad. In North Korea, due to the absence of a genuine corporate sector, the few international NGOs, the complete lack of local NGOs, and the omnipresence of the military, there are no such problems.

Chapter 6

* * *

Some days, surveying can be rather trying. Today, I had Mr Yang, who is not the best translator, along with me. He knew zero about surveying before today. So, trying to give instruction to Koreans, to go here, there, over there, and then there, through Mr Yang, is a challenge. When I ask him a question, he invariably answers, 'Yes,' and then just stands there ... waiting ... until I realise he has not understood what I said at all. I ask him again, emphasising that this is a question, which prompts the reply, 'Yes.' Whether he means, 'Yes, I agree,' or, 'Yes, I don't understand,' or, 'Yes, go away and stop asking me questions,' I have yet to figure out. So he doesn't know what I am saying, and then he tells someone else to do something which is not what I had asked, and the result is a little Korean running around a hill with a red-and-white pole, not knowing what he is supposed to be doing, but knowing he is supposed to be doing something. By the end of today though, three days into working with Mr Yang, it all started to come together. Mr Yang is figuring out how to use the theodolite, and is starting to get a handle on my Irish accent. His instructions to the FDRC officials are getting more accurate. They are all getting the hang of the rudiments of recording the data on the theodolite and sighting the next point. I am learning that if I let them press the buttons, while I run around to the places I know I need to go, then everyone is happy, and the work gets done twice as quick.

Sometimes it tries my patience though – especially in the cold, or when I input the data into a spreadsheet and convert it into points on a map, and then realise the map looks nothing like the town we just surveyed. When six houses appear on the map on the wrong side of a river, I realize ex-poste that there is something wrong with the survey and maybe, just maybe, we need to do it all again. Sometimes it is just my calculations. We got through three surveys over fairly large distances yesterday, and two today by lunchtime, before heading back to Pyongyang. I was reluctant to head back – I felt we were on a roll, and

The Big Freeze: 2005

wanted to keep going. In the end though, with the sub-zero temperatures plummeting further, I was happy enough to leave it all behind until next week. I slept for about an hour of the journey, because I had a terrible sleep last night. The electricity kept going on and off in the hotel. It went from freezing to roasting to freezing, because the underfloor heating is run by electricity. I ran out of bottled water and was parched all night. I also had what seemed like a mild asthma attack in the middle of the night. I am not sure if it can be attributed to the strange menthol cigarettes that I took off Mr Wong. It passed and never came back.

* * *

I have something to admit. At lunch yesterday, I was eating away, bits of roots, bits of cabbage, cabbage soup, sinewy chicken, *soju*, and some other strange meat. Another bowl of meat arrived. Mr Yang said to me, 'Eat that, it's hot.'

I said, 'What is it?'

'It's hot,' he said. So I ate it. It wasn't hot at all; barely lukewarm in fact.

I said, 'It's not hot.'

'Yes it is,' said Mr Yang. 'Dog hot.'

Dog hot? Dog heart.

The food is getting stranger and stranger. It is a few months after the harvest, and I guess stores and stocks are reducing. I don't want, or expect, to get fed well when I am outside Pyongyang and a guest of the various counties. Honestly though, I have no idea what I am eating a lot of the time, and I have given up asking, as I don't understand when someone tells me. I had pine-nut soup the other day. It was quite bland, but it was good to know it was pine-nut soup. I wish I knew what pine-nut is.

* * *

Chapter 6

Just as I was getting a bit depressed, thinking about Christmas passing and an empty Christmas stocking, a DHL delivery arrived from our head office. It contained a lot of nice cards and packages from Mam, Dad, all the many brothers and sisters and some of my old Ethiopia buddies. There was even a litre of strawberry-flavoured milk. It is nice to be remembered; I just hope my cards made it in the opposite direction. That staved off a bit of the sadness, though it nearly made me sadder temporarily, reminding me of all the people at home. It was especially good to get a letter from Dad, as he is not one for sending letters. He said that he missed my impromptu visits, and probably my help with the house, which seems to be coming along nicely.

* * *

My computer just shut down, so I have lost about three pages of writing – my most descriptive, of course, full of hilarious tales and anecdotes, including some of the best insights into life in North Korea. I doubt I will be able to replicate that again.

* * *

I was talking about the local currency before the computer stalled. It is called the Won, and foreigners are not allowed to deal in it. We get to use the euro, or sometimes dollars. A short while back, the dollar was put out of commission here and we were all told we had to use euro. I think that was pretty soon after George W made his 'axis of evil' statement, which, unsurprisingly, didn't go down too well here. The Won is officially exchanged at 160 to the dollar, but the story goes that it can go for as much as 3,000 on the black market. Again, I cannot substantiate this, but it is probable that it is true. The low rate is only maintained officially for some reason.

I have been reading the *Economist Intelligence Report* on the DPRK, which our HQ sent out here with the Christmas DHL package. It makes for interesting reading, though it is a little surreal reading about this place that is part of my everyday life yet still

The Big Freeze: 2005

feeling like an outsider, looking in. The *EIR* made reference to Tongil market, the only market area open to foreigners at the current time. I have yet to go there, but plan to have a look on Monday. It also mentions the Pyongyang Number One Department Store, which is famed for its peculiar brand of false economy. When important visitors come to the country, they are brought there, to see what are apparently lots of transactions taking place. People are busily buying nice items, indicating a thriving economy. I can confirm that transactions can and do take place, and that the skepticism is not entirely warranted, but I imagine that these particular transactions are put on for show.

The *Economist* report referred to continuing political uncertainty in the region, and the precarious relationships the DPRK has with all the surrounding countries – the South, Japan, China, and even countries such as Thailand and Vietnam, which are potential places of asylum and transit for North Korean refugees who escape the country through China. There was a recent DPRK clarion call to all asylum seekers, to 'return to the land that you love so dearly; do not fear that you have committed any crime'. Some who have sought asylum, or have been sent back from a neighbouring country, escape again as soon as possible, telling of the harsh welcome they received on their return. The report also pointed to the lack of an apparent heir to Kim Jung Il. He is now well into his sixties, and there is no one being clearly groomed to take the throne, though he has three sons and a daughter. The impression is that the youngest, Kim Jong Un, is his favourite.

7
Day After Day – Getting Into A Routine

> *The political form of a society wherein the proletariat is victorious in overthrowing the bourgeoisie will be a democratic republic.*
>
> **Vladimir Lenin**

My days have become fairly typical in their routine, though slightly varied in the events that fill them up. I am either working in the office or I am out in the field. If I am in the office, work is from nine in the morning to six in the evening, with a ninety-minute lunch from half-past twelve to two, coinciding with official Korean lunch time. It is a pretty long lunch, but you learn to adapt. I usually go home for lunch – some tea and bread and jam. Sometimes I go to the Diplo – a small group of shops along with a restaurant, a hairdresser, a sauna, a bar and a pool hall, all rolled into one. You can get some nice soup there, and toast. But

Chapter 7

I can't afford it too often, as I am spending a fortune on phone calls. At a rate of five euro per minute, it adds up pretty quickly. Work in the office mainly involves designing rural water systems. I am getting the hang of this quite quickly, so now it's just a matter of seeing if they actually work. Will the water get from A to B, and then to C and to D?

In the evenings, after making dinner when I can be bothered, there is television, sometimes visiting, writing a bit of a letter or watching a DVD, if the cheap Chinese DVDs work. Sometimes I go to the *Friendship* Health Service Centre for a drink. Sometimes I go to the WFP, to check emails or get the football results. Pretty non-eventful really. Not the excellent adventure you would be looking for? This is the controlled environment all foreigners live in here. There is not a lot of room for adventure, though you can push the boundaries of where you can go for a beer or a meal, and open up the city a little bit. I am just getting used to it, but too many people here seem to spend too much time hiding away in the Diplomatic Compound.

When I am in the field, I usually start work at eight in the morning to get a good run at the day. Because the places we stay in aren't too comfortable, there is no point lying around doing nothing. Breakfast is fairly minimal, and lunch can be either in the hotel/guesthouse for visitors to the county, or in one of the farms that we are working on. Dinner is usually in the hotel, and can be absolutely anything. Trips into the country have ranged from one day to one seven-day trip. Work usually consists of checking up on projects or surveying for water systems. Evenings are very quiet. After the formalities of dinner – which can be entertaining or can be a struggle – with some of the FDRC people, they usually try to coerce me into drinking *soju*, which I am only starting to like. Familiarity is not breeding contempt, I am glad to report.

Friday night is usually drinks in the RAC. On Saturdays, I try to do my five-mile run in the morning, usually with a small bit of a

Day After Day – Getting Into A Routine

hangover, and then maybe go swimming. There used to be volleyball, but now it is too cold. I went running yesterday afternoon in shorts and a T-shirt. My fingers had pins and needles from the cold, and it took me about an hour to get back to normal. I am not sure why I do it sometimes. Saturday night is beers in the *Friendship*, Sunday means football at three in the afternoon, and that's my weekend.

* * *

Christmas never ends this early at home. I am back out in Rongchon, home of that big ugly polluting power station, to have a look at a few water systems in the sticks. It is cold out here, and that's one of the reasons that work on these systems is taking so long. It is too cold to do any cement work, because the cement will be weak and crumbly. It is too cold to dig the ground to bury pipe, and it is too cold to be getting wet. So, it looks like these will not be finished properly until the spring, when temperatures start to reach above freezing. I am fed up with the cold already. I was out running in minus-eleven a few days ago. That was cold, but it is a lot colder up here in the hills. Fortunately, there is not much wind, which makes a huge difference, and even more fortunately, it is not bloody raining or snowing. But I have my thermals on and can still feel it in my bones. This type of cold takes forever to get out of your body, no matter how warm the room is. And this hotel in Rongchon is a great big concrete nothing, with big rooms and no heating, so I am not really getting warmed up at all.

* * *

There is a woman from Dublin here, who is married to one of the German embassy people. She wanted to come to the countryside with me at some stage, to see what it is like 'in the field'. She seems to think it would be a great adventure to get out of Pyongyang. It probably is if you spend all your time cooped up in the Diplomatic Compound. Her two children (aged about twenty-four and twenty-one) arrived about a week ago to spend

Chapter 7

Christmas, and I have been taking her son to play football with us. He is a good footballer, better than the rest of us here. She wanted to know if she and the two kids could come with me at some stage, so I said I would see what I could do. I checked with our Liaison Officer, who said that the embassy had to go through its own lines to request this. I told them that, and then it became a little complex – they couldn't go this day, but could go another. I went with it, and told our Liaison Officer, and then they changed again, and made a 'verbal note' (??) through their embassy to see if they could go. I told them I would need to know in advance if approval has been given, and their Koreans would need to talk to our Koreans to sort out the details. But they never got any official response, and reckoned they would only get told if it was refused. This was starting to annoy me, as I needed to know everything was arranged properly. I would get an ass-kicking and it could put the frighteners on the FDRC if I was to turn up unannounced with three strangers in a country town. It could affect our 'freedom' to have regular monitoring visits of our projects, as we have a lot more freedom than some other organisations, especially the Italians.

As time went by, the Germans weren't trying very hard to find out anything. They were saying it would be okay, only wondering whether they could take photos or not. I had heard nothing concrete, and our Liaison had heard nothing at all, but the Germans were asking me what time we would leave at. I had to say no, not until I got confirmation in the morning before we left could I say whether they could go or not. In the morning there was no sign of our Liaison, and at 9:30, around our anticipated departure time, I called the German embassy and they were only out of bed. 'Ah, sure, we will cancel it,' we decided. As it turned out, the Central FDRC had informed the FDRC in Rongchon that they were coming, and they were surprised when no Germans turned up. They had got the message that there were diplomatic people coming, and an entourage was arranged to meet them. They got only me.

Day After Day – Getting Into A Routine

* * *

On Sunday, I found a magazine in one of our offices called *Juche 93*. It is currently year ninety-four on the *Juche* calendar, which commences its chronology at the year of the birth of the Great Leader. One article in the magazine was about great North Korean sports people. One of these was a footballer from the 1960s, a member of the team that beat Italy in the World Cup. Another was a wrestler, and the last was a marathon runner who won gold at the World Championships in Seville not too long ago. According to the article, after sixteen miles this runner was in third place, behind a Japanese runner and a Russian. She had an injured ankle and was hitting the wall. She felt that she would surely collapse, but then the image of the Great Leader came into her head. She saw him and felt restored. Feeling great love for him, she ran on, overtook the Russian and finally ran past the Japanese, who had been the favourite to win, just before the finish line.

* * *

One of the most fun days so far was had yesterday. A few of us drove down to Morambong Hill, with some old, inflated tractor-tyre tubes. We took turns 'tobogganing' down the hill on the tyre tubes, having races, sledding down head-first, even bringing Kiki, the little dog that has been adopted by an aidworking couple, down sometimes. It was a bit strange. There weren't too many Koreans around. The few that did pass by didn't really pay us any mind, except for a few kids who were too scared to have a go. There were a few small shrubby plants that had been recently trimmed along the side of the path, and I hit them a few times. I even put a little puncture in my thigh, but it was so cold I didn't notice until I got home and started to thaw.

* * *

The electricity in the hotel has just got up and left again, and the battery in this thing only has thirty-seven minutes remaining. Today I feel like I have a lot to say, even though I am tired and

Chapter 7

very, very cold. I like using this quiet time in the field to catch up on my writing, and to get a good night's sleep if it isn't too cold for sleep. Fingers crossed. Legs crossed too, because it is too cold to be getting out of bed to go to the toilet.

I had to drive an employee of the Laos embassy home from the *Friendship* last night, as he was blind drunk. He was trying to drive his rickety old Volvo back to his embassy, but couldn't seem to coordinate himself. He would be a danger to himself more than anyone else, as there wouldn't be a soul on the roads at that time of night in Pyongyang. I drove his car, with him in it, to his embassy, parked it up and got a lift back with a helpful Croatian who followed us down. The car had the strangest gear system I have come across, and a light flashing on the dashboard that ominously read 'brake failure'. I chose to ignore it, and he fell asleep instantaneously for the duration of the five-minute journey. I drove slowly.

* * *

I should probably spend some time describing the North Korean landscape. The countryside in places is quite spectacular, as the country is approximately eighty percent mountain. I could attempt some flowery prose on the interlocking spurs and the undulating valleys, but in truth, there are so many places, and places in Ireland too, that are on a par, or more spectacular, that it would be false to be fawning for the sake of fawning. Sometimes, when you wind up a mountain pass and finally get to the top, you can turn around and look down on a vast expanse that can be pretty impressive. But the nature of the mountains does not allow for views over great distances, such as you would get from the top of a mountain in Afghanistan. Korea seems to be made of endless rolling hills, with scrub-lined mountains here and there. The little trees hugging the edges of the hills add a shivery, slightly unreal quality to the view. Perhaps it is because I am accustomed to the spectacular mountains from my time in Afghanistan that I don't appreciate them as much as I should.

Day After Day – Getting Into A Routine

Perhaps it is because I associate mountains with the twenty-mile walks I used to have to do, up and down the hills of Pushti Ban to visit projects, that I associate them with cold and mud and tiredness. The novelty of spending nights in small, isolated Afghan villages, getting fed and watered by really hospitable people who had never met me before, ought to create a favourable impression of mountain terrain. That is one of the most admirable parts of Islam – the requirement placed on people to give travellers food, shelter and safe passage to the next village. It certainly made my life easier on cold winter days. There were days that oily rice and flat brown bread, despite what it would do to my digestive system, was the most welcome meal in the world. The fried eggs with sugar even went down well once.

It is so cold now that the tunnels we have to pass through are covered with stalactites, hanging from where water drips through cracks in the concrete. Some are up to four metres in length, deadly if they were to drop on an unsuspecting cyclist. Not being used to such cold, I am taken by the formations of the ice in different places. Sometimes I see a sort of plume of ice, in a fantastical shape, teardrop-esque though much larger, which has been taken by the current, floating down a stream like a giant leaf.

Sometimes water that is flowing shallowly over a surface freezes, and then more water flows over the new ice and freezes again, creating a layered effect that not only looks unusual, but which creates a strange refraction when you look through it. It can be spectacular and eerily beautiful, and can be up to a few feet deep. Then there is snow-covered ice, which looks safe as I walk briskly down a hill. Then, as on one occasion only last week, I realise there is no traction and find myself skating for tens of metres, trying to keep my balance, much to the amusement of the Koreans. There are also dams, holding frozen-over lakes and reservoirs, making huge ice rinks. There is one I think I should stop to look at on my way back in a town called Unsan, to see if

Chapter 7

it will hold my weight, and to see if the water continues to flow underneath the ice or not. It is funny to see all the little Korean children, on their improvised skates and sleds, whizzing across these masses of water. I want to have a go, too. There can be hundreds out at once on a frozen dam. They don't seem to slide down any hills, though, and I think I finally figured out why. Every hill and slope, wherever you look, is ridged and terraced for planting and irrigation. There are no nice, grassy, snow-covered slopes to slip down. Any tobogganing would be a bumpy ride.

* * *

I just noticed again today, as I did in Songchon last week, that the faces of the towns are changing, even in the short time I have been here. Maybe it has to do with the seasons, or the time of year, but there seem to be many more street-trading stalls in the towns. Market areas seem to be very peripheral, well away from the centres of towns, but there are definitely many more of them than before, with much more bustle in these little areas than anywhere else. The stalls are very basic, selling grain or chillies, and maybe cigarettes. A lot of shopfronts seem to have been restored. Maybe it is a subjective thing, but I don't think too much emphasis is placed on aesthetics just yet in places outside Pyongyang. There doesn't seem to be much interest in preserving the unique Korean building style. The main street in Pyongyang got a total makeover over last year, and the highlight of this was that all the buildings got lovely new PVC windows and doors. Many of them got painted in a variety of pastel colours as well. There are an increasing number of shops in Pyongyang, and an alarming amount that only seem to sell alcohol.

In sharp contrast to all of these spruced-up buildings, I have just come back from a health centre that we are providing water to, and refurbishing slightly. It has plastic, like that off a polythene bag, for windows, with most of them torn, and only one bed (with no mattress) for patients. It is in a terrible condition, and

Day After Day – Getting Into A Routine

from what I could see, its only claim to be called a health centre is that the health centre manager, a medical person of sorts, works there. He was out on his rounds when I arrived. Some of the conditions in institutions are pretty appalling, especially in critical service areas like health.

* * *

I have been getting a little more daring recently, driving just that little bit further each day into different places. I have adopted the philosophy that in this country it is easier to apologise than to ask. Within reason. It is only a little thing, but it challenges me to do stuff I normally wouldn't do here – taking a chance when deciding which streets not to drive down, which shops and restaurants to go into, where to linger and where not to. The little market places are more and more interesting, because I don't usually get to see them. Nothing seems to happen when I stop by for a wander. I don't have any local money and these markets don't take dollars, so I cannot do any buying. Sometimes I feel a bit like a ghost, as people tend not to let on that they see me, yet I know my presence is felt. I guess it makes people a little nervous. There was one market with little wooden stalls, like the ones in Knock on the way down to the car park, selling meat and rice and *soju* and other little things. People along the side of the road selling cigarettes are becoming more common, which to me indicates that there is some illegal cigarette smuggling going on. Far be it for me to speculate, but I do anyway. Such criminal activity may mean that people are taking more risks, which may possibly mean they are less fearful. Perhaps the grip of the State is weakening. On the other hand, it could mean that people are merely more desperate, or that the illegal sale of things like cigarettes is being tolerated as a necessary evil, to let steam out of a pressure cooker of hardship that is building.

I even drove to the edge of the city a few times, but chickened out of going any further. The city seems to end very suddenly, and people need permission to enter and leave, with checkpoints

Chapter 7

on all roads in and out. Being foreigners, with Korean drivers and translators who work for the Ministry of Foreign Affairs (MoFA), and because we are registered to travel on certain days, we don't get hassled at these checkpoints. Sometimes we have to show travel passes, depending on the seasons and the mood of the system. The FDRC and MoFA people we work with are very much subject to the whims of the army and the Military First policy. Were I to pass them in either direction on my own on a weekend, I reckon there would be trouble. One time, I went driving out of the city northwards, and all of a sudden found myself on a big, three-lane dual carriageway with no options for turning. I was getting a bit worried as I passed the Mausoleum, and kept going for about two kilometres more. With fields all around, eventually I reached a roundabout. Relieved, I spun back towards the big pointy thing that says something about the Great Leader in Korean and acts as my compass on this side of town.

Every time I travel outside Pyongyang, usually approaching a big town, I see people pushing or pulling bockety old carts. These carts are often full of big bags of maize, or absolutely loaded with cabbages for *kim-chi*. Often it is a withered old woman, dragging a cart up hills and then down hills, wheels wobbling in and out; a terrible-looking task. The stone roads are far from smooth, and the hills are steep and long, winding their way up the sides of mountains. They are a struggle for a Toyota Landcruiser at times. If it's not an old woman, it's an old man pulling the cart, bent double, putting his full weight behind it, maybe with his wife walking in front trying to drag them along. It is not too long since we were doing work like that in Ireland. Not too long, but the country has changed a lot since then. I wonder sometimes whether Irish people, as they get wealthier and more materialistic, will be able to empathise with poorer countries, without any personal experience of the poverty and hardship that is experienced in places like this.

Day After Day – Getting Into A Routine

If people aren't pulling carts, they are carrying bags on their backs, be it a sack of wheat, a bundle of sticks or a baby. Women with babies on their backs seem to have a government-issued hooded coat that covers mother and baby. They make a strange picture from a distance, a lot of 'hunchback' women in red coats walking the streets. There are also many old women and men who seem to be extremely physically crooked, probably from years of hauling up and down hills, and from years spent bent down, working in rice paddies.

I have been reading *Angela's Ashes* by Frank McCourt over the last few days, full of descriptions of poverty in the Limerick and Ireland of the 1930s and 1940s. There seem to be many similarities with the North Korea of today. This is especially true for town dwellers, living in ten-by-twelve-metre apartments and relying on the public distribution system (PDS) for regular food, with few other alternatives for subsistence. The PDS is not like the dole, providing a back-up in times of difficulty. The PDS has to cater for everyone. It is not social welfare, but a State-imposed

Chapter 7

system of redistribution. When it is empty, well, you can't make something from nothing.

There are different levels of wealth in the DPRK. The majority of the population are in the lower sections, and even the middle classes are struggling. When government-controlled services cease to function, huge numbers of people suffer. And it is not possible for the people to protest the poor performance of the State. They can't vote for the opposition, and they can't form mass demonstrations, whether they would want to or not.

* * *

Today is the type of day when I feel I am wasting my time being here. I could be doing something more worthwhile, somewhere that my skills could be put to better use. I don't feel like there is any major pressure on me. In fact, life here is almost comfortable. I don't want to be comfortable just yet. I want to be under pressure, pushing myself. I am too young to be coasting. It is a weird place to be living, with many restrictions, and the work can be frustrating, but the hardest bit is that it can be dull. Mind-numbingly so from time to time. Take last night as an example: I went with a couple to a restaurant, a nice one, for beef and duck *bul-goggi*. It was nice, and we had a beer or two and came back and played darts for about two hours in my flat, and had a few more beers. I went to bed at midnight, then rolled into work for nine. I sat at my desk most of the day, designed a few water systems, detailed them, and headed home at around six. I could be living just like that in Dublin or Galway. It is good to be doing the water systems for people that need them. The water pipes will probably make some positive difference in their lives, maybe reduce the drudgery a little. But I don't feel that I am necessary to the work here. It would get done without me. I want to be where the difference is a difference that wouldn't be made without me. Perhaps that's selfish.

8
The Man Behind The Stories

Let the ruling classes tremble at a Communist revolution.
The proletarians have nothing to lose but their chains.
They have a world to win. Proletarians of all countries, unite!

Karl Marx

Before I came to Korea, I had very little idea of the place – the people, the politics or the system. I honestly could not have told you when the Korean War took place. I didn't even know that M*A*S*H was set during the Korean War. My knowledge was limited to the quirks of the country, and its leaders, that were reported in the news. Just before leaving for here, my minimal research dug up lots of interesting 'facts' about Kim Jong Il:

He was apparently born beneath a double rainbow in the north of the country, though more informed sources believe he was

Chapter 8

born in Siberia. It is said that his birth was prophesied by a swallow; he produced a 100-part documentary; he is scared of flying and always travels by train, thus apparently narrowly missing the Ryongchon explosion in 2004; like many height-obsessed politicians, he wears high shoes to make himself look taller; he could walk when he was three weeks old; he scored eleven holes-in-one, for a round of thirty-eight, in his first game of golf; he wrote over 1,000 books while at university; he loves films, and has a huge collection. Apparently he had two South Korean directors kidnapped to make a monster film for him. He likes cognac, Hennessy in particular. He can control the weather. He has a lot of official titles in North Korea – aside from being the Lodestar and the Dear Leader, he is the Guiding Sun Ray, the Great Sun of Life, the Invincible and Ever-Triumphant General, Generallisimo, Our Father and more. He is leader of just about everything in the State apparatus – Supreme Commander of the Korean People's Army, Chairman of the National Defence Commission and General Secretary of the Workers' Party. He has never been president, because Kim Il Sung is the Eternal President.

I have just read the last chapter of a biography of Kim Il Sung, written while he was alive. The level of propaganda that people here are forced to ingest is incredible. Can people really be taken in by this? This last chapter is the summation of three volumes on the life of the man – how Korea had such a complex and unusual problem in its quest for independence that it took someone of the genius and intelligence of Kim Il Sung to make it all happen. No living man could have carried the country to the glory of the present day, it claims. He defeated America and its stooges, and successfully imported a Marxist-Leninist doctrine into the country, adapting it to the principle of *Juche*. He is now acknowledged around the world, in countries such as Cuba and Libya, as the greatest Marxist-Leninist revolutionary ever (this is around 1987, I think). Then he had to pull the country through the post-revolutionary phase, and he successfully did this in a

The Man Behind The Stories

way that no other man could do. He had to deal with usurpers in his ranks, and people who tried to sway him from his path. This he successfully completed like no other man could do. He set about the development of the country, transforming it into one of the most glorious countries in the world. It must have changed a lot since the book was written.

* * *

Since I stopped smoking, I am eating non-stop and am in danger of getting fat. I spend too much time in the *Friendship* - my *Cheers* Bar, where everybody knows my name. Somehow the waitresses have decided my nickname is 'yoangii', short for 'coyoangii', meaning 'cat'. It is kind of endearing. I sit at the bar and everybody greets me with, 'An yong ho sim ni ka, yoangii tong-mu,' which means, 'Hello, Comrade Cat.'

* * *

No smokes. Only beer and fingernails. And crisps. But no smokes.

The last week has been the most stressful and longest of my time here, all because I am not smoking any more. Time really does go slowly when you are thinking only about cigarettes. It can drag. But I can't. I find I have little or no attention span without the smokes. It is worst at work, because those convenient cigarette breaks have been taken away, and there is nothing to fill the gaps. No matter. It is for the best. I am just starting to cough up all those months of tar now.

* * *

I went swimming today for the first time in a while. I swam ten fifty-metre lengths and I was wrecked. That's not very good. Then I spent fifteen minutes in the sauna. I am not a big fan of saunas, but after a few beers last night this one was welcome. Then I decided to get a haircut, Korean style. As well as wading pools and the individual baths that Korean people seem to like, the swimming-pool complex houses a barber's shop (with a lot

Chapter 8

of barbers) and a beauty parlour. The last time I went to the barber, I wanted to get my head shaved, but the woman refused to shave it, adamant that it had to be cut with scissors. It took an hour, non-stop. Snip snip snip snip snip, like watching *Edward Scissorhands* in action. It was the same this time.

After leaving the pool, I cursed myself for not having my camera with me. It was a really good day for photographs. For some reason there were hundreds of kids out and about, maybe on a school excursion. There were kids on ice skates, skating around on the compacted snow in an idyllic little park with stone landscaping. They skated in circles around a big fountain, lots of them on what I would describe as uni-skis, like a mini sled with only one blade. Crouched down on their hunkers, two feet on the homemade ski, they propelled themselves along with little sticks with nails in the bottom of them. I spent a nice hour walking around, simply observing the city and its people. I don't usually take time out to do it. Lately I have been watching too many DVDs in the evenings.

There was a woman outside one big building with a Pooh Bear teddy perched on a chair, and a display of photos a few metres away. She was taking and selling photos of people posing with the big teddy bear. Different places, different ideas.

We went for a burger in a fairly new restaurant, which I will call *KimDonalds*. Apparently the big man was in Russia recently and had a Big Mac. He liked it so much, he commissioned his chef to make him one, and then decided that a restaurant selling burgers should be opened. When we got in there, five waitresses were crowding around the only heater in the place, laughing at me ordering everything in poorly practised Korean. I had a beef burger, a chicken burger, fried chicken and fried potatoes. Big deal, says you. BIG DEAL, says me. Simple pleasures, but that was the nicest burger I have ever had. They skimped a bit with the meat, but were very generous with the cheese. No one ever

The Man Behind The Stories

seems to go into this restaurant, and I don't know how it stays open.

* * *

I was annoyed with my boss the other day, when he was complaining (he complains a lot) about the woman who cleans his house. These people are called *domos*, derived from *domestic*. He was worried about a big tender for pipe materials that we are in the process of preparing, and the *domo* was trying to tell him where she put the cooking oil, in case he needed it. He was very disdainful, saying that it is amazing what some people lose sleep over. I don't think he understands that if he was to complain that he couldn't find the oil, she could lose her job in an instant. The cooking-oil issue was more important to her than our half-million-euro tender is to him.

* * *

It is an awful thing to live without dreams and aspirations, as I feel many people here live. But when it is the only life you know, and you are not exposed to any alternative life choices, I wonder is ignorance a good buffer? Does it help to make life more bearable? When you have a little, you want more. If it is outside your grasp – you know it is there, and other people have it, but you can't – perhaps that is worse. Life is living you; you are not living life. I wonder what kind of dreams for the future a Korean teenager from a work farm has. With so few options, is there more or less chance of disappointment and disaffection?

* * *

Two days ago, Tom, my boss, and I had the privilege of being allowed to visit a motor factory in the DPRK. This was not a motor factory as in Skoda or anything like that, but industrial motors for water pumps and the like. Outside there was a big mural of the old man visiting the factory to give on-the-spot guidance. I am not sure what he would have told them, but I imagine it was something along the lines of 'make more', or

Chapter 8

'work faster'. The factory looked how I imagine Irish Spinners in Kiltimagh was years ago – a big, warehouse-type building, with great industrial cranes and huge transformers, dark and gloomy, really greasy and outdated-looking. But that's me speaking from my Irish viewpoint, where health-and-safety practices have dictated the quality of workplaces since before I ever had a job. It would probably look familiar to someone a couple of generations ago. There are no unions to stand up for the rights of the worker here. You do what you are told and that's that. It is supposed to be a Workers' Party and a workers' paradise. I wonder.

Not many foreigners get to see the insides of such places, and Tom pondered why we were being allowed to see the place. The truth is, of course, that they think we are going to spend twenty grand on their motors and bits and pieces for our programmes in Songchon, so they gave us a glimpse inside. However, we weren't allowed to view any of the motors or the starting compensator that we were hoping to see in action. There are a number of pump stations in Pyongyang using this equipment, but not even our Liaison Officer is allowed to visit, as they are considered security-sensitive for some reason. Pump stations? Seriously? I imagine the problem is that they are all in a great state of disrepair, and the Koreans don't want us to see this. They like to give the impression that Pyongyang is thriving. Pyongyang is not thriving.

I had to laugh when Tom wanted to know if it was the only factory of its kind in the DPRK. Of course they weren't going to tell him it wasn't. He was probably hoping for directions to a competing factory. Not that it really matters, as they are all government companies, producing what they are told to produce. It was interesting that, when asked, they were able to give us prices for various items in euro and dollar, so obviously they were expecting us to be purchasing. Considering that they should only be dealing in Korean currency, and should really only produce on government demand, this was quite unusual. I

The Man Behind The Stories

do not know the internal workings of all of this, but I am sure the chance for the factory to get access to hard currency would be an opportunity not to be sneezed at.

* * *

I will have to start Korean lessons soon. I keep postponing them. I have heard stories of foreigners learning with government-appointed teachers – you couldn't possibly find your own teacher. Apparently the methodology is very regimented and slow.

* * *

I think I am getting acclimatised. It was minus thirteen today, and I really didn't feel that cold. There was no wind and that's a help, but compared to a week or two ago, this feels practically mild.

* * *

I keep missing out on big celebrations in the city centre. There was another a few days ago, marking the new year. About a quarter of a million people were in Kim Il Sung Square, doing I don't know what, but that's the second mass celebration that I have heard about retrospectively. Apparently there will be a sixty-year anniversary celebration of the founding of the Korean Workers Party sometime this year, which I am told will be huge. There is some other milestone anniversary this year – something about the greatness of the Korean army – but I am not sure what it is or when.

* * *

Zlatan was showing me pictures of a beach in a place called Wonsan. It looks quite nice. To go there, however, I would have to go through the usual palaver of getting permission from the various government factions. There is also a beach in Nampo, only forty-five minutes' drive away, near that pump factory I visited, but it isn't quite as nice as the one in Wonsan. It is really

Chapter 8

just a stony inlet, but within the limits of where foreigners can travel unhindered, unaccompanied by Korean colleagues and without the need for permission. Many of the beaches facing Japan are closed off from the public, and the coast is apparently mined, so I probably won't be doing much swimming there.

* * *

Today I am tired and cold. I spent the afternoon playing football. Well, I spent most of it standing around in sub-zero temperatures, waiting for people to turn up. Eventually we had seven for a game with small goals, but it was hardly worth it for the sake of the hour and the quality of the football. I had the misfortune of getting hit on the side of my head with the ball when I wasn't expecting it. Not only did I look stupid, but my ear was already practically frozen. It's still ringing, and now it is hot and red. That was four hours ago and I am still struggling to get any warmth back in my bones. Even though it was freezing, I managed to break a sweat. After a while, the sweat at the edges of my hairline started to freeze, and I had a halo of ice-sweat around my head. Strange.

When I had thawed a little, I went walking around town, ambling in and out of alleyways and making myself noticed. I spent a few hours sitting on the steps in Kim Il Sung Square, reading to myself and discreetly watching the world go by. The square is right beside the Ministry of Foreign Affairs, and who did I meet? Only our Liaison Officer, who has to work in the Ministry on Saturdays, doing much of the fixing for our work the following week and probably filling in various files and forms on who did what, and who said what to who, and when.

Then I went to get some provisions. There are a few shops in Pyongyang that we can shop in, and there seem to be more and more all the time, so I presume I haven't seen them all yet. There are a few Japanese-owned shops, where I sometimes find cereal, and nice, but expensive, food. There isn't much of a selection though, and as I am too lazy to cook most of the time – bangers,

The Man Behind The Stories

beans and mash excepted – I don't usually buy much. There is also an Argentinean shop, which is fairly popular and sells random stuff, like kitchen utensils, cosmetics, some foodstuffs and beer and wine. Then there is the Rakwon Store, which was the only one yesterday to have any milk in stock to have with my cereal. I was about four weeks here before I found any cereal, and when I finally got some, there was no milk anywhere, until yesterday. I had eaten the Frosties in dry form over a period of about two days (small boxes, I promise), and most of the Choco Crispies. Now I have the milk, but no cereal.

I remembered to bring my camera with me today, and I was determined to take pictures of as many billboards, murals and mosaics featuring the Great Leader as I could get away with. In the end, I only took a few, as I am a bit nervous. First, I went down to near the swimming pool to see if I could get any photos of the kids skating. They must have known I was coming, as there was no one there today. Off I went to the Theatre, and parked up outside it. There was no one else parked there, but that's not unusual. I don't really know yet where it is acceptable to park, or not, so usually I just see what I can get away with.

By parking there, I attracted some attention. A big black car pulled up fairly close beside me, which was a little unnerving. I ignored it, and took a picture of a big mural of the big man on the theatre front wall. Then I moved along, noticing that someone was watching me at a distance. I wouldn't normally notice, but I was bit self-conscious because I was taking photos. My senses were a little heightened, and I wondered if maybe I was wrong about this Korean watching me. I went over to the Pyongyang sports hall, where a lot of teenagers seemed to be knocking around, and I aimlessly wandered about, looking at the soldiers marching. They weren't really soldiers, more like reserves, but they had military uniforms on. They were stopping to take photos of each other with a snowman in military garb, and were as amused by me as I was by them. I didn't dare to take photos of them taking photos of each other.

Chapter 8

Off I went back to my car, and no sooner had I sat in it than the other car pulled away and parked at the end of the car park. I was planning on going to the statue of the Great Leader to take a few photos, but when I pulled out, so too did the other car. I decided I would go for a spin to see if he really was following me. Lo and behold, for a few miles through the city he stayed a safe distance behind, and then just disappeared. I kept driving, out toward the west end of town, until I came to the place where I had had my driving test, on the road to Nampo. This is a huge pointless ten-lane highway, with a few little cars on it and lots of pedestrians. I headed back into town. I wasn't going to drive on that road with so much ice around – I would have some explaining to do to my boss and the Koreans if I came a cropper ten or twenty kilometres outside the city.

Feeling quite happy with myself, I carried on driving in the direction of the big rocket-shaped building. This is apparently 105 stories high, but has been sitting half-finished for the last ten years. It is a great landmark for getting my bearings in the city – it stands out a mile because it's such an ugly monstrosity. I suppose it could be quite impressive if it was ever to be finished. Maybe.

After passing the big rocket thing, I drove past another place I hadn't seen before. A quick turn and spin around, and I saw that it was a lavish memorial garden commemorating the Korean War. As I walked up to the entrance, I was met by a guard, talking in Korean at me. I hadn't a clue what he was saying, but it was something along the lines of, 'Where are you going? What are you doing?' After a lot of gesticulating, he let me by. I suppose, given that it was a landmark war in the history of the peninsula and the Cold War, and that the North Koreans are under the impression that they defeated the might of the American army, the Memorial Park is justified. As with all the other military propaganda, with the incessant calls to fight for the country against 'America and its stooges', to 'protect the fatherland' and so on, this is just another attempt to manipulate

The Man Behind The Stories

the people with rhetoric and exaggeration. Perhaps it is no different from what you see in most countries, even in Ireland with its own Garden of Remembrance and monuments to Wolfe Tone and the rest of them. There are monuments in London and the States commemorating military achievements. Even the current state-building project of the EU is pushing to revise its own history, gradually erasing national discourse and replacing it with a completely secular, pan-European narrative.

Korean nationalism is being moulded through the re-writing of the tale of the formation of the North Korean State. This is used as a means of maintaining the status quo, of keeping the people down and living in fear, in need of a fatherly figure to keep them safe. In the DPRK, there is no space for an alternative. Discussion and debate is not stifled; it simply does not exist. This is what you are given, and you have to accept it. However, unlike the statues of George Washington standing to attention, or Wolfe Tone looking into the mid-distance, the statues in the park are really impressive. They depict Koreans, teeth gritted, fists clenched, dragging cannons up a hill, mouths shouting, arms raised, muscles pumped, veins bulging from arms and eyes bulging from sockets, men and women fighting for the cause of … of … Korean reunification, I think. But I am not sure. The biggest statue at the end was of a soldier, not dressed like a soldier, but in farming clothes, gripping a Korean flag and calling back, beckoning his comrades on. Tongmu. Many Koreans address each other as Tongmu, meaning comrade.

Duly impressed, I thanked the guard for letting me in, just as I saw a wedding party entering the garden for photos in front of the monuments. I gesticulated to see if they minded me taking their photo, and they weren't bothered. It is the norm for newly-weds to go to the statue of the Great Leader, present flowers, take photos, and then amble off to some of the other great monuments for memories of their special day.

Chapter 8

I still had plans to go to see the Great Leader, but I kept getting sidetracked along the way. Moving on down the road, I ended up facing the Arch of Triumph. This sits right beside Kim Il Sung Stadium, where the DPRK play their home international soccer games. At this stage I was not lost – I knew where I was – but I didn't know how to get home.

After pausing to think for a few minutes, I parked up and went into a small restaurant near the junction. The little old lady inside looked a little stunned to see me. I don't think she knew what to do. This was definitely not a place that catered for foreigners, so I quickly said, 'An-yong-ho-ga-ship-sii-oo,' before backing out the door, more for her sake than mine. She may have had a heart attack.

I still intended to go to see the big guy, but ended up going through a tunnel that I had never been through before. This brought me out onto a road I hadn't been on before, yet everything around the road was familiar. I was close to the city centre, and near the Diplomatic Compound, but something looked different. Somehow the road was higher – the roads I usually travel on go under this road at junctions. It felt really strange, like I was on a different level, and not just physically … As I was in no hurry, I followed the road, and it turned into another ten-lane highway, with not a soul nor any cars on it. I kept going for about five kilometres, past high-rise apartment block after high-rise apartment block, until all of a sudden, this huge road just ended. Abruptly. I had no choice but to turn back. The road was so wide and empty, I was able to practise handbrake turns on the ice for about half an hour.

I was still on a hunt for propaganda billboards to photograph, and I spotted one off this big road, so I took a slip road that brought me onto another unfamiliar road. I was far from familiar territory, and didn't want to travel outside city limits, so, as the road was quiet and quite empty, I decided to U-turn. No sooner had I turned than I saw a traffic cop, in his deep blue uniform (it

The Man Behind The Stories

wasn't one of the pretty lady traffic cops), indicating for me to pull in. He gesticulated in the way that all cops do, indicating that I shouldn't U-turn. I just nodded and agreed, and sat there, while he said it again in Korean. I could see he was wondering whether I had a clue what he was saying. Then he just walked away. So I waited, and waited, and then drove off, only to meet another traffic cop a few kilometres down the road. He pulled me over at a junction, and I was thinking, 'Oh feck, I shouldn't have driven off.' This guy was gesticulating excitedly. It looked like he wanted to talk to me, but in fact he was trying to tell me to turn off my headlights. In Sweden, the law states that you have to drive with your dips on during the day. Here it is the opposite.

It was still only two in the afternoon, so I decided, to hell with it, one last chance to go and get a picture of the big guy. I finally found my way there, parked and strolled up to the statue, not

Chapter 8

entirely sure if I needed permission to be there. There were a few wedding parties, all paying their respects, and a few other random visitors. Normally when you visit, you buy flowers and lay them at his feet. No chance of that, I just wanted to see how big the statue really was. The location of the statue is probably its best feature – though it isn't a landscape-dominating monument, it stands slightly higher than everything else. The big hammer-sickle-pen monument is about two kilometres away, in a direct line across the river from it. The big guy looks out over the south of Pyongyang, the father of the motherland. At night when it is lit up, it is, along with the *Juche* Tower, the dominant feature. Everything else is in darkness.

Beside the statue of the old man, there is a statue of a horse called *Chollima*, the great Korean steed of legend that could cover 400 kilometres in a day, or something like that. It was a great symbol for the Korean people at the time of the Korean War. To compare anything to Chollima, or to address something or someone with the adjective Chollima, is to say that they are extra fast, or possessed of a superior quality, a type of verve. I was hoping to get a photo of me giving the big man a high five – using perspective – but that's for another day, when there is someone with me who isn't Korean to take the picture. I don't know any Korean who would appreciate that. Sightseeing for the day done, off I went to play football in the cold.

* * *

I was reading a bit of the young lad's book today – the young lad being Kim Jong Il. It is called something like, *Why it is Still Great to be Socialist*. It is an unending diatribe about how Leninist Marxism was a great idea, but it was flawed because it didn't take *Juche* into account; and how *Juche* is about the masses; and that the masses have the power to decide history. This is the philosophy Korea is built on. Some of what I was reading was written in 1990 for a speech. The young lad says the future of socialism in Korea is assured, because the people live in a

The Man Behind The Stories

country without fear or worry, and that it is not totalitarian, as described in the West. Abuses against socialism must not be tolerated, he says.

In the DPRK, there are numerous little restrictions and controls on the people, that seem to exist to make life that little bit less easy – like randomly placed barriers, and laws restricting travel, such as who can and who cannot drive a car on a Sunday. Music blares out of little minivans driving around the city early in the morning, pumping out *spirit-lifting, chest-thumping* music through megaphones as people get ready for their day's work. I don't know if there is truth in the rumour that there are household, State-issued radios that cannot be turned off – the volume can be lowered, but not quite to silence, so that the propaganda is unceasing and inescapable. Individual choice seems to be taken away here – there is no religion; no vote; no choice.

The book goes on to say that the Government must ensure that it nurtures the proper people, who are totally in line with the socialist *Juche* idea, so that it will continue to prosper. The reason socialism fell in Eastern Europe, the young lad argues, was because of compromising, weak-willed people, along with stooges of the US in the hierarchies of these systems. That cannot happen here. There can be no perestroika or peaceful abandonment of socialism in Korea. The highlight of the book has to be where he says that the *Juche* idea states that it is the masses who decide history. It cannot be driven by one leader. This is a great irony, coming from the cult leader of a country where free will and decision-making are hugely curtailed.

I cannot wait to read the rest of it. Then I'll have to read the old man's *Reminiscences*, another great work in three volumes. It should be interesting to see whether there is any intelligence in the writings, because to do what the old man did – to build his leadership and establish his immortality – there had to be something exceptional about him. He was certainly no fool, and he wasn't a puppet for someone else's agenda. Certainly, good or

Chapter 8

bad, he was his own man and created his own legacy. Maybe he was just a thug and opportunist, but in the end, it was him and no one else who ended up as Eternal President. I am hoping the book will reveal a bit more, but somehow I don't think I will be reading the deepest thoughts of the man.

I couldn't find anything in the writings of the young lad to suggest he inherited any sort of exceptional ability. Nothing he has said so far gives any idea of what *Juche* really is either, apart from saying that man is in charge of his own destiny, and that *Juche* is why socialism will not fail. He says it is a great idea, and, 'Down with American imperialism.' Marx had a Communist Manifesto, with some form of a shape to its ideas, however flawed. What do the Kims have? I have yet to see.

9
Inspiration For The Masses

Communism needs democracy like the human body needs oxygen.
Leon Trotsky

I have started reading a book, by an economist called Marcus Noland, discussing the possible outcomes of the current situation in the DPRK. He thinks there are three possible outcomes that can be achieved:

1. The collapse of the system in the DPRK, and chaos ensuing; people feeling aggrieved both about the life they have been living for the past fifty years, and the lies and manipulation that have been taking place.

2. Reform in the DPRK, and the opening up of the economy in a slow and careful manner, slowly reviewing systems of operation, both economically and institutionally.

Chapter 9

3. The current governmental set-up in the DPRK 'muddling through' the current 'crises', coming out the other side intact, and tipping away for another forty years.

The future will require muddling through with the tacit support of China. It would be unfair to say that the DPRK rode on the back of China previously – for years, the DPRK was economically and developmentally far ahead of any part of China, with living standards higher, and health, education and life expectancy far more positive. As Mrs Ri told me, they looked down on the Chinese as being dirty, uneducated and uncultured, and generally a lesser species. In fact the North Koreans had, and still have, a superiority complex. This is fed by propaganda such as the New Year address by Kim Jong Il a few days ago, which I found fascinating.

The speech revolves around the *Juche* idea and *Songun*, the *army-first* policy that exists in DPRK. Throughout, the young lad insists on the maintenance of the status quo in the country. The opening paragraph is this:

Now, our army and people are entering on a grand march of the new year with an emotional retrospect over the glorious victories of the Party and revolution and a great optimistic view of the bright future of our thriving nation. Last year Juche 93 [2004] was a year of fruitful endeavours that made a fresh breakthrough in the building of a great prosperous powerful nation by launching a revolutionary offensive on the three fronts – political-ideological, anti-imperialist military, and economy and science.

There are numerous phrases like this, saying very little in terms of fact:

Last year saw a fuller display of the faith and will of our army and people who, rallied around the leadership of the revolution, were determined to move on straight along the road of the Juche revolution opened up by President Kim Il Sung.

And then lots of this sort of stuff:

Inspiration For The Masses

The whole country was brimming over with a high political ardour to live and work in the same spirit as in the 1970s when the ear of the Workers' Party attained the highest stage of prosperity under the banner of modeling the entire Party and the whole society on the Juche idea. The ample demonstration of the might of the WPK's Songun politics and the overall strengthening of single-hearted unity of the Party, the army and the people – this is the most valuable achievement.

One of my translators asked me to give my opinion of this speech. What am I supposed to say? 'It's great that the single-hearted unity of the Party, army and people has been strengthened.' At least the speech acknowledges – albeit circumspectly – that things have gone downhill since the seventies.

One scary element is the promotion of what is called the *soldier culture*. Sometimes I wonder if intelligent adults listening to this take it seriously. One has to remember that the North Korean state was born from war. It started as a military movement to oust Japan, became socialist under the influence of mother Russia, and developed in the 1950s on a wave of emotion. Defeating, or at least not being defeated by, a number of powerful armies, an independent State was secured and the destroyed country was restructured. But the times have not been allowed to change. These military ideals, relevant in the search for independence, are still maintained, and the lie that the war is still on is maintained and used to fuse the people's spirit:

The revolutionary soldier culture developed in the People's Army has passed through the whole society, so that everywhere the militant spirit and zeal are throbbing and our work and life are permeated with greater joy and optimism.

Even the industrial fervour that played a central role in restoring the country is being kept alive on artificial respirators. Heavy industry, the rock on which the country progressed initially, is still being held up as the way forward:

Chapter 9

The key fronts of the national economy including the power industry and railway transport witnessed a rise in production which was rarely known in recent years.

It all seems so dated and antiquated to me, but as the Koreans know nothing else, it is merely a continuation of what has been said over the past fifty years. Considering much of the population knows little of how the external world has moved on from the era of heavy industrialisation and dated methods of production, it could nearly seem rational. A similar line is taken regarding agriculture:

… great progress made in carrying out the Party's policy of bringing about a radical turn in seed production and the rapid promotion of large-scale land realignment.

There is something to be cheerful about when the leader mentions that,

… gravity-fed waterway projects have laid solid foundations for striking development of agriculture in the era of Songun.

This is a departure from the mentality of having industrial-sized pumps feeding water systems in every single little village – a system that is not sustainable, and is unnecessary in a country with an abundance of mountain springs. The young lad gives other snippets of advice to various sectors of the country:

The power, coal and metal industries and the railway transport sector should advance in high spirits in the vein of the effort to effect an upswing. The construction of large-scale hydropower stations should be accelerated to bring earlier the day of their operation, coal production be put on normal track and the capacity of thermal power generating facilities be raised to increase power generation markedly.

So now everyone is under no illusion as to what is expected of them. Do more, faster, and better. Simple, sound advice. Your country needs you. *Citius, Altius, Fortius.*

Interesting also is a brief mention of the light industry sector:

Inspiration For The Masses

The light industrial sector should reconstruct and update factories and produce a variety of high-quality consumer goods in large quantity.

Light industry, and a move to consumer-based products, is clearly not given the same importance as heavy industry like steel, construction or mining. Farming is particularly promoted, unsurprising given how the country is struggling to bridge the food gap:

Agriculture is the front of main efforts in socialist economic construction this year. We should concentrate all our efforts on farming this year. All the people should subordinate everything to farming and supply manpower.

On the way home from Namchong, Mrs Kang pointed out to me how all the work teams are taking this invocation seriously, holding New Year natural fertiliser-spreading competitions. There are red flags all over the countryside, identifying the boundaries for each competitor. Whether this is because the people feel inspired by these wise words I don't, and can't, know. Probably they are holding these competitions because they are told to by the work team managers, who are also following orders from above. What little guy is going to resist the call of the Dear Leader?

A large section of the speech is devoted to the army and its merits. In fact, most of the speech revolves around the army and *Songun,* and it attempts to create the impression that the army is actually fighting battles and doing something:

The brilliant victories and successes attained by our army and people last year are fine fruits borne by leader Kim Jong Il's absolute authority of leadership and ever-victorious political ability.

If they are fighting wars, then the international media are not picking up on it. Maybe it is us here in the capitalist West that are being lied to?

There is a great love of slogans evident in the speech. Kim Il Sung had to come up with many slogans during his lifetime, and

Chapter 9

the practice has been maintained, with the following slogans being adapted for the year ahead:

Party, army and people, give fuller play to the might of Songun in single-minded unity!

And the slogan for this year's national reunification movement:

Let us hold high the banner of cooperation for national independence, peace against war, and patriotism for reunification!

The speech emphasises the 15 June 2000 Joint Declaration, as a historical moment on the road to reunification. I'm not sure what the Joint Declaration was, but Kim plays on it like it is a joint statement of both peoples that they want to come together as one. He also uses it as ammunition to throw at the United States:

It is the nation's intolerable disgrace that the other half of the country's territory has been subject to the violation of sovereignty by foreign forces for over a century [forty-odd years of Japanese colonial rule, and then apparently 60 years of US military occupation]. Last year our army and people resolutely foiled the crafty moves of the United States to stifle the DPRK.

Well done, boys.

But I think my favourite part has to be Kim Il Sung's founding of a union called the 'Down-with-Imperialism' Union:

President Kim Il Sung brilliantly accomplished the cause of founding the revolutionary party of Juche type on the strength of the deep and strong roots of the Down-with-Imperialism Union.

This year is the sixtieth anniversary of the liberation from Japan, and the founding of the Korean Workers Party. There will be dancing at the crossroads and big marches in the Square this August. The tone of the address sounds antiquated to my ears – in European countries we are not accustomed to hearing such rhetoric any more. But I would imagine that if you took a North Korean out of Korea and parked him in front of our politicians and leaders of society, he would see through some of the inanity

Inspiration For The Masses

that we have been weaned on. Some of the self-evident truths that our societies are gradually becoming blind to would be obvious to a society that continues to value the family and the old, and responsibilities as much as rights.

* * *

I was struggling this morning when I went running, feeling a little the worse for wear after another Friday night in the *Friendship*. I think the repetition, as well as the drink, is starting to dull my brain. Another Saturday mid-morning run, and the streets are absolutely choc-a-bloc with Koreans, going here, there and everywhere. Human traffic seems quite organised: people walk on the footpath; people cycle and drive on the right-hand side of the road, with very few exceptions. People pulling and pushing big heavy carts follow suit. It is impossible to run on the footpaths, because of the crowds, but also because they are made from little square concrete tiles that are subsiding irregularly and deadly dangerous for the ankles. It is a battle of wits and widths sometimes with the crowds, as I am forced to dodge whatever they are carrying on their backs, or avoid cyclists that veer in my direction. One day I was running past a tram queue, and about six men decided to spit about a foot in front of me as I passed. Call me paranoid, but it was a lot of phlegm. Kids tend to stare at me or laugh, which is fine, and some soldiers have even given me a wave while they are standing around. Sometimes when I run past Korean runners, going considerably faster than me in the opposite direction, they acknowledge with a nod the sad state I am in. They run fast. I plod. One day I was even wolf-whistled by two Korean girls, which I thought was nice. It sounded like a wolf-whistle anyway. To my ears. For me.

* * *

The DPRK has been drawn in the same group as Japan, Bahrain and Iran for the final stages of the World Cup qualifiers for the Asia region. They play Japan in Japan at the end of February, and home games against Bahrain and Iran in March, right when I am

Chapter 9

going to be in Thailand. Then they play Japan some time in June, and there is no way I am going to miss that game. That will be an emotionally charged match, to say the least. Forget Windsor Park – this will be a cauldron of a different colour. I can't wait.

I was out on one of my solo drives around the town, looking for somewhere new to eat, when I saw the lights on in the Kim Jong Il Stadium, the second of the two Pyongyang soccer stadiums. I had never seen the floodlights on before, so I drove over, parked up and wandered to the entrance. I was stopped from going in, and thought that this was game over for me, but when I was about to turn away the doorkeeper said 'dollar', and I realised that I was expected to pay to get in. I gave two dollars and walked in. There was a game on, with only a small, fairly disinterested crowd watching. It was cold and the stadium seemed to be acting like a wind-tunnel. After some gesticulation and miscommunication, I managed to discern that the DPRK under-seventeen national team was playing against an army team. This was the under-seventeen team's preparation for the Asian games or something. The army team won three-nil. I left, cold but happy with my new adventure.

* * *

Kim Jong Il is sixty-three now, I think. No one really knows what he is like. Some of the people who were close to the first family of the DPRK and have managed to get out of the country have written books describing the man, but they end up being quite contradictory. He is fairly reclusive, and apparently is keen on Cognac. Madeleine Albright reckoned he was on top of everything when she met him, and that he covered his brief quite well, though she thought his plans for economic improvement in the country were a bit absurd. She didn't say what exactly they were. The BBC states:

A series of recent memoirs by former cooks, a bodyguard and the sister of one of the lovers of North Korean leader Kim Jong Il have all served to conjure up a lurid portrait of a mercurial and extravagant dictator.

Inspiration For The Masses

I think perhaps that this could sum the man up quite well. He is known for his love of Hollywood movies, and is said to have kidnapped a South Korean director and his wife in 1978, to make films for him. He likes dancing girls. He likes burgers. He has a few kids, though no one is sure how many, and has had them by various different women. It is unconfirmed, though widely accepted, that his apparent favourite consort, a former army troupe dancer, died from cancer a while back. He has two sons with her. His first wife suffered from depression and died in Russia, I think.

* * *

I finally found the Catholic church in Pyongyang. I didn't have the nerve to go looking by myself at Christmas, and was a little too shy to ask around. It is quite strange that this even exists, because it is well known that there is little religious freedom in the DPRK. It has been described as having a system of enforced atheism. There are a number of cases of chaplains who used to be in the DPRK, who have since gone missing. I was told about a book by a priest, one Father Crosbie, who was taken by the socialist North forces during the Korean War as the Northerners retreated. He spent three years in captivity, and the book is called *Three Winters Cold*.

The church actually looks like a church. It is fairly big, and inside there is an altar. The Stations of the Cross are there, and there is what looks like a tabernacle. There is no priest, but there are three lay people who look after the place, and they have a Korean Bible and a Missal as far as I know. A guy here, who grew up in Yugoslavia in the time of Marshall Tito, says it was much the same there, though not as bad as here. In communist Yugoslavia, Catholics were looked on as 'black sheep', and there was no open religious practice. There might be Christmas and Easter Mass, and a celebration of certain other days, like the feast of St Anthony. But like here, a lot of it was State-managed farce. This church is really here so that the Korean authorities can say,

Chapter 9

'Look, we have a church. We don't stop people practising religion; they just don't want to.' There is supposed to be a prayer meeting at ten every Sunday morning, so I will have to check that out. A word in my ear reckons that if I go to the church, my next visa extension will be refused on some pretext or other. It will be interesting to see if that happens.

* * *

I am off to Japan tomorrow, for a week. Brilliant. I am tired and feeling sick, and I want a break. I went bowling last night in the Yang Dak Doh hotel, the big Chinese hotel in Pyongyang. Zlatan scored 205 in the last game, a record for foreigners here, two days before he leaves for good after nearly four years here. It is a nice way to go, especially as he seems to be struggling with moving on to somewhere new. A nice guy, who helped me settle in here more than anyone else when I arrived.

Zlatan is being replaced by an old Englishman – forty-nine, wife, one kid – who will be leaving his family behind and living in the 'team house' with me. It will be interesting to live with somebody again, but he'd better be a bit of fun. I won't be able to play my loud music loud and throw stuff around the place like I usually do.

I am also becoming a parent for the first time. I am taking responsibility for Kiki, the little ball of fur that belongs to Zlatan and Ninh, once they leave. He is a small, white, fluffy dog that I will have to feed and water every day, bring for walks and clean up after. I may look a little effeminate walking this poodle-esque mongrel, but I'll just have to deal with that too. I can hardly look after myself, so I don't know how I'll manage with a dog. Maybe a bit of responsibility will be the making of me. I doubt it, and I pity the dog.

* * *

Just before I left for Japan, Zlatan and Ninh had a little farewell party. It was in the Old Diplomatic Restaurant, and was just for

Inspiration For The Masses

our office. I thought it would be very emotional, as the pair of them have been here for so long – Ninh almost eight years and Zlatan about four. All in all, everyone was quite sad, and the dreary North Korean music did not help. The restaurant did not help either. It is an old place, and used to be only for diplomats, before there were aid workers in the country. Everything is dark red, musty and bleak. It was a sombre affair all in all, a night that could have done with a couple more beers to help put people at their ease. I was glad to be heading to Japan the next day.

* * *

I am back at work after a nice, relaxing holiday in Japan. Actually, no, I didn't find it that relaxing most of the time – it is quite an intense place, with lots of people, cars, noise, traffic lights and bright neon signs. Everything is packed into small spaces, and there is very little greenery. Interestingly, it seems that people in Japan have as little idea about what goes on here in the DPRK as the people here have about Japan. Most of the Japanese I met seemed quite nervous asking me any questions about this place. One of the girls wanted to know if the people were still starving here.

Mostly the immediate question was about some Japanese citizens, mostly in their twenties, who were kidnapped by North Korea and never seen again. I was asked if I had seen any Japanese people here. Nope. Would I be able to tell the difference if I did? Nope. Everyone I spoke to was quite surprised to hear that I am living in North Korea – none of them had ever met anyone who had been here before. It is nice to be a novelty. Mind control was something they all seemed to have a bit of a fixation with. None were interested in a trip to the DPRK.

* * *

I went to the post office yesterday to post a few letters. This is usually a simple process, but not this time. One letter was slightly bulky, so the woman behind the counter wanted me to open it. I

Chapter 9

did so, and when she saw two pairs of socks in it (gifts from Japan, though I did not tell her that), she just handed it back to me and wouldn't take it. She was just talking away at me in Korean, and I was talking away at her in English, getting quite annoyed. I asked her to reseal the envelope, seeing as it was her that had asked me to open it. She refused, and then sent me to another woman further down the counter, an employee with equally as little to do. I was getting annoyed, and a girl from the German NGO was laughing at me for getting annoyed. Usually I don't display emotion. The second woman looked at the parcel and pointed to customs, and I went down there to a man who didn't speak any English. He looked at my letter, in tatters at this stage, and wouldn't do anything, not even go and talk to the women at the counter. I went back to the second woman to remonstrate again. This time, she took the package and wrapped it neatly in brown paper. She got me to address it again, and gave me a little label in French that needed a signature for customs clearance (why it was in French I can't fathom). I went down to the customs man again, and he refused to talk to me. He eventually went back to the first woman, and got me to sign the label. He stamped it, and I filled out another French-language form, writing 'socks' on the customs label. This entire time, one Korean woman was laughing at me, because I was in a T-shirt and it was about minus five outside and no warmer inside. I was starting to shiver with both cold and rage. She thought it was funny, which it was ... in hindsight.

* * *

My adopted dog keeps barking at people outside the apartment during the night. I am not sure how this relationship will develop.

10

The North, The South And The Economy

Communism is the perfect system, in theory. As are Monarchy, Fascism and Democracy. The only reason they don't work, is because of human nature to pervert the situation into the best one for them.

Samuel Webster

In Japan I spent a lot of time travelling on high-speed trains, and when I wasn't staring out of windows I was reading *Avoiding the Apocalypse: The Future of the Two Koreas* by Marcus Noland, which, as I mentioned, has some ideas on what the future may hold for the peninsula. It contains some interesting facts and figures relating to the two countries. It made me realise that I am quite ignorant about South Korea, probably even more so than I am about North Korea. South Korea in my mind has always been quite a developed country – similar, I would have thought, to

Chapter 10

Japan in terms of technological advancement. From reading the book though, it seems that Japan and South Korea are worlds apart. This observation, however, is based on a five-day visit to Japan and extracts from an economics book, and so should be taken with a pinch of salt.

The South Korean government was, for a long time, very closely linked with the major conglomerates in the country, and also with many of the financial institutions. This created an unsustainable and uncompetitive financial situation, to the initial benefit of the major conglomerates. There were four main ones, mostly names you would be familiar with: Daewoo, Hyundai, Kia and Lucky Goldstar. These conglomerates, or *chaebol*, owned, operated and dominated most sectors of the Korean market, from electronics to automobiles to the plastics industry. The streets are full of Daewoo, Kia and Hyundai cars, and nothing else. Only recently have foreign companies been allowed to compete in the Korean automobile market.

South Korea was, for a long time, a military state. Numerous coups resulted in changes in government and successive undemocratically elected leaders. Until recently, in some respects it was not dissimilar to the DPRK. Though it wasn't a socialist state, it had very restricted and corrupt market practices, which eventually led to its downfall and economic crisis. The enduring Asian economic crisis, at the time of writing, is putting such a social strain on South Korea that the people are losing interest in reunification with the North. The economy is the number one concern. Nationalism is gradually becoming a dated concept in a globalised world, and promoters of national solidarity are antiquated in the modern positivist discourse. That is not the case in North Korea, where there is no real affluence among the populace. The vast majority of the people here have not known wealth or comfort. They have not been able to enjoy the fruits of modern technology or of someone else's labour. Life has been the same for a long time, and reunification remains the overriding priority. A united Korea is still viewed as the

The North, The South And The Economy

Motherland. Estimates from economists (and economics mean very little to me) suggest that, given the difference that existed between the two countries in 1999, the cost of bringing the North into line would be an investment of $60 billion per annum over ten years. Needless to say, the gap has widened considerably since then, with the South more prosperous, and the North still in decline.

South Koreans, when surveyed, showed only a passive interest in reunification if it was going to be at a personal cost to themselves, leaving the quest for reunification in the hands of the North. I met a South Korean when I was walking up Mount Fuji, and had a bit of a chat with him after he got over the initial shock of meeting someone who lived in Pyongyang. He said that he would like a united Korea, though he didn't seem too wildly enthusiastic. He was more concerned with getting to the top of Fujiyama. As was I. I didn't make it.

* * *

I have started smoking again.

* * *

I stumbled upon a huge public mosaic today, showing a great big Korean bayonet skewering a United States soldier. Quite violent, but it tickled my black sense of humour. It is not too different from some of the graffiti adorning the walls and gables of Belfast or Derry.

* * *

When dreaming up, or modifying, the legend of the Kims, the propaganda machine seems to draw very heavily on Christian symbolism. When Kim Jong Il was born at Mount Paektu (he wasn't really born there; he was born in Siberia), it is said that three guiding stars and a swallow appeared to an old man and guided him to his birthplace. He is described as 'superior to Christ in love, superior to Buddha in benevolence, superior to Confucius in virtue and superior to Mohammad in justice'. What

Chapter 10

a really nice guy. He drinks too much apparently though, and watches more cinema than those others.

A strange story I came across recently recalls when Kim Il Sung decided that every person in Korea should have meaty soup. He came up with the great idea that everyone should have hens. Then everyone had to buy hens, but the hens ate all the grain meant for the people, because there wasn't enough chicken feed. Then the big man said that worm and maggot production had to be increased to feed all the hens, and so worm and maggot farms were set up all over the country. Twenty years later, it was eventually deemed that everyone had had meaty soup. Sometime.

* * *

That big spaceship hotel I talked about earlier, half-completed and destined to a future as an eyesore, is called the Ryugyong Hotel. It has been inspected and deemed irreparable. I find that hard to believe, and a terrible shame. At the moment it is solid concrete and is still standing. I am not sure how the inspectors came to conclude that it is structurally unsound. I wonder what the Koreans think of it – whether they have any opinion on why it is in the state it is in, or if they are in any way embarrassed by it. The Koreans I work with understand the economic woes of the country probably as well as I do, though we probably have different assumptions as to their causes. The prevailing view here is that the United States and its stooges are undermining Korean industry and the economy, resulting in the hardships affecting the poor and the middle class. This narrative filters down and resonates with the masses, fuelling further resentment of the imperial powers.

* * *

Another inappropriate edifice here is the West Sea Barrage, the longest dam in the world. This is causing the Taedong River to silt up, and contributed to the flooding that so badly affected the country a few years back. It is a very impressive sight – you can drive out to the dam and along the eight-kilometre barrier, with

The North, The South And The Economy

the sea on one side and the river on the other. The barrage is designed to regulate the river and its tidal action. However, it has virtually reduced the Taedong's flow to stagnation, causing the river to deposit its silt load far upstream instead of carrying it out to sea. The river is filled with sediment as far back as Pyongyang, more than forty kilometres inland. There are cranes on the river in Pyongyang, dredging the sediment for gravel. It is loaded onto trucks and taken away for building works. The river is no longer navigable even by the smallest boats.

The Taedong is now extremely static, and tends to freeze over. At the same time, the Barrage attenuates the tides in the area, so the sea tends to freeze in a really unusual manner. While the river on one side freezes flat, the sea freezes almost in wave shapes, as the ice breaks due to the wave and tide motion beneath it. Huge

Chapter 10

chunks of ice stick out of the sea in parallel at twenty degrees to the horizontal.

* * *

The DPRK invented its own synthetic fibre, called *vinylon* or *binylon*. The authorities then built a huge factory, the biggest vinylon factory in the world. Apparently there are others in China, but this factory is the pride and joy of the country. There is one more factory underway, but looking like it will never be finished. The fabric is really only suitable for mops in my opinion. I have also heard that it is not a discovery of the DPRK, but a stolen idea. Again, this is unsubstantiated.

* * *

Much of the oft-lauded development of the DPRK is now being undone. The country is finding out that its rise is now unsustainable, with vanity projects and reliance on heavy industry leading it on a one-way trip to ruin. According to national news, the way forward and out of the present mess is to emulate the army's 'undying and absolute sacrificing spirit'. This is similar to a motto from the South in 1968: 'Fight while working, and work while fighting.' It could be argued that the North is following the example of the South Korea of the 1960s and 1970s in pursuing *Songun*, its military-first policy. The two countries weren't too far apart until very recently in terms of development and living standards. It could also be argued that rigid military rule in the South paved the way for a managed economic boom in the late 1980s and early 1990s. This argument could hold some weight regarding China too. It is debatable whether following such a path could work for the North in the way it did for the South. I don't know.

The country will need to learn about 'development' economics (a woolly discipline of a woolly science) and all that goes with it. At present, these things are not taught in universities as a learning discipline, only as a study subject, often qualified with the dangers and evils of such approaches – how they exploit the

The North, The South And The Economy

weak, perpetuate feudalism and keep the workers of the world downtrodden. I don't know how open the country is to a more rational approach to economics. In 1997, a group of students travelled to Australia to learn economics. On returning from their studentships, they had to undergo 'intensive re-education'. I wonder what that involved.

*   *   *

The Korean Workers Party says:

Our own style of revolutionary planning law, which thoroughly bars the wind of economic liberation, and reflects the immovable will of the party, the state and the people ... will deal a heavy blow to those who plan to destroy the socialist economy.

That quote comes from *Rodong Sinnum*, the newspaper of the Central Committee of the Korean Workers Party. They are pretty sure that the collapse of the Soviet Union and the Eastern Bloc was the result of giving an inch, allowing a little opening of the economy through *Glasnost* and *Perestroika*. The Koreans say they will never give that inch. The dogma is that total avoidance of outside integration is what is needed to maintain socialism 'in our own style'. This is ironic, given that there are small markets, selling foreign goods, opening up across the country, in big towns and small.

North Korea has not been the most reliable when it comes to paying its debts. The State has defaulted several times on loans, even after requesting rescheduling on a number of occasions, and now they use the nuclear issue to try to wangle further concessions, whether through more loans, debt write-off or food aid. The nuclear issue is being used as a stick to get carrots from its neighbours and from the US. In response to other states and the 'international community' complaining about them and their inability or unwillingness to pay debts, the machine states:

It is a morally negative thing to make bad rumours about a few pennies of debt in this country. If you lose this time, you may gain next time.

Chapter 10

Worth noting is that there is a conglomerate of DPRK business people in Japan, known as the *Chochongryun*. This group was set up in 1955, and apparently sends more money back into the DPRK than the Gross Domestic Product of the country at the moment. Many of these people left Korea soon after the Second World War and the Korean War. It is reckoned that there are 8,200 of these business people, and some more who have moved back to the DPRK with Japanese wives. Those who have moved back cannot now visit their homes in Japan, a situation that further heightens tension between the two countries.

There is a lot of bitterness in the DPRK regarding the colonisation of Korea by the Japanese. The Koreans, North and South, rightly resent how they were treated under Japanese colonial rule, and this will be a bone of contention for a long time into the future. Japan has already compensated the South somewhat for the damage it caused, and the North is expecting something similar. The Japanese refuse to pay this while North Korea remains as it is: a belligerent state. This refusal to pay compensation is used by the North Korean State as further propaganda to keep the populace bitter. The Korean propaganda machine, which was headed up by Kim Jong Il for many years, is happy to fuel this animosity and maintain the great rift between the two countries. It can engender an upswing in military fervour every so often, when the Japanese say something that can be deemed belligerent.

The militarists of Japan are thirsty for revenge to make up for the defeat.

I learned recently that a few American companies have wanted to go into business in the DPRK, but were persuaded, partly due to the US 'Trading with the Enemy Act', not to do so. If North Korea were to be removed from the official list of US enemies, it could help to further the Six-Party Talks in the region. Removing their name could act as a concession to appease Pyongyang, and might gently encourage them to move a little on the nuclear issue. The countries involved in the Six-Party Talks are the

The North, The South And The Economy

DPRK, the United States, South Korea, Japan, China and Russia. China is generally considered the DPRK's closest ally, a type of cajoling Big Brother. People wonder how much longer China will remain patient with Kim Jong Il, and when it might change from cajoling to some tough love. The DPRK has long reneged on loans, insulted the Chinese and generally leaned too heavily on their goodwill. The Chinese are increasingly trading with South Korea, to the extent that trade with the North is not now nearly as important. The *realpolitik* of this scenario is that China is probably now more concerned with maintaining relations with the South than the North, outside of maintaining regional stability.

* * *

Another rumour I can't substantiate, but that is repeated regularly, is that the DPRK sends thousands of workers to Russia to work in what are supposed to be appalling conditions in logging farms in Siberia. The Korean State seems to place so little value on its own people inside the country that the logging companies must feel that they have free reign to do as they wish with them.

* * *

Whether the South actually wants a union with the North is an ongoing topic for debate, and could render the possibility of a North Korean collapse irrelevant. Its absorption into the South may just not be countenanced by the people of the South. The longer the separation goes on, and the wider the economic, and also social and cultural, gap grows, the more difficult it will be. As it is, the South struggles to absorb the small number of North Koreans who escape through China into their society. How much would it upset the fabric of the country to attempt to integrate this very different society? And is the South strong enough, economically, after the much talked-about collapse of 1997, to absorb the mess that is the DPRK?

Chapter 10

In present joint economic ventures, there is a small and cosmetic, but increasing, interaction between the countries. There is the tourist venture at Mt Kumgang, in which South Koreans get a chance to go to the North, though in a very controlled environment – this venture seems to be coming to an end now. There is also talk of Hyundai developing a Special Economic Zone (SEZ), to generate capital in the North. During the build-up to the Hyundai-organised Mt Kumgang project, the CEO of Hyundai drove 500 cattle through the DMZ as a gift to the North. This was followed by a number of cars. The North Koreans later stated that the cattle died very quickly, as they had been fed plastic, vinyl rope and nails prior to being driven to the DPRK. Hyundai is the leading *chaebol* in trying to start business ventures in the North. Not everyone in the North is keen on this interaction. Hyundai's efforts are being characterised as a Trojan horse by the DPRK authorities. This is possible, but I think that the high rankers have to be seen to be taking this stance, politically, though they realise that the country needs the money.

The thing is that there isn't a huge amount of money being made anywhere else. There is suspicion that the foreign currency the DPRK does make is coming from weapons and missile sales, to the likes of Libya, Egypt, Pakistan, Congo and Syria. Reports vary on the amount of money the DPRK is making from the missile trade, anywhere from one billion to five billion dollars per year. This would make the DPRK the fifth-largest arms exporter in the world. I don't see how they could be doing that much and getting away with it. Considering the state of the army personnel I see marching along the hills and streets, it looks like the only arms they are exporting are their own. All of this is unconfirmed, and it still wouldn't be nearly enough to bridge the gap and allow for sufficient food imports to feed the people. Economists are clear that investment from outside will be far more effective than the missile trade, which is probably just lining the pockets and stomach of li'l Kim.

The North, The South And The Economy

I have also heard that money is being made through the drugs trade. I was really surprised by this, as I haven't seen any sign of poppies growing around anywhere I have been. I saw a lot of poppies in Afghanistan, often hidden behind rows of cotton, but I have not seen a single one in Korea. That said, I haven't seen one fiftieth of the country. For some theorists, the drugs trade is the reason why so much of the country is inaccessible to foreigners. To me, this is more credible as a reason why there are so many areas restricted to foreigners, and North Koreans, than arms and missile depots all over the place. Only recently, some DPRK embassy representatives were arrested in Turkey on suspicion of drug smuggling. By 1999, more than forty North Korean diplomats had been cited as being involved in drug smuggling operations around the world, many of them comical, botched attempts. There has been speculation that the DPRK is the world's third-largest opium producer, way behind Afghanistan and Burma. The only drugs I have seen in North Korea were a few lonely marijuana plants growing inoffensively in the Diplomatic Compound, unnoticed by most.

Allegedly, counterfeit money is another big industry. There was one former Red Army official, from the DPRK and carrying a North Korean diplomatic passport, stopped in Macau, in a North Korean naval convoy, with $200,000 in counterfeit notes. Another official who was caught is reported to have been director of 'Bureau 39', an 'X-Files'-type government department in Korea, responsible for li'l Kim's personal funds. It seems that counterfeiting is something the United States is very interested in – they suspect that the DPRK is involved in the reproduction of super-notes: one-hundred-dollar bills that are very difficult to detect. There is also suspicion of an Irish link in this.

I was at an artist's shop in Pyongyang where there were very good reproductions of the *Mona Lisa* and old religious paintings, including Caravaggio's *Doubting Thomas*. *The Last Supper* was there too, and quite expensive at that. It would seem that any artist here would have to be quite brave, and this old man is one of the

Chapter 10

few who has managed to survive until now. Apparently he used to work in Russia, drawing cartoons and caricatures! The nature of Korean art, which is essentially reproduction, seems to provide a good basis for counterfeiting. Some authentic Korean communist art, such as on the enormous murals, is very impressive though. The men are always depicted with strong jaws and broad shoulders, and are very intense-looking.

Artists here are controlled rigidly. They can do reproductions of the classics, but only a few are allowed to create representations of the Dear Leader and the Great Leader. There are strict guidelines on how each of these should be represented in art, and anyone not adhering to these guidelines risks serious repercussions. Every household is supposed to have State-issued pictures of each Leader on their walls, and another picture of both together. When images of the leaders appear in a newspaper, everyone has to be very careful that these images are not damaged in any way. There cannot be any tears crossing the bodies of the leaders. I am not sure whether folds are permissible. I have read about someone getting in serious trouble for standing on a coin that had the Great Leader's face on it.

11

The Nuclear Issue, Kidnappings And The Pyongyang Times

But if thought corrupts language, language can also corrupt thought.
George Orwell, 1984

A major debate regarding North Korea at present is on the nuclear issue: what are the intentions of the country? What nuclear capabilities exist already? Are there real plans to produce nuclear weaponry? Is it a bluff, or should it be taken seriously? These questions dominate the narrative surrounding the country. No one is really sure of the answers.

It is well documented that the DPRK has a certain capacity to manage some aspects of the process, and they may slowly be getting to the stage where they could be functional as a nuclear

Chapter 11

state. There are a few different missiles in development. They have some short-range ones that worry Japan and the South. Then they have some longer-range ones that people reckon could reach the States, or Alaska at least. These are called Nodong and Taepodong missiles respectively.

The Koreans fired a missile directly over Japan sometime in the 1990s. The US had to tell Japan about it, as the Japanese had no idea what was happening. Apparently, since the end of the Second World War, they have had no defence or detection systems in place. The incident definitely scared them. There is debate over why the Koreans did it. Some reckon it was to remind people that they have the capability. Others think it was an error – it wasn't meant to happen at all; a result of a trigger-happy technician. Others believe it was a sales pitch, to demonstrate to potential buyers what was on offer. It may have simply been a test. The North Koreans say it was a scientific satellite launch, and that hymns to the Great Leader are now being played in space from this satellite.

Three light-water reactors have been long promised from the United States, under the 1994 Agreed Framework, in exchange for ceasing the development of nuclear capability. Suspicions abound that the DPRK will use these after a time to aid production of weapons-grade plutonium or uranium, in some way or other. I don't remember how that works – I do regular-water work, not heavy- or light-water. The Agreed Framework was a framework of intent. Rather than a contract between the DPRK and the United States, it was a tacit understanding that the States would fund the construction and initial operation of the light-water reactors (LWRs) if the DPRK shut down its graphite reactors (which are suspected of being used to manufacture weapons-grade nuclear materials) and agree to abide by the Nuclear Non-Proliferation Treaty.

Yongbyon is the name of the place where everyone reckons all the nuclear stuff is going on. There are satellite images of what

The Nuclear Issue, Kidnappings...

looks like a serious piece of work. Nuclear inspectors have been there, though I am not sure what they found. There is nothing conclusive, but impressions are that technically, the place seems to be fairly modern and capable. I will have to ask our Liaison Officer if I can go there. I wonder if he would see the funny side of that request? I am told you don't usually get kicked out of this country officially – your visa is simply not renewed if you stir up trouble.

The US has claimed that certain sites were missile-testing spots; the DPRK has responded that these areas are 'military recreational areas'. The US remarks are 'slander and blaspheme Korea' apparently, and the Government here has demanded that 'they must of course pay reparations for the slander'. The DPRK seem like opportunists, seeing what they can get in terms of concessions, and how far they can push things using the nuclear issue as leverage. They seem to be doing quite well with this approach. After the missile launch over Japan, the US warned that another missile launch would have 'serious consequences'. The DPRK responded that the person who said this was a 'crazy war maniac'.

* * *

I was out running this morning and saw one hundred identical buses, numbered from one to one hundred. They passed by in numeric order, carrying a lot of Koreans, from where or what I don't know. There were traffic-cop escorts with them, who were as amused and baffled by me, in my shorts and T-shirt in sub-zero temperatures, as I was by their entourage and accompanying propaganda vehicle. It was like an Enda Kenny convoy a few days before a general election in Ireland. Everyone got out of their way.

* * *

There was an accident today playing football. At the *MayDay* Stadium, Mario, an Italian agronomist, got tackled by a Polish person whose name I don't know. He was in a lot of pain. We

Chapter 11

brought him to a Red Cross doctor, who didn't even leave his apartment to look at him. He just said to bring him to the *Friendship* Hospital, the hospital in the Diplomatic Compound. I did not even know it existed. We went there, and had a bit of a language-barrier problem, trying to get the receptionist, and then a doctor (he looked more like a patient, with a limp, so we were beginning to wonder why we were brought to him) and then a nurse to understand the situation. We eventually dragged the nurse out to the car to see Mario lying there, in agony, and she figured out what we wanted fairly quickly after that. Unfortunately the 'x-ray' doctor was not there, so they cleaned the small cut on his leg, gave him some antibiotics and painkillers and agreed that he should come back tomorrow for an x-ray. I don't think it's broken.

* * *

My new flatmate has arrived. George, a forester from England, moved in with me last week, and stayed a day before deciding he wanted to go live where Zlatan and Ninh used to live. I like to think it wasn't because of me, but I'm not entirely sure. He said he couldn't cope with living with Kiki (my dog, who has been living with me for a few weeks now, and has managed to poo and pee and puke all over the place, to the extent that I am seriously thinking of letting him off his lead next time we go for a walk. He could be dinner for some needy family). George thought the dog was lovely at first, and cooed all over him and laughed and played with him for a few hours. When Kiki made a mess on his bed on consecutive days, he changed his mind. I had warned him to close the door. George was ruining my attempts at training the dog by laughing all the time, and encouraging him up onto the wrong couch. One of them clearly had to go.

Kiki gets me lots of attention when I bring him for walks downtown, and can be an ice-breaker with severe-looking Koreans. Today, when we went walking, I saw lots of shops that I wanted to go into, but I don't know if I am allowed. It is always

The Nuclear Issue, Kidnappings...

a bit frustrating, because I see things that I want to ask about every time I go down a new road, but I have no one to ask. I can't really ask Koreans – especially our translators, as they aren't the most forthcoming with information. On one street, workers were cutting down all the trees along one side of the road. One thing Pyongyang has going for it is its nice tree-lined boulevards. They looked fairly picturesque, but now the Koreans seem to be getting rid of them all. Probably to facilitate the new PVC-window look.

* * *

Very recently, the daily ration on the public distribution system (PDS) was reduced from 300g per person per day to 250g. I am not sure what the ration consists of, but I have heard that it is only half the recommended calorific value required for a regular person. In 1991, the government launched a *Let's eat only two meals a day* campaign, in response to decreased yields. The decreased yields were not a result of droughts or floods, as this was before the time of the floods, but a result of over-cropping and misuse of agricultural land. The soil was being stripped away, with its productivity thereby reduced considerably. They have attempted to increase yield on the land by cropping absolutely everywhere – on ridiculously steep slopes, in flood-risk areas and on forestry land. I have seen people tilling land on slopes that I would not feel comfortable walking down.

* * *

For those interested in North Korean medical developments, the *Pyongyang Times* has announced that the Korean Oriental Instant Medicine Centre has recently developed Neo-Viagra-YR (for rejuvenation). Apparently, it is better than the original Viagra – it works twice as quickly, and lasts twice as long. It produces little side effects and no fatigue, the paper reports. It is especially effective for lumbago, arthritis, obesity, hepatitis, nephritis and cerebral arteriosclerosis.

Chapter 11

Also in the news, li'l Kim visited an army unit and a pig farm recently. He went to KPA Unit 347, who were being trained as 'one-beats-a-hundred-foes' combatants. He gave the unit a pair of binoculars and an automatic rifle as gifts. He must have an endless supply – he gives those to everyone.

* * *

I went to see a factory today in a town called Dae'un. It makes control boxes for pumps and motors – kind of similar to the fuseboxes with the trip switches you have in your house – for controlling the operations of a pump and motor. In Ireland, these would often be automated, designed to switch on and off depending on water levels. In the DPRK, they are not so high-tech. Ones that come from China can be quite snazzy and simple to operate, but the ones made here are monsters. They still operate with big levers and massive magnetic coils. It is interesting to get to see places that you wouldn't normally be allowed inside. In reality, it is the EC funds that grant us this opportunity for voyeurism.

It is hard to figure out what is going on with this factory in general. I have a strong feeling that the wool is being pulled over my eyes somehow. The Korean translators aren't much help either. We are buying some pumps and motors for the water system in Songchon, and, after putting the material out to public tender, we have reluctantly agreed to give the contract to a North Korean supplier, on the proviso that we can go to see the places where all the bits are manufactured.

This factory apparently makes control boxes. Now they are saying that they only usually make transformers – and this is only done on special request from the Government. They made two transformers last year, and have no samples for us to see. The transformers look suspiciously like the *compensators* that we are getting from another factory I visited a while back. We are getting the pumps in another place not far from here.

The Nuclear Issue, Kidnappings...

I think there is something fishy going on, but there is little I can do, as the test of the cake is in the eating. There is only a short time until we need the materials delivered, so I will see what they are like when they get to site. The problem is that I am not an expert on these electrical issues, and if the local technician is told to tell me they are fine, then I may not know the difference. It was a nice day out though, and we got to drive along the West Sea Barrage in Nampo.

* * *

There is quite a lot of anti-Japanese and anti-American vitriol as usual in the *Pyongyang Times*. This is balanced by reminders of diplomatic ties with Vietnam, and back-slapping of Cambodia and Guinea. There are complaints about the Japanese desecrating Korean monuments somewhere. The paper decries as false, Japanese accusations about photos and kidnappings of Japanese citizens.

Japan must earnestly apologise for the occupation and military rule of Korea and its past wrongdoing as a legal and moral obligation.

Probably right too. There is also an article claiming that US military bases are the root cause of environmental destruction and degradation around the world. There is apparently a river in the South that is so polluted with oil from the US military that it can burn all day if it catches fire.

Kim Jong Il says:

As the struggle for the masses cause of independence, the socialist cause, is accompanied by the confrontation of power with the imperialists and all the anti-revolutionary forces, the military affairs are the key factor to the victory of the revolution and the prosperity of the country and nation.

* * *

There are stories of people selling food aid in informal markets around the country, at prices much higher than in the public distribution system. So, either someone is hijacking the system,

Chapter 11

siphoning off the aid before it is distributed, or people are selling their food aid. The implication is that the need is not food aid for some people, while others are not receiving enough and have to resort to paying extortionate (or non-subsidised) prices in order to meet their needs. It shows that, despite all efforts to enforce a communal and social system, market forces do find a way around the controls. I have read that in recent years, people caught foraging for food have been sent to concentration camps. I don't know if I believe this. It seems very severe, but I wouldn't rule it out. Another tale I have heard is that only certain people were allowed to live in Pyongyang, in order to maintain the beauty of the city, in line with the face of the socialist ideal. No people with disabilities or disfigurements, and even no pregnant women, were allowed in Pyongyang, or at least in the centre of it. It sounds quite extreme. I have seen plenty of pregnant women around the city. And one amputee. I saw a few in my one day in Nampo.

* * *

Kim Jong Il has a penchant for announcing new food-security measures capriciously. His officials then implement his decrees in programmes and policy across the country. He has just urged people to grow more vegetables, to 'increase military power'. He announced previously that 1999 was to be the 'year of the potato farming revolution'. He believed that if Koreans grew potatoes, rather than concentrating on rice and maize, the famine would have been avoided. He has not heard about Ireland in 1847, I guess. He also reckoned that they should 'make rabbit raising a national movement', because a rabbit can produce two kilograms of 'delicious' meat, and produce at least thirty babies, thus increasing productivity indefinitely. Food is such a serious issue here at the moment that, in order to ensure that rice aid would continue, the Koreans practically apologised to the South Koreans for accusing their crew on a rice shipment of spying. The North Koreans don't apologise easily. Usually they reply with a scathing attack and batten down the hatches even more,

The Nuclear Issue, Kidnappings...

before straining already tense relations with military movements or threats of some sort.

* * *

Last night: Japan 2, DPRK 1 in the World Cup qualifier. Unlucky for the boys. They equalised with a few minutes left, and then the Japanese got a late, late winner. There was no real violence or hassle. I didn't get to see it, unfortunately, and a Korean told me it would probably only be shown on television if they had won! It was still a good performance for a team that has not played much competitive football for a long time. After a dismal performance in the run-up to the 1994 World Cup, the team was told by Kim Jong Il to train hard for ten years, before they would be allowed to try to qualify for the World Cup again. There are two members of the North Korean team playing in the J-League in Japan. The rest of the team is from an army unit.

* * *

My boss is leaving at the weekend, and I am going to be left minding the shop. Good for me, but it means I will be ridiculously busy for the next while. He will probably have more to do where he is going than I will here. Dealing with a real emergency means lots of work, little sleep and less play. I am a bit annoyed, because he doesn't really want to go and I do. Still, he knows more than me at this point in time, and will probably add more value than I would.

* * *

It was Chinese New Year across the way, and 'big' Eid, Eid al-Adha, across the Muslim world, yesterday. Meanwhile, the DPRK were celebrating the birthday of the young lad on the same day. Strangely though, no one seemed too interested. I went for a spin around the town to see what was happening, but there was very little. I thought there would be hoards of people hanging around the big statue of the old man, but no. There did

Chapter 11

seem to be a crowd coming from the mausoleum, but I think that was just a regular requirement on a holiday.

* * *

North Korea has just announced that it is withdrawing from the Six-Party Talks for an indefinite period. They are upset with Condoleeza Rice, US Secretary of State, for labeling (libeling?) them an outpost of tyranny. This could be seen as another attempt to extort economic concessions. They have also stated publicly, for the first time, that they do have nuclear weapons. This is by no means confirmation that they do have nuclear weapons, merely another move in the ongoing game of brinksmanship. The Koreans say they need the weapons for defence, to maintain their 'independence and democracy'.

It is possible that they have everything, except perhaps the precision technology. The US believes that in 2001 they exported fuel rods to Libya, so they have the first piece of the jigsaw. Firing the missile over Japan a few years ago means they have the throwing arm needed. They may have the precision technology, given that it is accepted that the former USSR had the means for years. The Koreans were pretty close with the Russians for a long time, and there are suspicions that ex-Soviet scientists are contracting their services to the DPRK.

* * *

In the *Friendship* last night, there was a demonstration of Korean dancing, participatory of course. There was one Uzbekistani girl, here studying Korean dance, who gave an impressive demonstration of traditional dancing. I am not sure why someone would want to come here to study dance, but there are a few foreign students, particularly from China, Vietnam and former Soviet Bloc states, in the country. The Korean waitresses, who were also participating, dragged a few of us out to dance. I learned one Korean dance when there was a mass dance in Kim Il Sung Square a few weeks ago, and I do it very badly. Most Korean dances look very similar to the untrained eye, featuring

The Nuclear Issue, Kidnappings...

strange hand movements – a bit like ballet, but less strenuous. I wouldn't really be a fan, but I imagine Korean dance is to the Koreans what Irish dancing is to the Irish.

12

The Pen Is Mightier Than The Sword

Our country is well organised. There are no riots, no strikes, no differences of opinion.

Mun Sung, Committee for External Economic Cooperation

I received an email this evening containing the complete North Korean response to the US calling it an outpost of tyranny. I will pick out a few points to give an idea of the tone. It is important to remember that this statement is really directed internally – demonstrating a strong response is important for the credibility of the regime.

The second-term Bush administration's intention to antagonise the DPRK and isolate and stifle it at any cost has become quite clear. As we have clarified more than once, we justly urged the US to renounce its hostile policy

Chapter 12

toward the DPRK whose aim was to seek the latter's 'regime change' and switch its policy to that of peaceful co-existence between the two countries.

It is not far off the mark so far.

They have declared it as their final goal to terminate the tyranny, defined the DPRK, too, as an 'outpost of tyranny' and blustered that they would not rule out the use of force when necessary.

Again, they are on the ball. Force could be used, though when it could be deemed necessary is always tricky. The next few lines are almost poetry:

This is nothing but a far-fetched logic of gangsters as it is a good example fully revealing the wicked nature and brazen-faced double-dealing tactics of the US as a master hand at plot-breeding and deception...

The statement returns to a long-running issue with the Japanese, denying that human remains sent back to Japan were indeed false:

Moreover, it fabricated the issue of false remains over the 'abduction issue' that had already been settled in a bid to nullify the DPRK–Japan Pyongyang Declaration and stop any process to normalise diplomatic relations with the DPRK.

The statement proclaims a global dimension, preaching mutual understanding and tolerance, ignoring the irony in this regarding its own affairs.

It is the trend of the new century and wish of humankind to go in for peace, co-existence and prosperity irrespective of differing ideology, system and religious belief.

The next bit is the main tenet of the article, as the Koreans announce that they are increasing their nuclear arsenal. Whether this is reality, one can only guess, but who wants to play bluff with nuclear weapons, considering that, if pushed, the Korean regime may end up having very little to lose?

The US disclosed its attempt to topple the political system in the DPRK at any cost, threatening it with a nuclear stick. This compels us to take a

The Pen Is Mightier Than The Sword

measure to bolster its nuclear weapons arsenal in order to protect the ideology...

The language used in the statement makes it difficult to take seriously. Such statements are commonly viewed more as curios than as real statements of intent, in the international media at least. Political powers may take them more seriously, but if they do, they don't let on.

* * *

I am just back from a Water and Sanitation sector meeting at the UNICEF office, where all the *WatSan* people from the various agencies turn up and talk at each other. The main topic of the meeting was sanitation problems in the country, and how to address hygiene promotion using participatory methods, especially given that no-one can participate. Hygiene promotion – disseminating information on personal, household and community hygiene, respecting cultural practices – can be a sensitive issue in many countries. Mostly, you don't want people to get sick from faeco-oral transmission of bacteria. In layman's terms, you want to prevent faeces getting in people's mouths, whether it is through flies, fingers or whatever, somehow contaminating food or water. The question is what is the best method of getting the message across so that it has an effect, and this is where people are not really in agreement. In the DPRK, the Government is not happy with the idea of hygiene promotion, as they say that it is taught in school, and that's that. Maybe it is, but maybe it isn't effective. NGO expats can also be a little arrogant, thinking they can 'teach' hygiene and change behaviour wherever they go. If I were Korean I would feel more than a little slighted.

For the UN and the World Food Programme, huge-scale food distributions are the priority here in the DPRK. And in food distribution, the big issue is where the food actually goes. The aid is donated by the US, Japan and South Korea primarily, some directly to the country and some through the United Nations.

Chapter 12

Others, such as the Canadian Food Grains Bank are also involved. WFP is continually restricted in their monitoring of the distribution of the food. There are worries that a lot of the aid is going to the military, possibly the least vulnerable section of society, and being used to ameliorate military stockpiles (It is estimated that the DPRK has enough military stockpiles to last for about four months of war). Note: various reports claim that somewhere between 1.6 and 3 million people died in the famine – a huge percentage of the population if it is true. Korean sources say about 220,000 died.

There are reportedly camps, called the 9/27 camps, where people caught foraging or begging for food are sent. Escapees from the country that are returned are also sent there, often for hard labour and re-education. There are stories of cannibalism in the DPRK during the worst famine years, particularly in the far northern areas of the country. The country denies this strenuously, but such stories reflect how far the regime had let the situation deteriorate.

* * *

There is much discussion on the prospects for reform in the DPRK. The word 'reform' is usually taken to mean change to a more democratic system of government, as well as economic change, to a more capitalist, market-based economy. This will not happen quickly, as it did in East Germany, but will be a slow process. It is not necessarily true that capitalism is the best system, and *ideally* it probably isn't, but it seems clear that socialism and communism as economic models are bound to failure – human nature might idealise egalitarianism in philosophy, but requires autonomy that is ultimately restricted by such models. Qualified capitalism, social-justice models along the lines of John Rawls rather than Karl Marx, are more realistic. Centrally planned economies are inherently inclined to dictatorship.

The Pen Is Mightier Than The Sword

In discussions on reform, it is said to be more apt to compare the DPRK to former Eastern Bloc countries than to its geographic neighbours, China or Vietnam. These neighbours were far more agriculture-oriented than the DPRK, which is a highly urbanised, industrialised country, similar to East Germany in this way. There are also similarities to Soviet-era Albania, a country that did not toe the Russian line all the time, but attempted to create its own mini-world, with very little external access allowed, and where people were led to believe they were the best in the world. In China and Vietnam, there was a deep labour pool (low-productivity agricultural labour, available to transfer to other areas) to use in the transition to a market-based economy, which is not really available to the less-densely populated DPRK.

Should collapse occur too suddenly, and the whole structure that the society is based on disappears, there could be chaos. Militia groups could form, as there are many armed people. There could be anger at the lies of the last fifty years and the broken promises of the State, and fear at being abandoned by their invincible generals. The region and the rest of the world would have to step in to provide support. Whole new legal frameworks would be needed for commercial activities, property rights, wage structures, currency evaluation and so on. Much would probably fall under the responsibility of South Korea, much as East Germany was supported by the West. Though how welcome representatives of the South would be in the North is another issue, as there is long-standing distrust and enmity, which will not disappear overnight. Many would continue to see the US as the great Satan, and the South Koreans as their puppets. Sixty years of misinformation cannot be wiped out with one epiphany.

Unemployment could be phenomenal, once all the irrelevant jobs – in factories that are not productive, in ministries that are not relevant, and in the military that will have no more wars to prepare for – are cut out. A social welfare system of some sort would be needed. Private income would mean a tax base would

Chapter 12

have to be established. A lot of run-down and outdated factories would close, as South Korean industries would now have access to markets in the North. Investment in industry would be required, which is where all those big *chaebol* would come in.

The country's land management would have to be revised. Who would claim all the common land? How would it be distributed among the work teams? What lands would the State legitimately lay claim to? It would be difficult to privatise all the different industries, without actually closing them down or their being taken over by South Korean companies. In East Germany, because the East Germans had little or no spare cash, it was West Germans that did all the investing and purchasing of East German stock. In Russia, opportunistic oligarchs were able to take over State-run enterprises at rock-bottom prices, creating a super-rich elite while the masses queued outside supermarkets for bread that wasn't there. Could this situation be avoided in the DPRK?

13
Building Toilets And Diplomacy

Someone that you have deprived of everything is no longer in your power. He is once again entirely free.
Aleksandr Solzhenitsyn

We are working on a few small, innovative projects in Songchon and Namchong, building different types of latrines: Biogas, Eco-San and VIP toilets. A bit of technical background: a biogas latrine is a toilet connected to a big concrete tank, where all the human waste goes. As well as the human excreta, pig stuff is thrown in there too. This all ferments and creates methane or biogas, which is then siphoned off and can fuel some lights and stoves. The biogas digester is kept underground beneath a greenhouse, as it is necessary to keep the stuff fairly warm for it to biodegrade and create gas. The Eco-San latrine is one that

Chapter 13

separates the yellow from the brown, in order to use both for farming. The yellow can be added directly as nutrient for plants, while the brown, if kept separate, can be used safely as compost after six months or a year, depending on temperature. Thus you need three holes: one for the yellow, one for the brown in the pit that is in use, and another for the pit that is fermenting for six months before being used as fertiliser. Using the three holes is challenging, especially for the old and arthritic. If the yellow mixes with the brown, it doesn't ferment so quickly. The final one is the VIP latrine. This is not a toilet for important people, but rather a Ventilated-Improved-Pit latrine. It is fairly basic, but has a black pipe to take away odours and trap the dirty disease-carrying flies that tend to end up in the dung-heap. We have been installing these in schools and hospitals, but not in individual houses. They are not too cheap. That's the technical bit over.

We were trying to buy materials from the local FDRC through work team farms, thus reducing the costs of the latrines and providing some local money (though this seriously goes against the socialist ethic). If the projects are successful, we will study how to make them widely replicable. For a larger-scale intervention, we would like to see some buy-in from the people, giving an indication that it is something locally needed and valued. Anyhow, the Central FDRC doesn't want us to purchase materials from the local FDRC. They are stalling, so that we will go through them, so that they will get the money, or we go through a regular Korean supplier, who all seem to work for the Government in some way or other.

* * *

I have been reading a small book called *Dalai Lama: My Son*, about the life of the mother of the fourteenth Dalai Lama. It is incredible that a peasant boy, randomly born into the position, can become the leader of Buddhism, as an infant. The interesting bit for me was when the Chinese communists took control of

Building Toilets And Diplomacy

Tibet. The Dalai Lama's mother was back from a year in China, meeting old friends who were now under the rule of the communists. Asking them how they were, the response was, 'By virtue of Chairman Mao, we are very happy.' Though they didn't mean it, they had to say it, even when only in the company of close friends.

It seems to be the same story here. They say you can't have a conversation among three people here. Two's company, three's a crowd. When talking one-on-one, there is an element of safety. When there are three, people have to be careful what they say, in case they get reported. The system of reporting in the country is absolutely all-pervasive. Everyone has to give a brief on all the people they work with. This tight control is a feature of all communist societies, and fear makes it all work, at least until it gets to breaking point. Control here is almost total, and information control is absolutely total.

* * *

I watched *Goodbye, Lenin* last night, a German film based around the time of the fall of the Berlin Wall. It was very interesting from the perspective of living in this parallel world. There was one superb scene, in which an old woman, who had been a great supporter of the system, wakes from a coma and sees the outside world for the first time after the fall of the Wall. She looks out the window to see all the little changes around her – people with long hair, a pink lampshade, a BMW, and then a helicopter carrying the dismantled bust of Lenin flies past her window in slow motion. I guess I am awaiting the day the big man's big bronze statue is carried off in the same way.

* * *

In Romania, Ceaucescu attempted to create a cult around himself, mirroring Kim Il Sung's status in the DPRK. He, however, tried it all too late. He had no real heroic background to build on, nor any great affection from the people. He tried setting up statues of himself all over Romania, and was brutal

Chapter 13

enough to force the issue. The State never managed to seal itself off from the outside world, and in the end any perceived affection toward him was quickly exposed. When the opportunity arrived, the people's true feelings toward him were displayed in the most brutal fashion. It does not seem that he has been mourned in any corner.

Romania was also a semi-rogue Eastern-Bloc state, in that it didn't always bow to the Soviet Union. It didn't sign the Warsaw Pact, and it had diplomatic relations with West Germany, and it even hosted a visit by US President Nixon. Ceaucescu, like most communist leaders, gave government positions to most of his family, in an attempt to surround himself with a loyal and trusted cabal. He also tried to develop a *first family* thing, similar to the Kims in the DPRK.

* * *

One of our translators here noticed me reading a book about the IRA, and asked what I thought of them. He knew who they were, mentioning Sinn Féin and even pronouncing it correctly. He said he learned about them in university. They also seem to be quite well known in Afghanistan, where I had brief conversations about them with a number of people. It makes you wonder. The Republican movement has been supported by Libya in the past, and even attempted to import a shipload of arms from Libya. The DPRK has a history of selling arms to Libya, which is one of the reasons they have now pulled out of the Six-Party Talks, as the US accuse them of supplying Libya with uranium-something-or-other.

* * *

When comparing the future of the DPRK with the past of other countries, such as China, East Germany, Vietnam or Romania, there are similarities and differences. This place has been closed off for a long time now, about twenty years longer than East Germany was. Thus, there is less and less memory of a different era. Also, the previous era was the forty-five-year struggle against the Japanese. Those are bad memories. For many people, the early years of independence under Kim Il Sung represent the heyday of the country. Also, the level of control here, in terms of access to, and knowledge of, the outside world, is much higher than most regimes have managed, making it easier to run the propaganda machine. In East Germany, people could receive western television, and had an idea of what was immediately over the Wall – the curtain was never fully drawn.

A survey carried out by a South Korean think-tank found that 90% of Southerners thought reunification was 'somewhat' important. 50% thought it should be supported financially 'only to the extent that it does not burden the average household'.

The per-capita income difference between the two countries is huge, the North's being about one tenth of the South's. This is much larger than the difference between the two German states at the time of unification. In 2000, it was estimated that a $500 billion investment by the South into the North over ten years would be required to bring the country to about 60% of the wealth of the South. Infrastructure here is so bad that it may be better to slowly integrate the two countries, gradually building the economy in the North and restricting movement in a manner that would protect the South from being overloaded. If the borders were opened immediately, there would doubtless be a huge migration to the South, which could have catastrophic consequences, societally at least. I don't think either of the Koreas is quite ready for each other. After all, you don't wipe out one hundred years of oppression and propaganda too quickly.

* * *

I am trying to toughen Kiki up. No more walking around with a little blue jacket on him, the way he did with his previous owners. Last night he took a liking to a French engineer, who was wearing furry white shoes, and spent the evening trying to make friends with his leg. He never did that before. He is growing up.

Chapter 13

He needs a friend, or he will be the laughing stock of the Diplomatic Dog community.

* * *

It was the young lad's birthday yesterday, and a national holiday. There was lots of stuff happening around the town, but no one in our office told me. Thousands of Koreans were dancing in the square – men in their lovely Maoist suits and women in neon-hued traditional Korean dresses. There were also special exhibitions of ice-skating and synchronised swimming that I was not told about. I only happened to spot all of this as I was driving around town, looking for somewhere to have dinner. It is not permitted to watch the spectacles without a ticket, and I would have had to watch from a spot designated for foreigners. This could only have been organised through our Liaison Officer. I was not impressed with the lack of information.

* * *

I am now an old-timer here and know my way around the city as well as anyone, so I have to drive my agriculturalist colleague George around the city until he gets his license. We went to see the big man's statue. I joked that I would drive into the Forbidden City, which scared my passenger. There is no way of getting in there. George didn't seem too impressed with me breaking the rules of the road either. He is a bit nervous generally. Traffic cops must be getting fed up with me now, turning right when I should turn left and crossing double white lines. They are constantly blowing whistles at me. That scared my passenger too.

* * *

I learned how to write my name in Korean last night.

둘타

* * *

Building Toilets And Diplomacy

I should really be able to speak Korean much better by now. I have been a bit lazy with the language, and only have a few sentences. The script here, created in the fifteenth century, is called *hangul*. Bunches of three characters make each syllable or sound. Apparently there are 11,172 potential combinations or sounds, made from the twenty-four consonants and vowels. To the untrained, western eye, it may look similar to Chinese script, but it works very differently. Chinese script is *logographic,* meaning that the symbols are images or representations of an idea, and can be quite complex. In Korean script, characters make up syllables. The syllables are written sequentially, usually horizontally though sometimes vertically, left to right, top to bottom.

There are well-worn jokes about the Chinese cooking 'flied lice'. In Korean, there is the same problem. There is no character that makes either an *L* sound or an *R* sound. There is something in between that can sound like both or either. When I say it, I get laughed at because I just can't get it quite right.

* * *

It is very difficult to get an idea of the military capabilities of the DPRK. There is very little information available, and much of the country's operations take place in networks of tunnels all over the mountains of Korea, out of sight of prying satellites. Driving around the countryside, I see camouflaged entrances to tunnels that would not be easily visible from the air. How do you fight a war against a country that is essentially a network of catacombs?

The North bought a freighter full of old helicopters and fighter planes from Kazakhstan in 1999. I don't know what it has bought since, but the perception is that the country is still upgrading its army, under the banner of *Songun*. I wonder if there are any Libyan armaments that, having spent a holiday in Ireland, are knocking around the DPRK now. The North also has

Chapter 13

rockets pointed at Seoul at all times, ready to blitz the place at the push of a button.

* * *

It just got really cold again, and it is going to get colder tomorrow. So much for starting my training to run the DPRK marathon. Winter here seems like it never wants to end. I went swimming today in the Olympic-sized pool, instead of going running in these Arctic temperatures. It is huge. A few Koreans were in there as well, but we still had a lane each to swim in. I am still building up to jumping off the ten-metre diving board. I climbed up and had a look. Maybe next time.

* * *

Every year, all the NGOs and the European embassies here have to go to Koppensang Guesthouse to partake in some diplomatic formalities. These formalities largely involve singing. The idea is that pretty much all foreigners turn up, along with their Korean counterparts. Some representative of the European embassies gives a speech, and the Korean Foreign Minister gives a speech. There is a buffet dinner, and each NGO or embassy or other sort of group sings a song or two. At least one of these songs is in Korean – a eulogy to the socialist state, one of the leaders, unification or something along those lines.

The Ministry of Foreign Affairs went first. There were about thirty of them – diplomats, former diplomats or wannabe diplomats. They are polished performers, perfectly practised, forming a booming ensemble of basses and baritones. This, unfortunately, was followed by the English contingent – ambassador, first secretary and administration staff, as well as a few British aid workers – singing the Beatles' 'I Get By With a Little Help from my Friends'. Luckily they have a sense of humour. Then all the NGOs went up in turn to sing. I will spare the details.

Building Toilets And Diplomacy

We sang an upbeat Korean song, which was better than most of the others. I don't exactly know the translation, but it was about pride in the motherland. We had plans to sing 'I Don't Like Mondays' by the Boomtown Rats, but the only one of us with any musical talent left for Indonesia a week ago. I had also thought about having a go at the tin whistle for a bit of light entertainment, but chickened out, as this was going to be my first diplomatic venture and I didn't want to make a big splash. I had to wear a shirt and nice shoes and trousers. These don't sit easily on me.

The best performance was probably from the Swiss, who were harmonious and well-rehearsed. ADRA, the Adventist Development and Relief Agency, did a mime, which seemed emotional, but no one really knew what it was supposed to represent. The Koreans introduced it as a 'Christian performance', and it was apparently about giving your heart to God.

The highlight of the evening was the British Ambassador's speech. Usually at these things, people will just be polite and schmoozy, but he didn't hold back. He came on right after the Korean Minister, who had tried to give the impression that relations with Europe were rosy, saying how great it was that representatives from so many noble states were there. Then the Ambassador stood up. He said it was great to be having dialogue, but that he wouldn't pretend that things were perfect. There were lots of issues and problems, in particular the recent announcement that the DPRK were pulling out of the Six-Party Talks. He also referred to new restrictions placed on NGOs back in September, further curtailing travel and access to certain areas. Sometimes these things need to be said. It is not a job I would like to do and it is not easy to get that balance between playing good cop or bad cop in international diplomacy- though more often than not it is the DPRK determining whether it is the carrot or the stick that is to be used.

14
Prayers, Rugby And The Cold

An army of the people is invincible.
Mao

I have just come back from a 'prayer meeting', with a few people from ADRA and PMU (Pentecostal), and some other people I don't know. It was good to be able to say a few prayers with people. I am not really into the whole singing songs end of things, but there were a few good stories from people – in particular, one from a Swedish aid worker who has a farm and some forest in Sweden. A month ago there was a storm and a lot of the forestry in his area was wiped out. He only lost a few trees, and trees are the bread and butter for a lot of people in those areas, so he was lucky. When he came back to Korea a few weeks ago, some of the Koreans had heard about the storm, and asked

Chapter 14

him about it. He told them he was lucky, and one of the Koreans said, 'No, not lucky. The man up there was looking after you, because you do good work here.' It showed that there is religious faith in this country, despite everything. Or maybe they mean the Great Leader...

Life can be horrible for the North Korean people. Many of their liberties are curtailed, and there are innumerable restrictions. They must carry out ridiculous tasks at the behest of the State, often just for the sake of carrying out ridiculous tasks. They are told there is no God, and are not allowed to believe in one. They mostly live in grinding poverty. They know nothing about the rest of the world; about other possibilities. If they do know that something is not right, they don't know what to do about it. They are not able to fight back. The scariest thing about the place is that it is so organised, so clinical, that no one can put a foot out of line. There is no unrest; people can only accept their situation. They have to survive, and survival is the main concern for the majority in the country.

The national aims of the DPRK are to reunify the Korean peninsula through *Songun*, to immortalise the Great Leader, Kim Il Sung, and to wish a long life to the Dear Leader, Comrade Kim Jung Il. These aren't the aims of the common people, but the aims given to them by the machine. The farmer aims to produce enough food to make his quota, and hopefully to have some left over for his family, as he watches the rest get sent off to a central warehouse.

What does daily life consist of? Going to work in a field all day long, tilling crops you will never eat or sell; or mining coal in a dark and dangerous mine, and breathing dirty coal dust all day, because you live in a mining village; listening to the same music and propaganda on the radio that you heard forty years ago; feeling the constant pang of hunger, because the PDS ration has been reduced below the recommended calorific intake; and feeling the cold all day, every day.

Prayers, Rugby And The Cold

At the same time, I know that people have families and friends – they live, laugh and love, despite it all; they play sports and games; they drink and get drunk; they have dinner with friends; they court and hold hands; they marry and have children; they worry, and want the best for their families; they bleed and sweat, cry and smile, fight and fall out, and feel all of the same emotions that fill the lives of people everywhere.

* * *

Talking about the weather is as much of a pastime here as it is in Ireland. Football at the *MayDay* Stadium yesterday was almost unbearable. I knew it was getting colder, and people were saying it was going to be really cold, but nothing could have prepared me for that. At three o'clock it was cold, but I was still the silly Irishman running around in shorts (with gloves and hat as well). The rest were wrapped up really well, and looking at me a little strangely. I was sweating, and not really feeling the cold, after only a few minutes of running around. Then at five o'clock, reminiscent of the film 'The Day After Tomorrow', where there is a global freeze and temperatures plummet in a matter of seconds, the temperature just dropped a few degrees very rapidly, and everyone could feel their jaws stiffening up and their faces becoming sore. We decided to pack it in. On the walk back to the car, the sweat on the back of my neck, and on the waistband at the top of my shorts, froze. By the time I sat in the car, my backside was numb.

Today was no better. In my haste this morning, travelling to my home away from home, Rongchon, I left my jacket and my sleeping bag in the office. I think I looked a little ridiculous, standing out in the snow without gloves or jacket, trying to explain the basics of how to dig and build a well to the 'Afforestation' work team. I have never actually done it myself. It was cold. The only solution was to have a few cigarettes – my first in a long time.

* * *

Chapter 14

Snapshots from today:

On a community workfarm, old men weighing bags of potatoes on an old manual balance outside in the freezing cold, and loading the potatoes onto an ox-drawn cart in the farm storehouse, to take them to the central village;

On the road back to Songchon, four young children seeing a white 4x4 vehicle coming toward them, whipping their scarves and hats off to give a quick bow to the passing car in minus-twenty temperatures;

Two young children skating on improvised uni-skis on a frozen stream, snot running down their noses, hands going like the hammers propelling them home and faces full of smiles;

A teenage girl standing outside a health clinic, wearing an old jacket torn at the elbows, dancing on the spot to keep warm;

A health clinic locked shut; a health-clinic manager at home with a sore leg; in the health clinic, only a weighing scales, a bed with no covers, a table and an old pot in the corner, the wind blowing through the plastic windows;

An empty truck stopped before an old iron bridge; young soldiers and old people with loads on their backs rushing to climb into the back of the truck; some with children, some with tables, some bent double under the weight of a bag of grain; others, a hundred metres away, beginning a half-hearted run, knowing the truck will probably be gone by the time they get there; a red-faced teenager in army uniform, chubbier than your average Korean, trying to swing himself onto the back of the truck as it starts to move away, but unable to hold on;

A middle-aged woman trudging slowly up a long hill in the snow with a bag on her back;

My hands, blue and purple with the cold;

Inside the Central Building in the Central Village, a work-team manager, a farm manager, an NGO driver and translator, the

Prayers, Rugby And The Cold

FDRC chairman and an Irish engineer sitting cross-legged on a heated floor; the Koreans looking at each and laughing at the Irish engineer with sweating cheeks, eating pepper soup and gradually regaining some feeling in his hands;

Pictures of the big man and the young lad on one wall; pictures of the three stages of the big man's life on another wall; a picture of the big man and little lad standing majestically over Mount Paektu on another wall; and a picture of the big man with a crowd of children swarming round him, and his big, white *colgate* smile.

* * *

Where is my thermal underwear? I didn't leave it in Pyongyang, did I? I did.

* * *

The most recent Korean holiday was a full-moon holiday, and again it was on a Wednesday. A group of us went to Morombong Hill, the same hill we went sliding down on inflated rubber tubes, because one of the waitresses in the *Friendship* asked us to wish for a husband for her. The girl is twenty-eight – in North Korean culture, she is getting very close to her sell-by date. She gets very upset when talking about her marital prospects. I think she got jilted at one stage in her life, and took it badly. As she gets older, her prospects are becoming reduced to an old man or a divorcee, neither of which is desirable. Driving up to the top of the hill and looking at the moon, we all wished our hardest that she will not end up an old maid. We managed to do a one-eighty spin on the ice on the way back. We were going slowly, about twenty mph, and the car just gradually rotated, almost in slow motion, eventually coming to a stop facing the opposite direction. It is a good job it was late at night and there were no other cars around. My defensive driving skills let me down.

* * *

Chapter 14

The Government issued a statement last year that they were going to restrict foreigners carrying out monitoring trips to project sites in the countryside. Everyone refers to this as the September 15 Statement, which is a bit melodramatic. It hasn't really affected too many agencies, though a few ex-pats have been refused visas, or had them delayed. The statement was largely posturing, and I think the NGOs would be better served to ignore it and carry on with their work, unless there are actual practical implications. Creating a scene forces the MoFA, who often make these statements merely to appease hardliners, to actually act, when they really had no intention of doing anything. For the MoFA, NGOs and their work are a source of extra income, covering the cost of seconded staff, plus expenses. In a time of austerity, they do not want to lose that. One Korean official has justified the stance of the DPRK Government and the September 15 Statement by claiming, 'For years, my country gave aid to Africa, and we never did any monitoring.'

* * *

According to the European Community Humanitarian Office's (ECHO) external evaluation of the DPRK, there are a lot of institutions for children in the country. Most of these children are either orphans or their parents are just unable to look after them. Apparently all triplets get sent to these institutions, on the assumption that their mothers will not be able to cope. The story is that parents get to visit them only on their birthdays; at the age of four they return to their families.

* * *

The furore over the North's refusal to continue with the Six-Party Talks, and the claims that it has nuclear weapons, goes on and on. All the other participants are taking it in turns daily to make statements about the situation. The Southern president has asked his 'beloved citizens' to remain calm.

* * *

Prayers, Rugby And The Cold

I had a nice run around the *MayDay* Stadium in six inches of snow for about an hour today. A lap around it is about 1.7km. I could see one of the lady guards outside the stadium timing me each time I went past. Sweat was pouring out of me, despite the cold. It was all Guinness: Friday night Guinness will have to stop. (The RAC imports some of its beer from Beijing, where canned Guinness is available. The local brew, *Taedonggang* beer – a tasty, sweet beer and fairly cheap – is not sold there.)

* * *

Last night, I was talking to a Finnish aid worker who has been here since 1999. He is firmly of the belief that the country is changing very quickly. There are more cars, and more bikes; people are more open, and realise that their ways are not always the best, or even not often the best. I am noticing little things even in the few months I have been here. The number of shops, and the number of shops foreigners can go into, are increasing. I have seen Koreans dealing in Japanese yen and euro, as well as dollars, in recent days.

The official exchange rate of the Korean won is 160 won to one euro, approximately. I can't really buy anything in won if I exchange at the 'official' rate, because it costs a fortune. At the unofficial rate, and if I could shop in more Korean shops, I would be eating a lot more and possibly a lot better. When I go to restaurants that operate in won, and I have to pay in dollars, the price is always charged at the unofficial rate. Officially, they could charge me the official rate, but I'm not sure that any of the regular people in restaurants would even know that there is an official rate.

* * *

I finally made it to Tongil market, the only farmers' market foreigners are allowed to go to. I didn't have any Korean currency though, so it was a waste of time. There are official money-changers there, but the best thing would be to get a Korean to change the money for me. It would be a bit risky for

Chapter 14

the organisation if I was to be spotted exchanging at the unofficial rate, and it would put our Korean colleagues in a compromising position to ask them to do it for us. People working in other NGOs seem to have their means, so I am sure I will figure it out. It would be nice to somehow engage in local commerce and interact with people in a semi-meaningful manner.

Tongil is a real, lively, vibrant market, full of hustle and bustle, with stalls selling fresh fruit, vegetables, meat, clothes, shoes … anything and everything, even some branded goods. There is noise and haggling and bargaining. This is one place that makes Pyongyang seem alive. There are rumours that fifteen more farmers' markets will open in the next few months. That is a big step. Opening up. Glasnost.

* * *

The light in the *Juche* Tower has been switched off for the last few nights. Fuel must be running low.

* * *

I got a smile and a wave from more than one traffic lady today. This is good progress. There are a few of them at roundabouts I run and drive past most days, so they are getting used to seeing me. For a while, they wouldn't even acknowledge me. Now there is usually a little nod in my direction. I would swear one of them winked at me the other day when I drove past. I also got heckled by teenage girls when I was out running the other day. I think it was because there were four inches of snow on the ground and I was running in shorts and a T-shirt, with a big red nose.

* * *

A very gratifying experience last night: sitting in the British Ambassador's residence in Pyongyang, as the final whistle blew. The final score in the Six-Nations rugby international was Ireland 19, England 13. It was difficult not to gloat. So I didn't even try. Unfortunately, the time difference between here and London

Prayers, Rugby And The Cold

meant I was in bed in the early hours of the morning, and up for work at seven. As a result, I am tired today, and not doing too well at work. Mr Kang and myself are in Namchong, going through the rural pipeline systems with each individual work team. I am pleased with how thorough I have been in preparing everything – maps, distribution lists, drawings and so on – and then disgusted with my lazy communications onsite, thanks to my fatigue and mild hangover. I am finding myself thinking, 'Ah, sure, it will be all right,' rather than hammering out the details and making sure everything is understood. Partly it is the language issue that puts me off discussing things, but I could definitely pay better attention to detail.

* * *

I went ice-skating yesterday in a very ornate building in the centre of the city. It is referred to as the Pyongyang Ice Rink, but it has a long Korean name that I can't pronounce, spell or translate. I have never been ice skating before, but I will definitely go again. It was good fun, though painful. North Koreans do not have big feet. I was forced into sub-standard, antiquated ice-skates, about three sizes too small for me. The first half-hour was spent trying to walk to the ice rink, turning my ankle twice and falling over three times. I have purple bruises all over.

* * *

One of the Koreans working with me wanted to buy a television from a UNDP employee who was leaving, but couldn't afford the full cost of €150. He asked me if I would act as negotiator, to see if the owner would sell for one hundred flat. He asked me not to mention the words 'national staff' on the phone, or his name, but to act as if it was my purchase. No, it was just too risky. Everyone feeds the system here by watching and reporting on each other mandatorily. It isn't paranoia if it is actually happening.

* * *

Chapter 14

I wonder how many times Kiki will have gone to the toilet on the floor of my apartment by the time I get back. He is not taking well to toilet training.

15

The Demilitarized Zone And A Particular State Of Mind

The control of the production of wealth is the control of human life itself.
Hilaire Belloc

I have just spent the day at the Demilitarised Zone (DMZ), the border between the North and the South. On the way there, we stopped for lunch at Kaesong. This is the town with the Special Economic Zone (SEZ), managed by Hyundai I think. We didn't get to see the industrial park itself, but the town is not the ugliest I have seen in Korea. There is a spectacular statue of the big guy, just visible coming over a bridge to face a hill. The statue dominates the view as you approach, with a few hundred steps leading up to it.

Chapter 15

A really friendly North Korean tour guide/soldier showed us around the DMZ, laughing nervously after every sentence of his official talk. When I had a smoke with him afterwards, he was more relaxed. We had a much more informal chat about his perspectives on the future of the two countries. The people here are keen on reunification. Their faces drop when they talk about the separation of the country.

After becoming used to the demeanour of North Korean soldiers, it was strange to see the South Korean version across the half-metre plinth of concrete that divides the two countries. Or should I say, divides the country? The southern soldiers look much *tougher* than the North Koreans. They look really mean, like they have attitude. They have the proper khaki gear, the sunglasses and the big boots, and they seem relaxed and at their ease. In contrast, the North Koreans are stony-faced and glum, standing stiffly to attention, too serious looking. Two big buildings eerily face each other across the border, each with surveillance cameras trained on the other.

There is one building that straddles the border, which is sometimes used for inter-governmental meetings I think, or various sorts of talks, as well as for tourism. It is a single room, about ten metres long. When you are in it, you can walk back and forth across the border. This was my first time in South Korea. One of the *Friendship* waitresses had asked me to bring her watch with me, so it could go on a trip to South Korea, across the demarcation line. The doors on either side of this building are kept locked from the outside by the respective soldiers, and they coordinate people going in and out from either side. You don't get any crossover. During our introduction, we were told by the North Korean soldiers that they keep the demilitarised zone free of arms, just using it for agriculture, whereas the Americans on the other side continue to carry arms and threaten the peace. I didn't get this independently verified. The soldiers tried to build up the drama, saying we needed military escorts for our own

The Demilitarized Zone And A Particular State Of Mind

safety. There are many incidents at the crossover, they said – 'Who knows what might happen today?'

I am glad I got to see it. It is a very strange and sad place. One of my workmates was commiserating with the soldier/guide, putting his hand on the guide's arm and saying he is sure everything will work out in the end: 'If everyone is sensible, and the Americans leave the peninsula to let the Koreans get on with it sensibly, it will all be okay.' I asked the tour guide how he thought the two systems could be worked in one country – which would prevail, in his opinion, the socialist/*Juche* idea, or capitalism? I don't know how the translator translated the question, but the response was that they just want reunification, and don't care about differences such as religions or ideologies.

Chapter 15

We were given a tour of the building where the 1953 Armistice was signed. The original chairs were there, and the agreement is displayed in a glass case. We were encouraged to take photos while sitting in the signatories' chairs.

When I came back, Mrs Yang had tears in her eyes while asking me about the DMZ and what I thought of the separation. She says that people here only care for reunification. I don't know if the crowd down South are quite as keen. Both sides have a lot to lose by reunification as things stand. One identity will definitely have to go; one way of life will have to change, and I can't see the South being willing to give up its burgeoning economic model for a moribund one.

* * *

My former colleague from Afghanistan finally got his visa to come here and visit. He was very lucky, and saw more in a week than a lot of people actually living in Pyongyang get to see in a year. This was thanks mainly to the powers of persuasion of our Liaison Officer, who managed to organise permissions and travel permits in a very short time. He had a two-day trip up country to watch me work, and saw Songchon County and its beautiful, rolling hills. He got to see most of Pyongyang, as he had an able guide (me), happy to drive him around without the hindrance of a translator/driver. We took a trip out to Nampo on the coast, and he got to see the West Sea Barrage, the aforementioned longest dam in the world.

We even saw some amputees. I know that sounds a bit strange, but in Pyongyang, amputees, or disabilities of any sort, are not seen around the streets, only able-bodied persons.

He got to go to the Demilitarised Zone. He went drinking in the *Friendship* on a regular basis, and was hungover most mornings. He walked Kiki around town, which provided him with cover for being nosy, looking into shops and so on. He ate burgers in *KimDonalds* and climbed to the top of the Yanggakdoh Hotel – with its occasionally-rotating restaurant – for a birds-eye view of

The Demilitarized Zone And A Particular State Of Mind

the city. He swam in the fifty-metre pool with three German ladies, and he was privy to a performance of improvised Korean song and dance in the *Friendship* on the eve of International Women's Day. Not bad for a week's work.

The trip to Nampo was fun. It was nice to be able to walk unaccompanied down the street, in a place that isn't Pyongyang. I constantly felt like I was doing something wrong, and that at any minute someone was going to stop me. I brought Kiki along for the trip, and he attracted more attention than we did. How weird it must have looked for the locals – three foreigners walking down the street, with a furry little white dog on a lead and no 'minders' in sight. Last week, I asked our FDRC partners in Songchon if we could walk downtown, and this created a bit of discussion. Eventually it was agreed that we could; we got about fifty metres beyond the door before being told that that was really as far as we could go unaccompanied. They don't trust me yet.

The Yanggakdoh Hotel is a really tall building on an island on the River Taedong. It was built by the Chinese some time back. When I say Chinese, I speak in very general terms. I don't know if it is the Chinese government or independent business, but it is managed by Chinese people and pretty much staffed by Chinese as well. It suffers from frequent blackouts. It is triangular in plan, and has a revolving restaurant at the top. The Chinese that work there used to play football with us, until the Koreans told them that they weren't allowed to leave the island. Then we went there to play football, and then they were told that they couldn't play football any more. Disappointing. The top-floor restaurant doesn't usually revolve, and when it does it goes incredibly slowly. It has a great view of the city, up and down the river, and almost all the main landmarks are visible. Even when it is not rotating, it is worth the short walk around.

* * *

Chapter 15

I watched 'Team America: World Police' last night on DVD. There are parts of it that only someone who knows Korea could appreciate. A few of us watched it, with the blinds drawn, in an apartment in the Diplomatic Compound. We were nervous, because the parody of Kim Jong Il would be truly shocking for a North Korean. I wonder what they would make of the final scene, where he turns into a cockroach, climbs into a rocket and escapes to outer space. His virtuoso rendition of 'I'm So Ronery', mocking the Asian inability to pronounce either an *L* or an *R* will probably outlive himself. The DVD was a Chinese bootleg, with very bad subtitles, which only added to the humour.

* * *

For fertiliser here, they use poo – or dung, faeces, whatever you are most comfortable calling it. It is used everywhere. Now that it is springtime, people are out spreading the *manure* on the fields. There are huge heaps of it – up to five feet high – on every field, marked with red flags. Much of it comes from the town sewerage systems, if there is one. It is covered with soil over the winter, to allow it to ferment. Often it is mixed with the leftovers from maize production. Fairly fresh manure is used as well, meaning that the countryside will smell like a toilet for a while. It is not a bad thing to use poo for fertiliser, but only when it has biodegraded to the stage where it is not a disease carrier. Stuff taken straight from a toilet or sewerage system is liable to make people sick. I don't imagine they use all the protective equipment that would be used when messing around in metropolitan sewers in Ireland. Pressure to get the highest yield possible from the land means that, at this time of year, every bit of *natural* fertiliser is used as soon as it is available, resulting in some very unpleasant jobs for farmers.

* * *

I must see if my FDRC colleagues want to watch 'A State of Mind', a documentary about two Korean dancers preparing to take part in the Mass Games. The Mass Games is a gymnastic

The Demilitarized Zone And A Particular State Of Mind

display, in which up to 6,000 gymnasts perform a type of dance theatre, all in harmony and synchronicity with each other. The Games are symbolic of 'group theory', in which the desires of the self are sacrificed for the needs of the masses. This documentary was made at the last Mass Games, in 2003. There may be another one for the sixtieth anniversary of the liberation from Japan.

Though the producers state at the beginning that no efforts were made by the authorities to censor anything said in the film, it is clear that people aren't acting naturally. This may be attributable to the presence of the camera, or to the presence of foreign producers, or just to general nervousness at being the focus of a documentary.

Some of the insights in the film are spot on. The girls that are performing seem lovely, just eleven years old and devoting half their lives to preparing for this. It is scary that their greatest dream is to perform for 'the General' (Kim Jong Il) at the Mass Games. They say that they want to be daughters of the General, or daughters of Mount Paektu. It is clear when they talk that it means so much; that they want this very badly. Disappointingly, after all their preparation and sacrifice, on the day of the performance Kim Jong Il does not turn up.

Scary too is a classroom scene, in which the kids learn about the Great Leader and about the Americans: 'What are the three greatnesses of Kim Il Sung? Greatness in ideology, greatness in leadership and greatness in aura.' There is a lesson about the imperialist aggressors attacking, involving blackouts and air-raid practice, and the kids know that: 'We have to endlessly fight the Americans to the end.'

The games were held the day after the fifty-fifth anniversary of something or other. The day before the Games, there was dancing in Kim Il Sung Square, with 30,000 people dancing in unison. Then a choreographed torchlight student march in the evening, and a military parade after that. It is estimated that one

Chapter 15

million people in all took part. That is almost half the population of Pyongyang.

Mrs Wong, the hotelier in the place I am staying in Songchon, came in and saw a bit of the film. Though she couldn't understand the English, she got a kick out of seeing Pyongyang and listening to the two girls talking about the Mass Games. Travel around the country is not easy for regular folk, and getting permission to travel to Pyongyang is particularly difficult.

Another film by the makers of 'A State of Mind' is 'The Game of their Lives', about the 1966 North Korean World Cup team. There are interviews in the film with some of the players, who met the big guy before the World Cup. He told them to go to the competition and win one or two games; which they duly accomplished. They credit him with inspiring them. He should have said to them to win the competition outright. The players were in tears talking of the demise of the old man, saying they wished he was still with them now. The film is littered with comments from the players about the leader, and about their own part in the great economic march forward. The people of Korea asked them to carry the flag of *chollima* to the world stage, and the rest would look after the economy while they were away. Incidentally, after the World Cup, the South Korean press reported that many of the team were imprisoned upon their return for excess drinking and womanising while in England.

16
A Dagger Aimed At The Heart Of Japan

True enough, the country is calm. Calm as a morgue or a grave, would you not say?

Vaclav Havel

The Koreans like to consider the Korean peninsula as 'a dagger aimed at the heart of Japan', but it is more accurately characterised as 'a shrimp among whales'. The history of the peninsula gives an idea why.

There is a legendary figure called Tongun, who is often described as the Founding Father of Korea. A few years back, the old man decided that he wasn't merely a mythical figure, but would be given historical status. This was done in order to solidify a feeling of Korean nationality, and provide a historical focal point for orienting the demand for, and expectation of, a unified Korea. I

Chapter 16

suspect the old man saw himself as a modern embodiment of Tongun, helping to create immortality for himself.

A brief history of Korea would perhaps be useful at this point, to position the narrative. The history seems to consist mostly of war and fighting, and then a little more war, since time began. The story goes a little something like this:

Way back, five thousand years ago – hence the phrase 'five thousand years of Korean history' – there was a god called Hwan In. His son Ung wanted to be boss of all the people on Earth. Hwan In said okay, and sent him to the Korean peninsula. Ung established agriculture (it didn't start around the Euphrates after all!) and the laws of humanity. He met a bear and a tiger, who wanted to be human, so he made them human. The bear turned into a woman, who Ung married. They had a son called TanUng, who set up his capital in Pyongyang, and established his land, Korea.

From a more conventional perspective, there are remains of humans, settlers who came from Northeast Asia, dating back 400,000 years on the Korean peninsula. There is evidence that around 300BC, there were five main tribes on the peninsula, the largest being the Choson. The Chinese Han defeated this tribe in 109BC, and Chinese rule lasted four centuries, with much fighting. It was the fierce Kugoryo warriors from the mountains that gave the Chinese the most trouble. Eventually, together with the Paekche and Silla tribes, they wore down the Chinese. The Han on the peninsula were assimilated, and the 700-year 'Three Kingdom' period started.

In 668, the Silla kingdom, with the aid of the Chinese Tang, contrived to pretty much take over the Koryo and Paekche kingdoms. However, the Tang wanted to rule over the peninsula themselves, which didn't please the Silla at all. They collaborated with the defeated Koryo to oust the Tang. Until 784AD, living conditions on the peninsula continually improved. Then, for about 150 years, there were many revolts and uprisings by small

A Dagger Aimed At The Heart Of Japan

groups, eventually weakening Silla power. The Paekche re-emerged as the new power and eventually set up a new state around the Taedong River.

Next came the Mongols. They surprised the Koryo with their irresistible force as a fighting machine, and eventually Koryo became a Mongol vassal state. Using its newly acquired state as a pawn in its expansion plans, the Mongols got the Koryo to invade Japan, but with little success. Buddhism declined at this time, as the Koryo realised it was of no help in removing the Mongols from their shores. At this time, the Ming Chinese were on the ascendency on the mainland. Japanese pirates were also attacking the Koryo's shores. The Koryo sided with the Ming against the Mongols, as the lesser of two evils.

At this stage, the capital moved to Seoul, and a new Koryo leader became *Ri* (the Chosen – incidentally the same pronunciation as the Irish world for 'king'). Enjoying good relations with the Ming, Korea slowly expanded northwards and westward across the Yalu river. The Korean continent remained reasonably stable and calm for about two centuries, with its own unique class system and slaves.

In the meantime, Europe and the western powers were just embarking on their great seafaring adventures, expanding their empires. The Koryo, like the DPRK today, were distrustful of foreign powers. They saw attempted trade links as subterfuge, attempts to introduce new doctrines and untrustworthy ideals to the peninsula. It was in this period that the term 'The Hermit Kingdom' was first used.

The Japanese were also attempting to open Korea to foreign trade, and were also resisted. There were some bloody battles, until eventually the Qing (Chinese, again) stepped in to help out their Korean neighbours. The last thing the Chinese empire wanted was an aggressive Japanese power right on its doorstep. After repelling the Japanese, it looked as though the Qing would extend their domination to the peninsula. The Russians had

Chapter 16

other ideas, however, and were pressing from the northeast as well as by sea. The British, who wanted to curtail the expansion of the Russian empire, not wanting them to get a foothold in this important naval and trade peninsula, stepped in to repel the Russians at sea.

After all this to-ing and fro-ing, with the Koreans as pawns in the wars between empires, and a multitude of treaties and trade agreements, it eventually boiled down to the Japanese and the Russians facing off over the peninsula. They decided that all-out war was the best way to decide who would control Korea's fate. Japan entered Korea in 1904 and, with the help of some of the Koreans, forced the Russians out.

This brings us into the period of modern history. The Japanese controlled every aspect of Korean society. Korean women were used as 'comfort women' for occupying troops, and controls over industry, trade and education were total – creating the present-day Korean antipathy toward the Japanese.

All through the time of Japanese occupation, there were brief and impotent attempts at rebellion. All of these were quickly and brutally quashed. The First World War distracted global attention from the peninsula, and there was little the Koreans could do to improve their lot for a long time.

Kim Il Sung was born Kim Song Ju, on 15 April 1912, the year the *Titanic* sank. His name is first recorded in Japanese records in 1929, aged seventeen, when he was arrested in Manchuria for membership of the Korean Youth League. He joined a guerrilla band called the Korean Revolutionary Army. The Japanese broke them up, but Kim avoided arrest and joined various other guerrilla groups harassing the Japanese occupiers. He became leader of his own group, though he allegedly never had more than a few hundred men under him. The Japanese were too strong, and Kim fled to Russia, where he received further military training. There he married Kim Jong Suk around 1936. In 1942, Kim Jong Il was born in Khabbavorsk Camp (not

A Dagger Aimed At The Heart Of Japan

Mount Paektu, as the Korean revisionist mythologists claim). Kim senior became famous among Koreans in Russia for his exploits against the Japanese, but no more so than many others. However, he evaded capture, and at the end of the Second World War was free and able to emerge *victorious*. Opportunity knocks.

Kim Il Sung fought with the Russian Red Army, and impressed the hierarchy with his guerrilla tactics during the Second World War. He was handpicked as the most suitable general to look after the DPRK for the Russians. His close-knit bunch of fighting companions were his circle of safety over the coming years when consolidating his power base. He immediately proved himself to the peasantry, by encouraging them to sign up to the Korean Workers Party and dispossessing landlords and aristocrats of their land. He redistributed these lands among the peasants. For a brief while, North Korea had its own government, while the South had a US-backed administration from the end of the Second World War until 1948. From there on, the North and South went on diverging paths.

In 1949, after four years of babysitting and moulding respective governments in the North and South, both the States and the Russians left the peninsula. Separate elections had been held in both territories, heralding Kim Il Sung as the leader of the former, and Syngman Rhee as the leader of the latter. Rhee was also quite the strongman, enthusiastically quelling dissent and vanquishing anyone considered to have leftist tendencies. As soon as the Cold War superpowers had left the peninsula, it was the North, well organised and ready to go, that stormed across the thirty-eighth parallel, into Southern territory, and forced the ill-trained Southerners all the way back to Busan. Then in stepped the Americans, pushing the Northerners back into the North, all the way up to the Chinese border and across the Yalu River.

Chapter 16

The last sixty-five years of North Korean history is dominated by Kim's legacy, and the cult he developed around himself.

17
To China By Roads And Bridges

The Korean People have a tradition of fighting their way to victory with songs on their lips.

The Pyongyang Times

I was in Namchong today, and what a waste of a day it was. Our usual road was closed, due to 'road works', and we had to divert via Rongchon. A two-hour drive became a three-and-a-half-hour drive. We didn't arrive until almost one, and then we had to have the obligatory lunch. We were hanging around for an hour waiting for food, on a day when we had a technician from one of the institutes in Pyongyang with us; a day when we needed some productivity. We didn't actually start anything until three, and I was envisaging a three-and-a-half-hour drive back home. We are supposed to be back in Pyongyang by six at the latest on any

Chapter 17

evening. As it turned out, the farm technicians were actually in the place we were having lunch – we could have started talking at half-past one, but no-one had bothered saying this. We managed to travel the 'untrafficable' road on the way back, and saved lots of time. Thank goodness.

We took a diversion through the backstreets of Pyongsong, one of the towns en route to Rongchon and practically a satellite of Pyongyang. Despite similarities, such as big cubic concrete apartment blocks and an overall dull demeanour, each county town has a unique feel to it. The three towns I work in – Songchon, Namchong and Rongchon – all feel quite different, though it is hard to put my finger on what makes the difference.

Long hair in the DPRK is actively discouraged, as authorities claim that it is bad for intelligence – needing much nutrition, it starves the brain of energy. Styles between one and four centimetres are allowed. There was a television campaign discouraging long hair, as it is individualistic and thus goes against the thinking of a centrally planned economy. Reporters questioned men with long hair as to their motives. Free time, it seems, also leads to individualism, and so it is important that the State saturate the lives of each person. Incidentally, bald men are allowed hair up to seven centimetres long, probably for a comb-over.

Three units compete for power in the DPRK: the Korean People's Army (who are really in charge), the Korean Workers Party and the State itself (or the Assembly). Anyone can become a member of the Party. It contains many ordinary Joe Soaps, who show great loyalty to the cause. The Assembly is the select few from the Party who get to rubber-stamp legislation. People in the country can be split into three groups: the tomatoes, who are red to the core; the apples, who are not to be trusted; and then the grapes, who are irredeemable. Which of these 'classes' you belong to depends primarily on the family you were born into and then, secondarily, on your own personal records. There are

To China By Roads And Bridges

apparently fifty-one different levels of 'trust' you can be on, and you can move up and down between certain levels, depending on what you do and say. Records are kept about everyone.

* * *

I played a Korean version of chess yesterday. I enjoyed it, even though I couldn't figure it out. It is played on a board of eight by nine squares, but the pieces do not move in the squares – they move along the lines that make up the squares. And the place where the king and queen would be in real chess is made up of four squares, with added diagonals. There is only one major piece, like a king, which is limited in movement, and eight pawns and a few other irregular pieces. It is tactical, but I couldn't figure out how you are supposed to win.

* * *

We are supporting some health centres, in very rural, remote work teams, in building wells for clean water. I was in these villages today to see how digging is progressing. It has been three weeks since work started. Very little has been done in one place, and in another they hit solid rock after only a few metres. The health clinic manager said they would try to go another metre into the rock – they know the water is there, and really want to have it for the centre. Then, after lunch, I saw four women climb into the hole with hammers and chisels to restart digging. There were men standing over at the centre, looking on. This is supposed to be a community health centre, yet only the women are interested in it. It is fairly common that women take more of an interest when it comes to health issues. It is usually women who have to deal with sick children, sick husbands and sick grandparents. Because of the groundrock, I suggested that they check out the small spring up in the hill, about five hundred metres away. Perhaps it would be possible to excavate a bit more to find the actual source. I said maybe the men could do it. There was laughter from the women. Ironic laughter I think.

* * *

Chapter 17

From the *Pyongyang Times*:

Swinging and see-sawing are expressive of the national sentiment of the Korean people are being developed.

Seesaws were introduced to Korea during olden times. This was apparently so that women, who were not allowed outside their compounds, could use them to look over the high walls and get a glimpse of life outside, while pretending to play with children.

Korean traditional folk games include:

... shuttlecock kicking in which kids flaunt their talent kicking shuttlecocks or compete with each other to see who can kick more; stick counting game that increases counting ability and fosters the power of observation.

The cheerful looks of children playing folk games on holidays present a lively feeling to viewers.

* * *

Kim Jong Il recently paid a visit to the Russian Embassy in Pyongyang, to present a medal commemorating the sixtieth anniversary of the liberation of Korea. There is a picture of the embassy people, stony-faced and staring at the camera, with Kim looking very diminutive in the middle of them all. I meet some of these Russians regularly, in various restaurants and pubs. I have just extended an invite to them to come for St Patrick's Day drinks tomorrow evening, so they can tell us all about their close encounter.

* * *

Apparently, the dual pricing – where markets have one price, and State-owned stores have a different price – is to be scrapped. All businesses will have to operate on a real-cost basis, in the real world of supply and demand. Companies will also be allowed to determine their own wage rates, replacing fixed rates, which will really put the cat among the pigeons. This is a huge shift, though I don't fully understand all of its implications for the centrally controlled services.

To China By Roads And Bridges

Another change being considered is a 'field undertaking' system, which seems to be the first step in moving from collective farms to family units. This contrasts sharply with the recent Stalinesque policy of land realignment, in which huge fields were created, and vast tracts of land were cleared to be run as 'super-farms'. In 'field undertaking', villages undertake to manage small units of land, the outputs of which are partly distributed locally, and partly more centrally.

* * *

I am spending way too much time in cars, travelling to project sites. I try to use the time to read, but when the road gets bumpy, I get sleepy, and tend to doze off. Reading while travelling is where I get a lot of the useless information (or fascinating snippets) that build my knowledge of the DPRK. Doing this means I miss out on looking at the countryside sometimes. There is always something new to be seen, like these interesting, badly camouflaged tunnels, dug into the sides of hills on the way to Songchon. They remind me of the Batcave from the original Batman series, starring Adam West as Bruce Wayne. Are they here so that they can't be spotted from the air? What are they building in there?

* * *

I have to go home and prepare some Irish coffee for St Patrick's Day. We Irish have a responsibility to bring this day to people everywhere. There are five Irish people working in North Korea, and we are hosting a *semi-diplomatic* party in the *Friendship*. Representatives from the Korean Ministry of Foreign Affairs, as well as the foreign embassies, are expected. I am not sure what the Irish government would think of this *faux*-representation of Irish diplomacy on their behalf.

* * *

Literary classics of the DPRK include *Girl Chairman of the Co-operative Farm* and *The Flourishing Village*. Films include *Soldiers*

Chapter 17

Hear Rice-Ears Rustle, and *The Leader Comes to Our Village.* The themes of these can probably be guessed at from their titles.

* * *

I am just back from China. We had to bring one Toyota Landcruiser, an old one, to a garage there to get it repaired, and a new Landcruiser to get its first service in a proper Toyota dealer in order to maintain the warranty. There is no Toyota dealer in Pyongyang. So, we were bringing the old one to Dandong, and the new one to Dalian.

Dandong is a small city of 700,000 people, on the Chinese side of the Yalu River, facing the Korean town of Sinuju. The contrast is incredible. It reminded me strongly of the time I crossed the long, metal bridge from Afghanistan into Uzbekistan. Then I was going from one poor country to another, slightly less poor, country. Here, however, I was crossing from one strange, and very poor, country into a country that used to be similar, but has now moved on.

Looking from Sinuju to China, across a big metal bridge, you see tall, well-finished buildings, bright lights, lots and lots of cars, well-maintained roads, well-dressed people, lively shops, nice hotels, restaurants and a new, red suspension bridge. Looking across at the DPRK from Dandong, you see dull, very grey, four-storey monolithic apartment blocks, old lopsided electricity poles, old abandoned boats, and a Ferris wheel right beside the bridge, probably to show the Chinese how much fun they have in the DPRK. The wheel never turns.

For the journey to Sinuju, our entourage consisted of three cars, carrying seven ex-pats – three Italians, a German, a Swiss, an Irish and a New Zealander – along with a few Korean translators and drivers. We passed by Ryongchon, the small town where a train exploded in early 2004, just after the young lad had passed by, en route to China. There are many theories as to what caused the explosion, as apparently it was huge. Some say it was an assassination attempt, or a nuclear explosion. The generally

To China By Roads And Bridges

accepted theory now is that a railway carriage containing fertiliser nudged against another containing oil, which was heating up due to a loose electrical wire. As the fertiliser contained nitrate, once there was a sudden movement, there was heat and energy enough to make a big bang. It created a sixty-metre hole in the ground, killing 160 people and levelling buildings within a one-mile radius. The damaged houses have been replaced with poor quality, 'traditional' three- or four-storey apartment blocks. The remains of the wreckage are rusting nearby.

The bridge linking Sinuju to Dandong is the DPRK's main overland trade route. Customs opens in one direction at a time, and Koreans are not allowed to cross the bridge. The Chinese that cross aren't allowed any further. They have to unload all their wares at a stock control, and these are then reloaded onto Korean trucks.

I was the first person from our side to drive across this morning, at eleven. We had to leave our Korean drivers in Sinuju, to await our return. Crossing big border bridges always feels pretty special for some reason, especially in these kinds of countries. Plus, I was getting out of the DPRK for a few days, and looking forward to eating good food, having nice coffee and seeing new places. We had a five-hour drive to Dalian ahead of us the next day, and I was quite looking forward to seeing some of the countryside.

But for this first day, I was tired. I had to get up at five-thirty, after the St Patrick's Day party in the *Friendship*, hosted by the ever-welcoming Irish contingent of the DPRK. The party started for me at five in the evening, introducing Irish coffee, made with bad cream, to our Korean workmates. Guests arrived intermittently from about seven, including many MoFA and FDRC officials. They thought it was great to see all these foreigners dressed up in green, and were looking forward to some Irish Dancing. The planned Irish dancing never happened, unfortunately. At one in the morning, after a few hours of

Chapter 17

drinking our green cocktail, I ended the evening playing the tin whistle, blurting out a few ill-practised tunes on drunken fingers. Then I left and went to bed, with thoughts of the early start ahead of me. The phone rang at six, telling me they would pick me up in five minutes, and in the rush I forgot my jacket. It is still winter in the north of China.

I enjoyed lots of seafood, fresh from the fish tanks, over the four days in China. There didn't seem to be much else to eat, not that I am complaining. On the drive from Dandong to Dalian, the similarities with the DPRK were very evident, as the collective farms still cast a shadow on the landscape. Though collectivisation is effectively finished, people still live in the villages and work large areas of farmland, a lot of it by hand. The houses look very similar to those in Korea, and they have much the same greenhouses, though better maintained and more plentiful. For half of the journey, we drove on a secondary road through minor towns, which are being quickly built up with tall buildings. The smaller, more traditional houses are hidden from the road by the new construction, literally changing the faces of the towns. The rest of the journey was along a motorway. There was little activity, apart from the odd suicidal pedestrian – who would wait until the car was nearly upon them before deciding to idly amble across the road, eyes to the sky, being rudely disturbed from their reveries by the sound of car horns and screeching brakes. It was as if we had never left North Korea. People here seem to have the same great faith and trust in drivers to avoid them and give way.

* * *

I am back in the DPRK now, back into the frustrations of work, with poor suppliers, low-quality materials and late deliveries, and problems with this, that and the other. It feels like I have never been away. I am in lovely Rongchon again for the night, and I can't go to look at the pipes, fittings and fixtures that are supposed to be in a warehouse, because the 'keymaster' has gone

To China By Roads And Bridges

walkabout. No one knows where he is. This is not the first time this has happened. On a positive note, I am going to a World Cup qualifier tomorrow afternoon. The DPRK is playing Bahrain, in the Kim Il Sung Stadium. The ticket costs forty dollars.

I just went downstairs for dinner in this grey, cold and empty hotel, and experienced an air-raid drill for the first time. In the Diplomatic Compound in Pyongyang, we are spared this sort of thing (probably because if a real one happens, they will see the bright lights of the foreigners' compound and hit there first). Tonight, just when I sat down for dinner, there was a loud siren, like in a WWII movie. All the lights were turned off. Everyone seemed a little embarrassed for me, having to endure this, as if they know it is a charade. All the same, there was much rushing around, turning lights off and closing curtains, while my dinner was getting cold. They insisted I turn my computer off. It went on for an hour, and I eventually had dinner at eleven. Just in time, as it is Good Friday tomorrow, and I have to fast. I couldn't manage that if I didn't get a proper dinner this evening.

* * *

Today was the World Cup qualifier in the Kim Il Sung Stadium: the DPRK versus Bahrain, in the second round of the Asian qualifiers. On arriving at the stadium, standing outside, I was surprised at the lack of people. There was a substantial number of cars, the majority of them Mercedes, though not as many as you might expect for such a big match. My translator and accompaniment for the match immediately looked around, and said 'So many cars!' It is all relative, I guess. The Kim Il Sung Stadium, a big mass of concrete, is probably the main stadium in Pyongyang. Its competition is the Kim Jong Il Stadium across the city, which is smaller and not as well maintained. Both of these are dwarfed by the massive tin can that is the *MayDay* Stadium. The *MayDay* looks impressive from a distance, given its

Chapter 17

location on an island on the Taedong River, visible for miles from up and down the river. Up close, it's a shed.

Approaching the Kim Il Sung stadium, there were a lot of Koreans clamouring at the gate, trying to get in, without tickets. I was led to the foreigners' section, a small portion of the ground, where all NGO workers get seated, along with the Bahrain supporters, and the Korean-Japanese. On entering the stadium, I was impressed. The place was full of people. No bright replica shirts though, only the autumnal shades of Maoist suits. It was still half an hour to kick-off, and the two teams were on the pitch, kicking balls around. On the far side of the pitch, a brass band was playing music intermittently. A conductor was directing portions of the crowd, all clapping in unison, keeping to the beat.

The match got underway a few minutes late, and the Koreans maintained a controlled possession of the ball, attempting to break down a packed Bahraini defence. The Bahrain team seemed to be made up of fairly average footballers, bigger than the Koreans, falling over and play-acting repeatedly. But the Koreans, though in control, seemed very predictable and robotic; there didn't seem to be any life or passion in the team. When they went one-nil down from a counter-attack, the first attack by the Bahraini team, there was nothing. Absolute silence. The game continued in the same vein, with the Koreans quietly in control, never really displaying any passion or urgency. The Bahraini team looked comfortable enough, as the Koreans tentatively probed their rear-guard with attempted one-twos and quick interplays, never quite finding the goal at their mercy. In the second half, they displayed much more conviction and created a few chances. Only luck, and the short-sightedness of the referee, prevented them from equalising, as their skilful midfielders were first to every ball. The goal just wasn't coming though.

Then, all of a sudden, the same story again – a quick break out of defence by Bahrain; two passes, the Koreans all at sea, and the unmarked number nine slipped the ball into the net from eight

To China By Roads And Bridges

yards out. Two attacks, two goals. There was still half an hour left, and the Koreans continued to press, throwing everything at the Bahraini defence. With two attempts cleared off the line, they finally scored. A cross from the number fourteen, a mis-header by the Bahrain centre-half, and the ball was pushed over the line by the Korean centre-forward. Two-one, and the crowd, subdued for most of the match, was getting excited. A Mexican wave was attempted with initial enthusiasm, though it failed to make it all the way around the stadium.

The noise from the crowd was like nothing I have experienced before at a football match, going from deathly silence to a unified 'ooh' every so often, sometimes in tandem with a Korean attack, sometimes, seemingly choreographed for effect, indicating a late tackle or a spurned chance, where none ever existed. The Koreans continued pushing forward for the last twenty minutes, with some neat passing. They were unfortunate not to have a penalty given when the centre-forward had his jersey pulled. The referee saw nothing. The Bahrain team continued to frustrate, play-acting and feigning injury, but they held out for the five minutes of added time.

The end of the match was marred by abuse hurled at the referee as he left the pitch. Two bottles, thrown from the crowd, narrowly missed the hapless official. The North Koreans, playing with two J-League players, left the pitch to applause, and the screams of ten Japanese-Korean female supporters in the 'foreigners' section of the crowd, in contrast to the quiet and downcast exit of the regular grey-suited Koreans. One feels that if only there was a Roy Keane, to instil some urgency and passion in the talented, disciplined Koreans, they would have overrun Bahrain. I am definitely looking forward to the game against Iran in April.

18
Springtime, Bird 'Flu And Defeat

The US Government wants the young generation of all countries to set the disgusting uneducated pervert drug addict American movie stars and singers as their models.

www.korea-dpr.com (2005)

The temperature is rising out of the negatives, and the traffic ladies have nice, bluer, brighter uniforms, with skirts instead of heavy woollen trousers. It's springtime at last. Out of nowhere it was twenty degrees Celsius yesterday, and I am slightly sunburnt after playing football for a few hours. It is nice to feel warm.

I am in the wonderful little-big town of Namchong. Large or small is relative, depending on who you are talking to. I have had a really trying day. I woke up tired, and my stomach didn't feel too hot. I wanted a cigarette, and eventually gave in. I was doing

Chapter 18

so well until today. The plan was to do what should have been a very simple survey, if things were allowed to run smoothly. But no. We arrived at twelve, and had to wait until one to have lunch (you can't skip lunch here, it is not the done thing. The Koreans aren't happy if they don't get at least an hour, with a bit of a snooze thrown in).

At two, we were ready to go. We went to the pump station and talked about pumps. We measured a few things: the sizes of inlets and outlets, the types of valves needed, the number of couplings and bends required; and then we went outside and started surveying. All was going well. Then the battery on the theodolite died. *Mea culpa*. I went to charge it for an hour, and I said we could go to the other pump station and discuss the second pipeline while we waited. After leaving the theodolite in the hotel charging, I came back to find most of the FDRC people had disappeared, and we weren't allowed to survey this pipeline or visit the pump station. I have no idea why. There could be loads of reasons, but who is going to tell me? I am not privy to that kind of information.

So I huffed and puffed, and complained that it was the FDRC themselves who requested us to replace these pipelines and pumps. Why would they ask us, if they weren't going to co-operate? Some of the lads went off to talk to the County Chairman, but by this stage the battery was nearly charged. I suggested we get the battery and finish surveying the first pipeline, so we did. A young soldier diligently followed me to the water tank, where I had a great view of the city, looking down over the hydroelectric dam and the artificial lake behind it. It was a great photo opportunity, if I had had the nerve to take it. Then another young soldier boy came along, out of breath after climbing up the hill at pace. He grunted at us. He was clearly concerned about where we were, and what we might see. If I knew what I was looking at, he might have had reason to worry, but I couldn't see anything of concern. We finished quickly and

Springtime, Bird 'Flu And Defeat

were ushered back down the hill. When the survey was done, it was nearly six.

At the start of the day, I had asked Mr Bang how long he thought the day's work would take? He reckoned one or two hours. Four hours later, we were only half done, if even. On returning down the hill, I gently enquired whether we could do the other pipeline, and the answer was, 'Of course!', as if it had never been an issue. Apparently, this pipeline runs very close to a particular *institution*, which I imagine means a military barracks. There were a lot of young soldier boys and girls hanging around while I was surveying. They seemed as nervous as I was.

* * *

I am staying in a nice little guesthouse in Namchong. The big man stayed here three times in his life, when he was in the area giving a bit of timely, on-the-spot guidance. I think I will be sleeping in the same bed as he did. Not the most pleasant thought. The room I am in has a very interesting toilet. It is quite high off the ground. I feel like I am four years old again, with my feet dangling from it. It has a cushioned seat, which heats up when the electricity is on. I am not sure how I should feel about that.

* * *

I had another strange day today, after completing the survey of the troublesome pipeline. We headed off to Rongchon in the early afternoon, to meet the local FDRC men and go look at wells in Rimsan and Sinsok. We were a little bit late arriving at the meeting point, on the Rongchon–Namchong road. When we got there, there was no sign of the FDRC officials who we have been working with for a few years now. We spotted them down the road, and they hopped into the car. We were informed that we were not going to Sinsok because, I was told, the FDRC officials were in 'a bad mood'. The county FDRC boss was holding his face, and I thought maybe he had a toothache. Then

Chapter 18

we had to stop for the other FDRC official to get out and be sick.

At this stage, I was wondering what was going on. I was told he was bitten. Bitten? Dog? Insect? No, by some military soldiers. He was beaten. The two officials, while waiting for us, were beaten up by some young soldiers. Why? I don't know. It isn't something I am going to be told. I am still shocked, as these people are government people, though of lowly enough rank. By the time we stopped, they both had very swollen cheekbones, and one very black eye.

*　*　*

The DPRK Government has announced that bird 'flu has struck a number of farms around Pyongyang. It is a big thing for the big guys to admit something like that. Usually they pretend everything is fine, that the DPRK is immune to all these things. The State still claims that the DPRK has had no cases of HIV/AIDS. It is difficult for anyone to refute the regime's claims, due to the lack of verifiable information. China attempted a similar denial for some time. Avian 'flu poses a threat to the livelihood of the Korean farmer. Poultry farming is a big industry in the country, and eggs in particular are an important source of nutrition, as protein-poor diets are a big problem here. There has been a bit of a push to encourage bean-curd production, as a high-protein staple food. It is fairy popular here in the form of tofu. A lot of eggs are eaten in the countryside, and form a component of the traditional national dish, cold noodles. Apparently each family is allowed one chicken and one egg per month. When I travel to the county towns, I would probably eat a few eggs per day. I never realised the rations were so low. I will have to cut back. I must look like a glutton.

At the Inter-Agency meeting today at the WFP, everyone was talking about bird 'flu. It is being taken very seriously here. The military is adamant that it will keep avian influenza out of the DPRK. People coming through the airport have to spend a few

Springtime, Bird 'Flu And Defeat

days in quarantine at Koppensang. Not the worst place to stay. During the discussion, the Russian Embassy representative interjected, saying that a dead girl was found in their Embassy grounds. With respect to the avian 'flu, what should they do about it? There was a stunned silence. No one really knew what to say. Eventually the OCHA rep asked whether the girl was Russian or Korean. 'Nyet, nyet. Not a dead girl. A dead bird.'

* * *

The few days of great weather has made a huge difference to the landscape. Throngs of people are out in the fields, doing things to the land that I don't understand, and there is greenery – leaves on trees, and flowers in the places that have not been ploughed. Springtime can make you feel all warm inside, as well as out.

* * *

Rimsan, the other village we visited today, is also referred to as 'Afforestation', though I cannot figure out why. One would think the answer would be very evident, but I am starting to think the name is ironic. This is where the well-digging has met rock after three-and-a-half metres. It looks way more than three-and-a-half metres when you are looking down into it. I have been at the bottoms of ten-metre-deep wells, though I didn't dare climb down the wells we were digging in Afghanistan – they were about forty metres. The last time I was here, it was women doing all the work. Today there were a few men down the hole. It isn't easy work. I try to avoid pressuring people to do work because the FDRC wants to save face in front of an international NGO. I think that this wasn't the case here.

* * *

The drive between Rongchon and Namchong is spectacular, both for its natural scenery and for the industrial and mining eyesores that line the road. The road runs along a river valley, filled with old rickety trucks loaded with coal or coal-dust. The road then runs alongside a railway line, carrying lots of the same.

Chapter 18

All of these mines feed the ugly Rongchon power station. We could see the tall Rongchon chimneys, about ten kilometres away in the distance, with a big plume of smoke forming high in the sky, where the three individual plumes meet. Along the valley is an old place where Kim Il Sung hid during the war of liberation. Apparently there are bullet holes preserved from the fighting.

I noticed today that the murals along the roads, depicting happy agricultural rural life, have all been repainted in the last few weeks. I don't know how often this happens, but the new images are supposed to fuel pride in the peasants, to encourage faster farming or something like that.

* * *

I think all the FDRC people have received State-issued red scarves of late. Everyone is sporting one this week. There was a Pyongyang-wide ban on bikes ten days ago for no reason apparent to me.

* * *

Oh dear. Outplayed and outclassed. DPRK 0, Iran 2. Like the last game against Bahrain, DPRK played neat football, and let in silly goals due to sloppy defending. The stadium was packed again, so much so that I had trouble getting in, even with my official forty-dollar ticket. I ended up standing to watch the match, as they seemed to have double-booked some of the foreigners' seats. The Koreans kept giving the ball away, trying silly passes, instead of the more careful, controlled brand of football they played in the last match. Maybe it was because Iran put them under more pressure than Bahrain did last week. Iran went one-nil up in the first half, when a floated free kick got the slightest of touches and bounced inside the far post. The second goal, early in the second half, was a carbon copy of the goals given away against Bahrain. A quick break out of defence, the Koreans seeming to amble back; a quick pass inside, and a first-time shot into the bottom corner. This prompted the Koreans into life. They had two penalty claims turned down. The second,

Springtime, Bird 'Flu And Defeat

which I thought wasn't a penalty, resulted in one man being sent off, as the whole team did a Manchester United-esque intimidation of the referee, even physically pushing him a few times. Then the Korean fans started throwing bottles and cans onto the pitch, as well as ripping up some plastic seating and throwing them onto the pitch too. The game was held up for a few minutes while, from each entrance, in marched squadrons of about twenty teenage soldiers in formation, to calm the situation. It didn't have much of an effect. The linesman on the far side of the pitch was nearly hit by bottles.

After the full-time whistle, the Koreans left the pitch fairly quickly. The Iranians had to wait in the centre circle until they could be guaranteed safe passage to the dressing room. The referee and his assistants had to hang around for about half an hour, as there was an irate bunch of fairly old men above the exit in foul moods. After the Bahrain game, where bottles were thrown and spit aimed at the referee as he left, this was precautionary, if anything. Some sort of riot police were called in, and all these little soldiers with batons marched in from the exits, saying, *'Kapsuda, kapsuda'* (let's go, let's go), while I hung around to see what would happen. I had to leave the stadium, as one foreigner with a camera tried to take some photos and was subjected to much anger from some Koreans, until he took out his film and handed it over.

Outside, a few thousand fans were still waiting around (for the Korean team or the referee, I don't know which). They tried storming a few entrances, until eventually the Korean team came out to be hoisted 'victoriously' onto the supporters' shoulders. Then I left. Any Koreans I have talked to blame the referee for the result. The Korean news is claiming corruption and anti-Korean bias.

* * *

I have been trying for a while to get one of our Korean staff enrolled in a distance-learning course at Loughborough

Chapter 18

University's London campus, studying 'Low Cost Sanitation'. I don't think this has happened here before, though many of the elite get to travel, and diplomatic families might go to foreign or international schools. Distance learning would involve regular Internet access, browsing the web as well as independent learning. He may eventually get a diploma, which could give him the chance to work abroad if the opportunity could ever arise. Usually North Koreans can only use a Korean *intranet*, where everything is controlled, censored and State-run. Today I was told that all this was going to go ahead, and then a few hours later I was re-informed that there was no chance. No reason given. I was advised not to push it.

19
Mass Games Training, Surveying And One Lost Puppy

For us in Russia communism is a dead dog. For many people in the West, it is still a living lion.

Alexander Solzhenitsyn

I am just back from Thailand. There were complimentary copies of *Newsweek* and *Time* on the airplane. Naturally, I was quite pleased to have some English current-affairs material to read. Even better was to read that Kim Jong Il was in *Time* magazine's one hundred most important people of 2005, alongside other noteworthy personalities such as Mary Robinson and twenty-year-old basketball player LeBron James. A twenty-year-old NBA professional basketballer could be said to have the world at his

Chapter 19

fingertips, but Kim Jong Il claims to really have it at his fingertips, in the form of a big red button. And the two young lads who have made their fortune with Google have put the world at everyone else's fingertips.

More notably, *Newsweek* had a big section dedicated to the memory of Pope John Paul II. I made an attempt to steal it off the plane (the irony), and ended up losing it before I had a chance to read it. I was in Thailand when he died, and wasn't able, and still haven't been able, to ascertain the reaction to his death. I am sad, because he really did try to maintain the values of the Church, despite great opposition by 'forward-thinking' people, those who say that the Church should move with the times; that times and attitudes are changing, and the Church should too. I was fortunate, on the day after the death of the Pope, to get to go to Mass in Bangkok. It was my first time in five months, as there is no Mass here. That, for me, is a very long time. I was in no rush to leave, though I had all of Bangkok and Thailand to see. I was content to sit there, and enjoy what has been denied to me in the DPRK – partially by my own choice in coming here. The weather was warm, and the church was practically open-air, with open doors on all sides and birds flying in and out.

There was even a Mass in Pyongyang, the first in a long time, to mark the passing of the Pontiff. Apparently it was a Korean, now living in the States, who celebrated the Mass. I wasn't there, but I have heard first-hand accounts. There were about a hundred people present, in the bright, colourful little church just up the road. I missed quite a few things while I was away, including the Great Leader's birthday, on 15 April. There was much fanfare, I am told, and dancing in Kim Il Sung Square, with foreigners included. The highest fountains in the world, on the Taedong River, were in full spray, but I missed that too. I also missed a terrible drama involving Kiki. He went missing and got ill while I was away. It really was a big drama. More later. Right now, at ten in the evening, I am in the office. Kiki is here, and I think he is

Mass Games Training, Surveying And One Lost Puppy

constipated. Not to be crude, but he is farting furiously, and it stinks. I have to get him outside. I never thought such a little dog could make such a big smell.

My boss left while I was away. She was very upset, and let down the Iron Lady mask that she tends to maintain. Her leaving coincides with the departure of three other long-serving NGO personnel in the country. It will leave a big gap in terms of institutional memory, contextual understanding, and the social scene. They have been here for three years, directing the few NGOs, and have been the centre of the small expat community. Good luck to them. Their time is done.

One thing I didn't miss was the DPRK marathon. I got back just before it, but I wasn't in any fit shape to compete. My hip is hurting, and I have not been training. The men's and women's races were both won by Koreans. There was a Norwegian runner who, according to the *Pyongyang Times*, struggled on to finish the marathon despite injury, inspired by thinking of the Korean Sun Festival. I wonder. I ambled along to the Kim Il Sung Stadium to watch the end of it, and managed to walk right in, onto the running track, to watch the first seven or eight men finishing. The guards at the stadium just assumed I was with the crew of one of the international runners. Then someone came up to me and asked to see my ID card, and I was rumbled. I was asked gently to please remove myself from the stadium.

* * *

I finally managed to get hold of the book I mentioned many months ago, *Three Winters Cold* by Philip Crosbie, an Irish priest/missionary who happened to be here during the Korean War. He was taken by the communist Koreans as they retreated north during the first US/UN advance. It is a harrowing story, but written with no sense of bitterness or anger. Father Crosbie was one of many Religious taken at that time. Their lives were lived in parallel with a number of American POWs, who were treated far, far worse. At the same time, it must be pointed out

Chapter 19

that these were mostly old men and women, some in their eighties, and the conditions they endured were harsh. Father Crosbie describes the *Death March,* a one-hundred-mile walk along the Yalu River, in which the captives, in all their infirmity, were pushed along at a punishing pace. They were killed off if they slowed up or fell behind.

One enduring section of the book is a frank conversation the author had with one of his captors, discussing communism and the lack of freedoms involved. The captor disagreed, saying that there is freedom in communism, only that some freedoms are not compatible with the system. I think that humans, by their nature, cannot live in such a system. In communism, someone has to be in control, and with control comes power, and with power comes inequality, and once there is inequality - the system fails. Once one person wants out, and starts being entrepreneurial, then the system will fail – you can't expect everyone else to sit by, working selflessly for the common good, while some people move onwards and upwards, making money and owning material goods. Humans are flawed, selfish and prone to greed, envy and jealousy; we have aspirations and personal dreams. The communist ideal could only work once all of this is given up.

* * *

My first mission on returning from Thailand is to stop smoking and lead a healthier lifestyle. I started with a trip to the *MayDay* Stadium, to do a lap of the island – about eight kilometres. What a struggle. The run was made easier by the sight of thousands of youngsters all around the stadium, preparing for the Mass Games in October. There were so many. Watching them was a spectacle in itself. They are probably still at the audition phase. To give you an idea: to run around the stadium is a two-kilometre circuit. The whole two-kilometre circumference, to a depth of about one hundred metres, was filled with coordinated and regimented groups of kids, all wearing white (*Nike*) baseball caps. They were

Mass Games Training, Surveying And One Lost Puppy

there until eight in the evening. There must have been tens of thousands. They still need a little practice, but it is an arresting spectacle to see so many teenagers attempting to move in harmony. They are accompanied by severe old ladies, barking through megaphones, and cars with propaganda PA systems on top, keeping everyone in time.

* * *

There was much drama while I was away, with Kiki and his host of minders. The plan was that he would go to a good Korean home – with a Korean who works with the German NGO – for a two-week trial period while I was gone. The idea was that they would keep him if it all went well. He lasted one night. Her kids, who really liked the dog, were harassed by him all night. He wouldn't let them sleep and, after one night, he was returned to our office. He proceeded to go missing on numerous occasions, prompting the whole of the diplomatic community to go on a dog-hunt. He got sick, was given antibiotics by the UN doctor, and worried everyone to death. Much to my surprise, on reaching the airport in Pyongyang, the Swedish Ambassador gave me a full update on the dog's exploits and general wellbeing.

Then the strangest of all scenarios unfolded yesterday. Upon returning from Namchong, from a meeting with a disastrous Korean supplier, Mr Ri came up to tell me there was some bad news. He offered his condolences. Kiki had died. I was upset, even though I was looking to offload him to a better home. I went home to see the remains, if they were still there. I was thinking how it was all my fault – he had spent too much time alone in a fifth-floor apartment, and it was probably something to do with having to wait hours to go to the toilet every day. As I went to put the key in the lock of my apartment, there was a familiar whine of anticipation from inside the door. I was greeted by what put me in mind of a decapitated hen – a white ball of fluff, bouncing up and down, more full of life than he had been for days. Resurrection indeed. Kiki had what seems to have been

Chapter 19

a dose of constipation. When I brought him for walks, he would stop every hundred metres, grunt and heave, and then give up and lie down and sigh. He seems to have cleared all that out. I don't know where the story of his demise came from. I think it is time I found him a better home.

*　*　*

We received a delivery yesterday, a month-and-a-half late, from one of our Korean suppliers. The consignment, supposed to consist of pipes and fittings for rural water-pipe systems, was a complete disaster. We will now have to go through a whole process of threatening them with cancellation of contracts, and withholding payments. However, as they are a Korean company, they are essentially an element of the State at some level, so there will be vested interests that will make it difficult to cancel the contract outright or blacklist them with the other agencies. I am sure some *compromise* will be reached.

*　*　*

I heard stories today from two people who went to the DMZ separately. Both went to the *Friendship* Museum in Kaesong (that I was never told about). The *Friendship* Museum contains gifts from various countries to the DPRK. From Russia, with love. From India. From Vietnam. Most countries have an individual, dedicated room. When Gianfranco asked where the Italian room was, there was a delayed muttering, and he was told that it was under renovation. When the Swiss lady went there, she asked the same question about the Swiss room, and got the same answer. I never heard about an Irish room. I never asked.

*　*　*

Kiki is missing. He wandered off yesterday while we were playing volleyball at the WFP. He was sniffing around when I went in to play volleyball. He stayed outside, marking his territory and what have you. Volleyball lasted about an hour. When I came out, expecting him to be in the vicinity, there was no sign at all. Now,

Mass Games Training, Surveying And One Lost Puppy

a day later, there is still no sign. I spent about two hours this morning walking the backstreets and alleyways of Pyongyang, outside the Diplomatic Compound, places I would never normally visit, hoping to hear a bark or a growl or something. There were lots of barks and whines. There are numerous alleyways and backstreets around the back of the WFP, home to lots of regular Koreans, where foreigners don't ever go. Everyone always seems to be carrying something somewhere. I think this will be an enduring memory for me of Korea: the constant carrying of things.

Korean city dwellers seem to be somewhat envious of country folk, who have their own private patch of land, however small, around their house for cultivation. City dwellers only have a balcony, and most of these are covered with glass or plastic sheeting to create a sort of greenhouse for growing. I would love to be able to get inside a regular Korean apartment in Pyongyang, just to see. I imagine Pyongyang would be an anthropologist's dream, as the people really are environmentally moulded in a different way to any other country in the world.

* * *

I was in Songchon, the city in the mountains, last week, *monitoring* the progress of our rural water systems and latrines. The authorities do not like the use of the word 'monitoring'. They don't like the idea of anyone monitoring anything in the country. A preferable term is 'providing technical assistance'; though I think that is a bit derogatory, especially as the technicians there know better than I do how to manage the water systems. Whatever words are used, it was good to see some work being done, and pipes being put into the ground.

We went to see the spring for one particular work team, in Naedong. It was a long, tough climb. At the top of the valley was a sort of plateau, with a few houses. It was very, very serene. After all that climbing, to get to this beautiful area, and take in the clean air and look around, was really lovely. Even the Farm

Chapter 19

Manager remarked that I seemed to be enjoying the scenery. I was. And I was impressed with the existing spring box, protecting the spring and collecting the water. It was constructed locally from slabs of stone. This was easier than trying to get bags and bags of cement up there.

That same day, I saw an electrician putting up new electricity poles. Health and Safety would have been interested to see the process in action. The technician shimmied up these shabby, unstable poles, and, hanging off the crossbar, attached the wires, and then shimmied back down. He only has very thin plastic shoes, and no gloves. It can't be easy.

* * *

I am in Songchon again, waiting for the electricity to come back on. I am feeling thankful for battery back-up, so that I have something to do in the dark – it is too early to sleep, but too dark

Mass Games Training, Surveying And One Lost Puppy

to read. I haven't yet got myself organised enough to bring a torch. I came here to check on a delivery of large pumps, motors and control-boxes, from a Korean supplier that has been the cause of many of my headaches recently. It was supposed to be here months ago, and has finally arrived.

They are not the best. The control boxes look antiquated, though they could possibly have been functional if they hadn't been damaged in transit. I was expecting high-tech flashing lights and touch-control switches. These have large levers and manual cut-offs. No automatic depth sensors or current surge breakers. It seems to be the norm here that things get damaged in delivery – assuming they weren't already damaged before leaving.

This contract is a supply-and-install agreement, yet no-one arrived with the goods to do the installation. The local FDRC were told (by the Korean company, which is Government-run, as all companies are) to install the pumps and motors quickly themselves. I told them not to, because the control boxes are missing bits and there is damage to the outer casings. The pump and motor did not come on a single base, but separately, meaning there will be problems with relative motion and vibration. Though the two motors are the same specification in theory, they are quite different in shape and size, which makes me worry that they are not actually the same spec at all, and probably duds picked up on the cheap. Plus the control boxes are made for only one pump, rather than operating two pumps alternately, and the local technician says they are for powering sub-stations, not pumping stations. This could get litigious.

The lesson to learn here? Don't work with Korean suppliers. We chose them because they were the most competitive tender, and we also figured that locally made goods would be easier to maintain, and be in line with local expertise. They still got it badly wrong. I got it badly wrong.

* * *

Chapter 19

The rest of the day was spent surveying, or rather watching my newly trained Korean colleague and his team do the survey. I had to laugh at his organisation. He has things much better organised than I could if I was getting him to translate for me. He has four helpers from the local water board and the County FDRC at his beck and call. Two are carrying the targets, one is drawing maps and one is numbering each point on a stone and putting it in the ground. They have also created flag signals, with white and red flags to identify and instruct each target-carrier. Much like directing an airplane. This *technician* is actually a translator; he isn't supposed to be doing this job at all.

We went to a lot of trouble to get an 'expert' on water systems from the Ministry of City Management (MoCM) to assist us in getting this town's water system sorted out. He is no expert. He has no interest, and he seems to have a weakness for hard liquor, and not just in the evenings. This is hearsay so far, but he was dying from a hangover when I arrived today, and could barely sit for lunch with us before going back to bed. Yesterday, he was also hung over and unable to do anything. The local FDRC repeatedly tell me that they can't carry out the survey without our translator. They were practically pleading with me. They are being diplomatic about it, but apparently our 'expert' was in such a state yesterday that incontinence prevailed in the jeep. He was sober when I first met him. He seemed intelligent and interested, though that could have been for my benefit.

It was good to be out surveying. The authorities don't want me doing much walking around the town. It is a mining town, as most county towns in the mountains are, and apparently it mines for gold. According to the central FDRC, I am not allowed to look through the theodolite, in case I see stuff that I am not supposed to see. There were no objections from the local guys today, as they just want to get the water system built. The local County Manager and his officials have a difficult balancing act to maintain – keeping the national Government happy, but also responding to the demands of their constituents. One of them,

Mass Games Training, Surveying And One Lost Puppy

the designated responsible councillor for water, was telling me today that three old ladies were haranguing him about the state of the water system. There is little he can do about it without support from the Government. It is good to hear that local women feel they can hold local government to account, but it also highlights the impotence of local officials in a centrally planned system.

While we were surveying, crowds of kids were swarming around us. They thought the surveying equipment was some sort of camera, and wanted their photos taken. We duly obliged. The kids are good fun. They aren't completely aware yet that they need to fear the foreign devil. Usually the local FDRC official threatens them with a slap if they come too near. While we were surveying by the river, I noticed two girls washing their hair in the river. It exemplified why we are working on water projects in the town. The people here obviously take a lot of pride in their appearance, especially the girls, but in a city, with only river-water to wash in, it has got to be difficult to stay clean and look nice. I am constantly amazed at how sparkling white the school uniform shirts and blouses always are.

It is always warming to get a reaction from kids when in strange places. They usually oblige, but here it is usually from a distance. Today, even a few adults hung around and had a laugh at us, wondering what we were doing. Two old women asked what we were at, and when told that we were trying to do something with the water system, they were delighted. They said they would like to drink some clean spring water in Songchon before they die. The pressure is on. This is a town of about 60,000 people, with hardly a tap between them. Even our driver was getting interested in the workings of the theodolite; or so I thought, until it was pointed out to me that he was using it to look at a pretty young lady washing clothes in the river.

* * *

Chapter 19

I was running again yesterday at the *MayDay* Stadium, as an excuse to watch preparations for the Mass Games. I was quickly embarrassed by young girls, on an adjacent set of steps, running up and down their steps a lot quicker than I was on mine. This is part of their training for the Mass Games. There has been much progress in the two weeks since I was last here. The training is becoming more synchronised. There is much more gymnastics now, and it looks good. They have six months of practising to do before the big day, and they seem to do it all day long, six days a week. The conductors are belting out instructions with their loudspeakers and propaganda vans, and berating youngsters, en-masse, like military commanders.

20
The Manifesto And The Invisible Hand

Independence is an attribute given to man by society, not nature; it is not a natural gift, but has been formed and developed socially and historically.
Kim Jong Il

I made a point over the past few days of reading Karl Marx's *Communist Manifesto*. I had never read it. I said earlier in this diary that I thought communism, or the socialism that goes with it, has potential in theory, but is not practical. I take it back. It isn't great in theory either. It may have been a brave alternative to the *slave* labour of the industrial revolution, but really it just involves making people into instruments of industry and agriculture, feeding the system for no real reward except sustenance of the masses and the system. Ambition is removed. Hope and desires are removed. There is not even space for a God for comfort.

Chapter 20

* * *

I learned that in Korean, *zuckara* means 'go to hell' or some equivalent, and *kae-tung-gotchi* is sh*t', or more explicitly 'dog-sh*t', colloquially. I am pleased to have found a few swear words, though I will never use them. They are the extent of my Korean, besides *Heineken han byong megju doh chom jus ay oo*; and *tambay jus shipsee-ooo*. These mean, 'Another Heineken beer please,' and, 'Give me a cigarette.' It is difficult to learn bad words and foul language in Korea. The Koreans are very reserved when talking to foreigners, and get embarrassed at hearing swear words even used. Language here remains generally much more formal and respectful than in the South, from what I can gather. Manners are greatly prized here, and bad manners both offend and shock.

* * *

Kiki is still missing.

* * *

I downloaded the International Crisis Group report on North Korea, containing a lot of up-to-date information on the country, and some interesting opinions. It is titled 'Can the Iron Fist Accept the Invisible Hand?'

I had a really good chat with one of the waitresses in the *Diplo* last night, at twelve o'clock, as the place was nearly empty. She told me a bit about the DPRK's relationship with Japan. A lot of the hate for Japan seems to be manufactured and fed by the State. People are not allowed to deal with it, to grieve and let it go. Instead the regime fuels the hatred. I could see she was upset, talking about grandmothers of people she knows, who were comfort women for the Japanese, and how the shame, more than anything else, was hard to deal with. She told me her grandmother never learned to write in Korean, because the Japanese stopped any Korean-language education. Her gran would ask her to help write her name by guiding her hand. The Japanese won't say sorry, and this is what is really eating at the

The Manifesto And The Invisible Hand

Koreans. It makes it easy to feed the animosity. Though she uses the word 'hate', I don't know if she really feels it. I think it is a word that people are institutionalised to use.

* * *

The speed with which everything has changed from being dull and wintry to full-blown spring blossom and greenery is incredible. A week or two ago, we were playing on a yellowy straw football pitch, and now it is a lush, green pasture. The trees are all in blossom, and the flowers and trees lining all the streets transform the city. Today was May Day, 1 May, a much celebrated festival in Korea. It is a day for picnics on the newly arrived green grass, for hanging out by the river with family and friends, getting drunk and singing songs. I was told there would be lots of picnic-makers along the river, and decided I would spend the early afternoon ambling around among the people.

I bumped into one of our translators purely by chance, picnicking with his family by the river, near the *Juche* Tower. I sat down and met his parents, his wife and children. It is very unusual to meet colleagues outside of work, and more unusual to have access to any part of their private lives. He seemed totally unperturbed, and they fed me *bul-goggi* and beer. His father, with a bit of English, told me to teach his son better English. Quite nice, and unexpected.

Everyone seemed to have dropped their guard today. I received random invites from people having barbecues to join them; some of which I declined, but one or two I felt obliged to accept. I joined a surgeon and his family, and I was quizzed about what I am doing and how long I will stay. They made me drink Korean wine. The sun was out, and people were smiling and dancing. We toasted the working people of the world, and wished for their unity. At that point I was tempted to use my newly acquired knowledge of Karl Marx, and say that we have nothing to lose but our chains, but I moved on. The brother of the surgeon, who was getting drunk and obnoxious as I was leaving, asked if I was

Chapter 20

married or if I wanted a Korean wife, much to the embarrassment of the surgeon's wife.

Walking around was fun. There were women in bright Korean dresses, even old grandmothers, *hangmoani*, playing accordions and drums, and children entertaining the elders upon request. Some people were asleep on the grass, and some people were struggling to walk in a straight line. Generally everything was good humoured and happy. There were plenty of people – women included – making the outdoors their toilet. I walked past a young lad serenading his group of mates, singing enthusiastically and dramatically. I waved and walked on. About five minutes later there was a tap on my shoulder, and about two hundred metres from where he had been singing a few minutes ago, this young guy wanted me to go back and sing a song with him. What could I say – no? Well I tried saying no, but he was having none of it. I went back with him to his mates, a group of about twenty young men and women, all late teenagers I reckon. They wanted me to sing a song. I said nah, I couldn't, and when I said I was Irish, they said an Irish song would do. Unable to think of anything else, I ran off 'Molly Malone' and her wheelbarrow, totally solo. I only got to give a brief rendition before I was harassed into a Korean song. The only one I know is the chorus of '*Bangap simnida*' ('Nice to Meet You'). When I hummed it, immediately everyone was delighted and we had an international concert. Then I dashed off to play football.

I was twenty minutes late, and there was no one there. Not a soul. I guessed that people hadn't turned up because of the crowds of picnickers. My car, parked at the stadium, had its wipers stolen while I was away. Very unusual for here. I decided I would get changed and go for a run. Not wanting to upset any picnickers by indecent exposure, I went to the passenger side of the car, opened the door and got changed. Then I put down the lock, and closed the door. I had left the keys in the ignition. I decided I should have my run, and sort it out afterwards. So I had a nice run, jogging past lots of young couples sitting on the

The Manifesto And The Invisible Hand

grass, or walking hand-in-hand, and one young romantic reading something to a girl underneath an umbrella. This country does not give the impression that there could be any romance, but at times, the façade drops. I have seen young couples sneaking kisses under bridges when I have been out running around the island. Kissing in public is not really acceptable here, though holding hands is all right. I got back to the car and tried to figure out how to get in, but all the tried-and-tested ways failed me. I am not practiced at breaking into jeeps.

Now, as I write this, the car is sitting at the *MayDay* Stadium, waiting to be stolen, with my money and passport and camera inside. There is nothing I can do until morning, when I can get the spare key out of the safe.

* * *

The car was okay. So were my belongings.

* * *

Yesterday was the Russian Embassy's annual sports day – soccer and volleyball competitions, a bit of chess for those with such an inclination, and a lot of vodka. The sports event happened to coincide with the hottest day of the year so far. Twenty-seven degrees, and after a late night in the RAC (not planned, I might add), the high temperature and the humidity were not welcome. It was too early as well. We didn't do ourselves justice in either the soccer or the volleyball. I blame the vodka. The Polish embassy won the soccer, with a little help from the Czechs. There is one Czech guy who is a mountain; a machine; he will cycle fifty kilometres to Nampo, cycle back and then play two hours of soccer with us on a Sunday. The Russians won the volleyball, courtesy of another giant. Not quite an athlete, but he has a super smash.

The Russians are a really nice bunch of people, very welcoming and hospitable, though they have to live fairly enclosed lives in their embassy. An eleven o'clock curfew is imposed by the

Chapter 20

Ambassador, apparently because their representatives tended to go out and get drunk too regularly. It is good to spend some time with them, because they get a different view of the DPRK than we do. They meet Kim Jong Il. I doubt he will ever extend us that courtesy. There are about 200 people in the embassy; it is like their own little village in the centre of Pyongyang.

* * *

In the last few days, there was an American rumour that Korea would attempt an underground nuclear detonation (I haven't felt it yet). Then, yesterday, the Japanese said they are investigating whether Korea launched a test missile into the Sea of Japan.

* * *

According to the ICG report 'Can the Iron Fist Accept the Invisible Hand?' (I presume 'invisible' refers to economist Adam Smith's coinage regarding the self-regulation of the market. It is not really relevant to the question they are asking, but is a nice pun), Korea needs to become a more 'normal' country. Korea is at the bottom of many of the UN human rights indices, though this is a bit speculative, as they have had no real statistics since 1965. The author quotes the Soviet Union as having been the DPRK's biggest market, whereas I believe the largest amount of trade was carried out with the Eastern Bloc countries, not so much the Soviet Union itself. I could be wrong. Extremely high speculative famine casualties are included in the report, for effect I feel. One interesting point is that the North's GDP per capita is similar to that of Kenya or Tajikistan, though, given the abnormally high expenditure on the military, and the urban/rural population balance, the North Koreans could be considered to be much worse off. The report states that *Juche* does not preclude foreign trade as part of its ideology, so long as it is trade in goods that cannot be produced locally. This can be manipulated to suit almost any scenario, and the author reckons this lacuna will facilitate gradual change.

The Manifesto And The Invisible Hand

One of the critical stages of change is moving into light consumer industries. This is something the DPRK has never managed, and something, in my opinion, that is unlikely ever to happen in a staunchly communist system. Light industry and personal luxury goods are products of capitalism. A completely communist world, I feel, would never reach a stage where manufacturing would be driven in that direction.

1975 is presented in the report as a key year in the development of the two Koreas. In that year, North Korea defaulted on its debt repayments, and it was the year when South Korea first recorded a higher growth rate than its northern counterpart. That must have been a very hard pill for the people to swallow, and must be getting more infuriating as time goes by – South Korea now has the tenth-largest economy in the world, however tenuous its hold on that position may be.

One horrible day for North Korea came in 1996, when the Public Distribution System came to a standstill, with no food to distribute, and famine impending. The Government declared that the people were responsible for feeding themselves. After forty-five years of an extremely controlling system, all of a sudden it is dog-eat-dog. The great mother has decided to just up and leave, abandoning her children to their own devices.

The report recalls that during the worst periods of the famine, there was much freer travel into and out of China, to relieve some of the pressure on the population. As things picked up, however, the young lad put his foot down. A stringent ID card system was introduced, monitoring movements, such that it became difficult to get into and out of Sinuju, the Korean border town, never mind into China. I remember seeing queues of people outside the entrance to the town, displaying little white cards, when I was there. I had no idea what they were doing. ID cards and travel permits play a big role here. Even movement between work farms is controlled; between counties requires travel permits, and travel to any of the big cities, especially

Chapter 20

Pyongyang, requires central permission and often vetting of the credentials of the traveller. People have luggage and vehicles checked, while we, with our privileged registrations and pre-approved permits issued in Pyongyang the week previously, can speed right through these checkpoints most of the time. The old lady who has been coming and going all her life, week in, week out, must go through these rituals repeatedly.

* * *

A discussion paper was sent from Head Office a few days ago, examining the conflict in NGO circles between humanitarianism and human rights organisations – the overlapping of these two aims, and whether they were really compatible within an individual organisation. The prevailing argument is that a rights-based approach to aid is more appropriate than a needs-based one.

For me, the distinction is essentially semantic. The semantics may signal a paradigm shift in how organisations approach their work, but the reality is that rights encompass needs, but not necessarily vice-versa. For humanitarian work the needs must supersede the rights if resources are limited and organisations have to choose between the two. The issue is very real here in the DPRK – *Médecins Sans Frontières* wouldn't come here to work, because they felt they would be helping to support and maintain a corrupt and bad system. Does an agency stand idly by and watch people go hungry, and even die, in the hope that this stance will push the limits so that the regime implodes, or that the people are pushed so far that they will take no more? Can you justify letting one person die in the expectation that this will save another? The flipside is the question of whether the humanitarian work is actually saving lives. If it is not saving lives, even though it may be alleviating suffering, but it is potentially reinforcing the status quo, then the balance swings.

Here in the DPRK, a famine that may have cost two million lives did not unsettle the regime. What will? Are aid agencies actually

The Manifesto And The Invisible Hand

playing a role in maintaining the regime, or would it muddle through anyhow? By refusing to provide aid, are agencies missing an opportunity to alleviate suffering, even in some meagre manner? It is very hard to make these judgement calls.

* * *

The front page of the *Pyongyang Times*, as usual, has an update on an army unit Kim Jong Il visited lately. He presented the soldiers with a pair of binoculars, a machine gun and automatic rifles. What a kind, considerate and thoughtful guy. He said that all commanding officers should take good care of the soldiers. He says this every time. The writers describe anyone, especially South Koreans, assumed to be on the side of the imperialists as *flunkeys, stooges* or *lackeys*.

* * *

Today was an interesting day, spent looking at clinics and hospitals in industrial communities, places I drive past but usually do not have permission to stop in. We are working on a proposal seeking funds to rehabilitate a series of rural clinics. These industrial places are bleak when you are among the houses. If it is a dry day, like today, the layer of black coal dust is whipped up by the wind and sticks to everything. It gets in your eyes, nose and mouth. It is like sitting beside a paraffin lamp, inhaling all the black muck that comes out of it, and this is all day, every day. No wonder people smoke.

How do they keep clean? I know I couldn't, yet there are young girls walking around, hair and make-up immaculate, as if straight from some Second World War film. The popular look in the country – the dress, the style, the hair and the make-up – does not seem to have changed in decades.

I wonder, sometimes, what good are a few latrines? Is it just a drop in the ocean? Communications are so poor, I rarely get enough information to make informed decisions on what I do. I always have to keep probing, asking obvious questions, even to

Chapter 20

get the simplest answers, and that can be wearing. Information never flows. I have to ask so many questions to try to find out who uses the water, and if we upgraded the system who would we affect; and if we only served some houses, as limited by budget, how would this affect other people's access to the water? No-one has any answers. Because access to these areas is so limited, each visit is precious, and I know I need to find out more. But sometimes I haven't the energy to fight the wall of blankness I am always up against.

* * *

Kiki is still missing. All hope is lost I think. He is probably happy, in a big house somewhere, with a nice family, small kids and a little garden. Or he is soup.

21
The Rattlin' Bog

Democracy extends the sphere of individual freedom; socialism restricts it. Democracy attaches all possible value to each man; socialism makes each man a mere agent, a mere number.

Alexis de Tocqueville

I just got my phone bill. Two 20-minute phone calls in one month, and I owe one hundred and sixty euro.

* * *

People here don't make eye-contact very much, but after passing them, when I turn around, there are eyes on me, and then they quickly look away. Then there are the stony-faced traffic ladies – some of them are a challenge, very reluctant to respond to my charms. Old, wizened people are usually more receptive, and pleased or amused when I say hello. They stare at me, curiously. Then there are all the angry boy-soldiers, who are unflinching. There is a lot of rage in some eyes.

Chapter 21

I see the same few fishermen most evenings when I go running around the island. They are getting to know me. Mostly they are old men, fishing in the twilight with nothing more than a wooden spool and a worm. Others have improvised lines; some have about twenty lines going at once. We usually share a solemn *annyong ho sim ni ka* when I go past. They barely bat an eyelid, or miss a drag on their cigarette, but they say hello. Just an acknowledgement.

* * *

Some days I wonder about the driving in this country; and the cycling; and the walking. Nobody drives, cycles or walks in a straight line. It can be infuriating, as well as scary sometimes. People tend not to look as they cross the road. They tend not to indicate, follow the road, or yield at junctions, and they love cutting corners. Cyclists tend to meander in and out, and always choose to swerve the wrong way when they hear a car approaching. If you add in the trams and buses, it can be quite stressful to get from A to B. The only exceptions are the efficient traffic ladies. From time to time, however, they 'change from green to red' when I am within a few metres, and I have to slam on the brakes. The grumpy ones look at me, wave a disapproving finger and make me wait for about five minutes.

* * *

I went to Nampo, on the coast, for a picnic with the rest of the office today. Our Liaison Officer organised it, and I think he was the only one that really wanted to go. It was a Sunday, the only day of rest for the staff, and I don't think this was what they had in mind. Me, I wanted to sleep. Probably the Koreans wanted to be with their families. They all started singing after a few glasses of *soju*. They like to sing, and they like karaoke. I had to sing too. I never usually sing, but this was twice in one week, and in public too. The rest of the afternoon was spent kicking a football with some Korean kids on the beach. One of our translators seemed a

The Rattlin' Bog

lot happier playing football than sitting at the semi-formal meal. A bit like me.

*　*　*

Such a painful day. I was planning on having a quiet few days – walk around, climb a few hills, look at a few water systems and gather information on what materials are needed to complete each one. That went out the window the moment we arrived in Yangchun, our first stop in Songchon County. On enquiring about what extra materials they needed, I was presented with a wish-list costing probably as much as the original design. So the first half of the day was spent painstakingly measuring distances to each house, to demonstrate what needs to be done. The farm manager reckons he has the idea now, and will sort out the rest of the work teams.

On to Naedong. Oh dear again. No farm manager; just a face I had never seen before, claiming to be the Assistant Chairman in charge of the water systems. Okay, I thought, I can talk with him. He had no idea what had been done regarding construction, except to tell me that some pipe was used in the wrong place. We went to look at the place (this is a spot way up a hill that I found very serene and relaxing last time; that image is gone), heading straight for the water storage tank. It was connected up with old, clear plastic pipe that the farm had lying around, instead of the new, black, strong, polyethylene pressure pipe, manufactured to ISO standards, that we had purchased with EC money. It was also held together using bits of everything, including hollowed timber, tying wire and plastic bags. That was not good. Seemingly, our entire new pipe has somehow disappeared – no one knows where it is. Did it disappear in the farm, or at county level? What is it being used for? It is frustrating. How can I ask them what extra materials are needed, when what they have been given has disappeared? What will happen if we supply more to replace what has disappeared? If we don't, it is probable that the people who dug the trenches for the old pipe, and the old rusty

Chapter 21

fittings, will end up with no water, just the memory of digging trenches in the depths of winter to appease a young foreign engineer who is holding their country to ransom.

* * *

Well, the day finally took a turn for the better. I have just finished dining with our local FDRC counterparts. It was a more relaxed meal than usual, and conversation was good. The County Manager, who I find to be a really genuine person and has reasonable English, was in good form, and I was unusually conversational (probably because I had a good night's sleep last night). I had brought ten cans of Guinness with me to Songchon, and the FDRC team was impressed. The County Manager knew there was a drink called Guinness, though he was only familiar with the name through the *Guinness Book of Records* (possibly because Korea has the biggest Arch of Triumph, the longest dam and the highest fountains in the world). He downed his quota no problem, and was surprised the alcohol volume was only 4.7%. He was feeling a bit merry and very flushed, and even promised to keep the last can for his wife, who has good English and is really keen to meet me. That would be nice, and seems possible, as the people seem less guarded up here than in Pyongyang, so she could be joining us for dinner some night.

The County Manager was also delighted that we have allocated a small sum of money in the *WatSan* budget to be spent as the local FDRC see appropriate, which means they get to choose a small project they consider to be important for the county. This approach was not welcomed in Pyongyang. The central administration don't like giving autonomy or control of finances to the local level. The whole notion of having money to spend on something seemed really exciting to the County Manager. He readily admitted that he couldn't decide immediately – there were many things he would want to do. He says when he first arrived in Songchon, he had no latrine in his house, and he realises what

The Rattlin' Bog

a problem this is. There are too many officials – usually living in Pyongyang – who do not see the need, or care about it.

* * *

Pyongyang Times, 14 May. The Koreans are annoyed that the return match against Japan in the World Cup qualifiers has been moved to a neutral venue (Thailand). It is to be played behind closed doors, after the violence at the Iran game. This is prudence on the part of FIFA.

What cannot go unnoticed is the world opinion that the committee (to evaluate the need to relocate) took Japan's 'advice' into much consideration.

I don't know if it is world opinion, but it is a fair comment. I am annoyed about it, as it means I won't be able to go to the game.

There is another article in the paper about a resurgence in the wearing of Korean traditional dresses. Personally, I think they make the Korean women look like teletubbies. This article quotes women on their joy at wearing the dresses:

They say I look ten years younger than my real age in Korean dress.

Korean garment is popular among girl students. They vie to wear more excellent Korean dress.

* * *

The last few times I have been to the *MayDay* Stadium, I have been hassled by people wearing armbands about driving in the vicinity. They say I need a special permit to drive there. This cheeky guard wanted two dollars from me.

* * *

I have got roped into teaching English to one of the new waitresses at the *Friendship* Health Service Centre. I am not too keen, but it will be something different. I should try to get reciprocal Korean lessons from her. I get to have a beer while I teach.

* * *

Chapter 21

The saga of nuclear development in North Korea goes on, alongside a similar progression in Iran. South Korea has recently taken a more bellicose stance, China still remains fairly mute, while the US and Japan seem intransigent. I do not believe that the United States, even under the guise of the UN, would consider intervention here. From talking to local people, and even our new young, educated translator, there is a fierce dogmatism in their attitude towards the United States. Any attempt to intervene here militarily would spark not only military, but civilian reprisals as well. I could easily imagine regular farmers taking to the trenches with pitchforks, such is the ingrained antipathy toward the 'imperialists'. Any intervention would be viewed as the long-feared attempted domination by both Japanese and American forces that the regime continually tells the country to be prepared for. Reaction would be instinctive, and no appeals for calm, even from the Government here, would be effective.

* * *

In the news: The North has agreed to two-party talks with the South, possibly in order to get food and fertiliser concessions, as the agricultural season is well underway and fertiliser is in huge demand. The North still won't discuss the nuclear issue with the South directly, maintaining the same stance as when it entered the Six-Party Talks all those years ago: no direct dialogue regarding the nuclear issue. The DPRK uses this as an international bargaining chip, and will not gamble it away lightly.

* * *

I am in the guesthouse of Namchong County, where the Great Leader stayed a few times, with the elevated, heated toilet seat. With me is the new, temporary *WatSan* translator, Miss Chae, fresh from the University of Foreign Languages, seconded from the Foreign Ministry. Two weeks ago, we had asked our Liaison Officer if it would be possible to get a new translator – ideally one who could speak English reasonably well. Initially I found

The Rattlin' Bog

her quite unfriendly, but she says she has been told frequently that she has an aggressive accent. It's true, she sounds mean. She has an English accent, which apparently came from BBC news DVDs. I enjoy having her in the office. She is new to the NGO game, and very curious. She talks a lot, brings me to shops that she probably shouldn't and buys me ice cream. She seems a little innocent, and a tad spoilt.

* * *

I have just been reading an article that takes a different look at the DPRK. It is worth reiterating a few of its main points. The author states that many South Korean left-wing students believe that in the DPRK poverty is distributed almost equally, and that there is fairness in that. It is true that the majority of the population here share the poverty fairly equally. But the elite live a lot better than the rest. The army also lives a little better than the peasantry.

The author believes that it is useful to take into account the influences of Confucianism and shamanism when analysing the current system in the DPRK: that family stick together is a central Confucian value. When the father dies, the eldest son takes over as head of the family. As the big man set himself up as father of the country, it follows then that the young lad should take the mantle. Similarly, veneration of ancestors is central to the two beliefs, and partly explains the immortality of Kim Il Sung, who 'will always be with us'. I guess I need to read about shamanism and Confucius. They could both be key to understanding this place – or making excuses for it.

There is a brief discussion on religion, as the author is a former pastor from South Korea. A few Northern Christians (who they are or where they are I don't know – are they the ones who have to turn up at the Potemkin churches on a Sunday?) are asked what their faith means to them, and the response is that it helps serve their people and their country better. Not entirely un-Christian, but it doesn't get to the core of Christian beliefs. In

Chapter 21

fact, the big man's mother was Methodist, and the current president or chairperson of the Korean Christian Federation is a relative of the big man.

* * *

The electricity went off in the middle of the last paragraph you have just read, just before I was to go to eat dinner. For dinner were myself, Cho Bak Nam, Driver Pak, Driver Kim, a forestry official from Central FDRC and Miss Chae, our new translator. Just before dinner, Bak Nam toasted to 'an excellent evening'. He has a devious, mischievous look about him. You know that he is up to something all the time, but he is funny, smooth and charismatic.

Dinner involved lots of seafood and then singing and drinking *soju*. The drivers wanted me to eat lots of the seafood, because it is good for *manly things*. There was much gesticulating. Miss Chae was embarrassed, as she is young and has been cosseted by her parents. She hasn't been allowed to have a boyfriend, and was never allowed stay at her friends' houses, despite having lived abroad as a diplomatic child for three years when she was about ten years old. Her parents wouldn't let her go out to play with her friends from the international school, so she used to climb across a ladder to her neighbour's window, leaving a pillow in her place in her bed once her parents were asleep. I know it seems quite normal, but for a shy North Korean girl, it is rather daring.

The drivers were soon getting a little merry. Mr Pak told me he would like me to be his son-in-law, but he doesn't have a daughter. As the evening wore on, the drivers asked the waitress working in the hotel to come in and sing a song. She has a really good voice, a little like an Irish *sean-nós* singer. I was forced to sing, again, giving an ill-advised rendition of 'The House of the Rising Sun'. It sounded bad. The songs went on. None of the Koreans are shy of a song or two. It came around to me again, and I had to introduce 'The Rattlin' Bog' to Korea. If you don't

The Rattlin' Bog

know the song, it's an Irish one, and it goes on, and on, and on. It is the type of song everyone can join in after a bit, and all the Koreans who could understand what I was saying soon did.

I went to bed, feeling a bit nervous that the lads would be making advances on young Miss Chae. The lads kept singing for another hour. My English forestry colleague was in his sickbed, with a bad dose of diarrhoea. I think he may have been faking, because he wasn't up for a party.

The next day I had to go looking at latrines and water systems in Namchong. There is almost no progress on the water systems to date. Miss Chae, being quite refined, struggled initially when translating discussions about latrines. I was telling her about *EcoSan* (twin-pit) latrines, saying, 'you have to put the brown in here ...' She would start laughing every time she had to translate anything to do with bodily functions, because she would never say words like that in public. She couldn't even say the less formal word for toilet, *byonso*. That's my new word for the day. The more formal word is *wee-sang-siil*, which is similar to the Chinese word. I made her translate for the Koreans in detail how to use the *EcoSan* latrine. I didn't ask her to demonstrate.

22
The Looking Glass

From each according to his ability, to each according to his need.
Karl Marx

Pyongyang Times, 21 May: The Workers Party of Korea Publishing House has recently released a paper entitled:

Kimilsungia is an Immortal Flower that has Bloomed in the Hearts of Mankind in the Era of Independence.

The *Kimilsungia* was originally cultivated in Indonesia apparently, and experts had to adapt it to the soils of Korea. This flower is the special flower of the Great Leader. Another variant of this shrub is the *Kimjongilia*. There is a display shop in Pyongyang full of these. I don't see the attraction of them myself.

The main headline was 'Kim Jong Il Sees Performance', of a Korean drama by an army unit. He expressed great satisfaction over the fact that the officers' wives have vividly and truthfully

Chapter 22

represented their lives, and that they are another aspect of revolutionary soldier culture in the Songun era.

* * *

Today was the first time in a month playing football at the *MayDay* Stadium. Despite running five miles a few times a week, I am still wrecked. It has something to do with the lifestyle I am leading. I don't really eat that well, except when I am up country. When I am in Pyongyang, I tend to skip breakfast, lunch or dinner, or two of them sometimes. I smoke. Too regularly I have drinks in the evening, though not many. Perhaps I need to take a step back and get myself in order. This morning I got up to cook omelettes for a load of people. Somehow I got roped into being a sous-chef for a breakfast for people I hardly know, who are leaving on Tuesday. It was tough to drag myself out of bed at such an early hour. They were good omelettes, though.

* * *

I am reading *North Korea through the Looking Glass*, and there are a few things that I have found interesting, relating to a Confucian interpretation of recent Korean history. Confucianism helps to explain, a little, the regime that exists in the DPRK. I am far from an expert on this, but I gather that Confucian tradition believes in a patriarchal society, a society where you accept unequivocally the edicts of a benevolent leader – similar to old monarchic systems in Europe a while back. Kim Il Sung has exploited this tradition to the extreme.

The Confucian tradition of the eldest son taking on the role of the father when he dies has, of course, also aided the Kim dynasty. Kim Jong Il, though not necessarily the most suitable of the leader's sons, was groomed to be his successor. The only reason for his accession is his lineage – he has no political, military or other background that would qualify him as suitable to lead the country. To an extent, Confucian tradition has trapped the young lad in the system, where he practically had to accept accession. He has to be loyal to his father, and not

The Looking Glass

denounce him in any way. He has to maintain the system that is in place, and by further propagating the ideology of *Juche* and indoctrinating the masses, he has left himself without a window to escape. He cannot turn things around, as there have been too many lies.

I have read in *Through the Looking Glass*, and it does not surprise me, that the Government here are continually rubbishing aid organisations in their internal propaganda, which we non-Korean-speaking NGO workers, unable to listen to North Korean news and radio, do not even notice. They tell the people that we are not to be trusted; we are merely pawns of the imperialists. The term 'wolfish ravening lamb' from *Romeo and Juliet* springs to mind. I wonder whether the people really think that of us. Maybe they are correct – most aid is political, no matter what we think. I like to think that I am not political, but the truth is that I don't like the system here, I don't like the regime and I want to see it gone.

* * *

On a lighter note, the other evening in the *Friendship* there was a Westlife 'VCD' playing, and I was told I looked exactly like one of them. I haven't decided if this is a good or a bad thing. If only I could sing and dance ... A VCD is a poor man's version of a DVD, essentially a CD with video on it. Most of the DVD players brought here from China are only VCD-enabled.

* * *

There are a lot of stalls around the *MayDay* Stadium, selling drinks and ice-cream to the kids practising for the Mass Games. Youngsters with bundles of money go to these little vendors to buy a drink, or sweets, or some dumpling-type confectionary. It is good to see the kids with a small bit of money – the bundles make them look like they have loads, but it really isn't worth a whole lot. The sellers are probably State-controlled and not private enterprise at all. Some of the participants are getting used to seeing me running around the stadium while they practise, and

Chapter 22

there are some unsolicited waves these days, and hellos and goodbyes.

* * *

The air-raid siren is going off again here in Pyongyang. It is midday on a Sunday. Why do they bother? What do they expect people to do? Why not have one day to relax? Everyone works five days a week, with Saturdays devoted to forms of self-criticism, education in *Juche* philosophy, and mandatory reporting on each other.

* * *

It is farming time at the moment. New baby goats are jumping around; the few tractors are trudging around the paddy fields; and throngs of people are bent double, weeding the fields, tilling the ground, picking potatoes and transplanting rice. The paddy fields are an amazing sight. This is one of the reasons why irrigation is so important in this country – there is no shortage of water, but the paddy fields need huge amounts. With all technology breaking down, particularly pumps no longer working, it is more and more difficult to get the required amount of water to the fields. Drinking water is not a priority in comparison with irrigation water. The choice is between poor quality water with more food, or lovely water with less food. The obvious choice is to go for the discomfort that bad water brings – diarrhoea, dysentery, possible skin problems – above the discomfort of having no food.

Working the paddy fields and bringing the crop to harvest requires enormous work. In the DPRK, it is a massive, state-wide process, getting all the rice seedlings transplanted as quickly as possible across the whole country. Half the population is in the fields as I write, taking the rice seedlings from their nursery beds to the main plots. The populations of towns and cities are required to go and help with farming at the weekends at this time of year. School children from the city spend around a month doing this work. The irrigation channels are all opened, allowing

The Looking Glass

water to flow into the flat paddy fields. There are men up to their knees in water, reinforcing banks and ditches in the channels and around the perimeters of the fields to hold the water in. Women and children, mostly, stand in the nursery fields, where all the rice seedlings are packed together in specially prepared beds. They pick them out, using a special trellis to track the work in neat, straight lines, and tie them in bundles. In some places, lovely red flags of socialism are planted to indicate a job well done, and little sandwich boards with propaganda written on them are dotted about, encouraging the populace to work harder and faster.

* * *

When I was in Namchong, Mrs Chang explained to me the story of a film that we watched on television. It was about a fictitious Korean Minister for Heavy Industry, and the hardships of his life. During the Japanese colonial period, he went to Japan to get educated and trained as an industrial technician. When Korea achieved independence, some bad people tried to persecute him for having been to Japan and working for the Japanese, but the Korean Workers' Party looked after him – they knew he was a loyal Korean. When he was in Japan he met a Japanese lady. He fell in love with her, but would have nothing to do with her because she was Japanese. She followed him back to Korea, dressed as a Korean lady, and tracked him down, but he told her he could not love her because she was Japanese. She told him she was really Korean – her mother was Korean, and had married a Korean in Japan, her father. Her father subsequently died, and then her mother remarried, to a Japanese man. The girl had just found out she was really Korean, and made it her mission to go to Korea to find him. They got married and were subject to much discrimination because of their Japanese association. He struggled on, eventually becoming manager of his factory, and by sticking to the *Juche* ideology and being loyal to the party, he became Minister for Heavy Industry.

Chapter 22

* * *

Our country is the only one known for its ideological power.

The regime tries to justify itself by virtue of the ideology of *Juche*. No country, not Stalin's Soviet Union nor Mao's China, has dedicated so much effort to promoting, producing and disseminating ideology as the DPR of Korea.

The first mention of *Juche* occurred around 1958, in a Kim Il Sung speech. This could be doubted, as the DPRK government has manufactured speeches the big man *apparently* wrote way back in the 1930s to give more credence to the ideology and his status. The ideology of *Juche* kicked off to a large extent when the young lad was given a job at the KWP Agitation and Propaganda Department, and he spent his time thinking of ways to mainstream *Juche* throughout Korea.

The dream of *Juche* is that people live in a communal state, with everything they need – overflowing stores of food and a self-sufficient industry producing all that is required – without the need for, or use of, money. People are supposed to spend a set number of supervised hours a week reading politics and *Juche*, discussing and memorising the ideology. *Juche* is not really a science or anything; more of a dogma, and a very loose one at that. The only person with the authority to alter it, or interpret it, was the Great Leader, and now the young lad. Everyone has to be careful that their interpretations are not out of line with official policy, or else they get in trouble and it goes on their record.

The reason given by one Korean representative as to why *Juche* is not understood in the West is that it is not meant to be fully comprehensible. The irony of *Juche* is that the people are told they are the masters of everything, that the power is in their hands, when, in fact, it is very far away. Korean prisons are filled with people who have misinterpreted or cursed *Juche* in a moment of frustration. The opposite of *Juche* is 'servility' or reliance on others, or, more colourfully, 'flunkeyism'. Korean

The Looking Glass

people, apparently, have to undergo regular sessions of self-criticism, where they reflect on how their actions have failed the principles of *Juche*. In recent years, the young lad has put a military-first slant on *Juche*, justifying the pre-eminence of the army in the country. Through *Juche*, the socio-political life replaces both the physical and the spiritual life. In *Juche*, a man is nothing without social and political standing.

Building on his years at the Agitation and Propaganda Department, Kim Jong Il has spent the majority of his life spreading, defending and writing about *Juche*, in long, unclear and often contradictory statements. He has been the driving force in making it the powerful, country-wide ideology it is today. Critics often complain about its internal contradictions, but I am surprised it is given any serious analysis at all. One has to remember Kim is only the son of the big guy, and only in his present position by inheritance, not out of any spark of genius.

Only the masses who are united organisationally and ideologically can shape their destiny independently and creatively.

Kim Jong Il is referred to as 'the respected and beloved general', though he has never had any military training or experience. He is constantly giving on-the-spot guidance to troops. There are many *slogan trees* still being 'discovered' near Mt Paektu, which apparently proclaim the coming of the young lad.

If we weaken the dictatorial function of the government ... we cannot provide the people with democratic freedom and rights.

In Korea, they are always in a hurry: there was the Arduous March, and then the March to Victory, and now, in times of trouble, there is the March to Paradise. They will surely get tired of marching eventually. I see the soldiers marching at the *MayDay* Stadium. It is quite formidable when they are goose-stepping across the car park.

* * *

Chapter 22

Koreans are encouraged to be self-detonating explosives, to turn into *one-defeats-a-hundred* warriors.

* * *

The tears shed for Kim Il Sung when he died were real. On the anniversary of his death, in *The Game of Their Lives*, all the ex-football heroes from the 1966 World Cup were filmed, at the statue of the big guy at Mansu Hill. They were crying, saying they wished he was still with them. People feel that strongly about him, though the same is not true for the young lad. The old man seemed to like the people, and spent time among them, while the young lad looks uncomfortable in public. He rarely ventures out, and never speaks in public. His public persona is constructed from news reports of his on-the-spot guidance, and rare public appearances at the Mass Games, diplomatic events or anniversary celebrations.

There is a Korean saying: *tiger father, dog son*, expressing the sentiment that a great or powerful father usually has unappealing offspring. In Pyongyang, allegedly, the young lad is referred to as *that man* in order to avoid being overheard disparaging him publicly, knowing the punishment that such slander entails.

Some say that the North Korean populace have simply switched off, as can happen under totalitarian regimes. People stop thinking; they disengage to avoid dealing with the situation. They allow themselves to be ruled, and get on with simply surviving. On the flipside, if they don't believe in the Kims, what else can they believe in? The propaganda machine crowds out any other thought – there is no room for alternative philosophies.

One thing the young lad did very early in his political career was to launch the Three Revolution Team Movement – motivators, propagandists, and agitating teams were sent to every village around the country, spreading the word on *Juche* and cementing the old man's cult status among the masses. He has been very successful. These propagandists would promote new ideas and movements started by the young lad, such as the Consumer

The Looking Glass

Goods Movement, promoting frugality: 'Let's do more with less,' was the slogan. People were told, 'Let's eat two meals a day,' while at the same time, partly in response to the Seoul Olympics, the Government was spending $4.5 billion on white elephants to show off at the 1989 Thirteenth World Festival of Youth and Students, and building monuments and statues to mark the old man's birthday commemorations.

Meat was practically unobtainable during the nineties. One result of the great hunger in the country is a generation of stunted Koreans, smaller than their Southern counterparts on average by five or six centimetres. A midwife here, who had just returned from a trip to Tanchon in the northeast, told me that living conditions are far worse up there than around Pyongyang, or in the other counties where we work. She says there is widespread stunting of growth, due to the famine. Those children who grew up in the nineties – adults now, some soldiers – are extremely stunted, due to the malnutrition they suffered in their formative years a decade ago. Present-day soldiers would have been affected, given that the famine was around the years of their teens, when they should have been due growth spurts.

* * *

There are five types of housing in Korea: Special, Four, Three, Two and One, in order of quality - Special being the best. Special is for officials of deputy-minister rank in the KWP. Three are single-family detached houses, two-storey, with hot and cold running water. Working intelligentsia, such as clerks with no special skills, live in Number Two housing. There are three types of Number One housing – usually multi-family houses with one or two rooms. These are for the rank and file, peasants and so on. These are the houses we find in work teams and on farms in the countryside. Since the sixties, the dream of the people, and the promise of the party, has been 'to eat rice and meat soup, wear silk clothes and live in a house with a tiled roof'.

* * *

Chapter 22

Kim Jong Il is quoted as saying, 'Trying to move man by means of money contradicts the intrinsic nature of socialist policy.' He later states, 'Material incentives should be accurately applied as an economic means for better implementing the principles of collectivism on the basis of giving priority to political means.'

23
Summertime And The Living Is Not Easy

We cannot expect Americans to jump from capitalism to Communism, but we can assist their elected leaders in giving Americans doses of socialism until they suddenly awake to find out they have Communism.

Nikita Khrushchev

The traffic ladies (and the few traffic men) have new uniforms, heralding the arrival of summer. They are white and very summery. They all look like Tom Cruise in 'Top Gun'. The new uniforms are a talking point among the foreigners here, indicating how little we have to amuse ourselves with.

* * *

There was incredible lightning last night, for half an hour. The night was lit up like daytime as I was walking home. It was actually frightening, and I was happy to get back inside. It seems

Chapter 23

this is commonplace in summer, with high rainfall, high humidity and high temperatures. The lightning came with monsoon-type rains that flooded the streets up to a foot deep, as the storm sewers are either blocked, collapsed, or not capable of dealing with the DPRK's weather.

* * *

The North Korean economy, rather than turning around, continues to deteriorate, especially in relation to agriculture. In many places far from Pyongyang, State policies are turning the people into hunter-gatherers again. People are being forced to fend for themselves, yet the State's centralised system means they are limited in how they can actually do this. For many, the only recourse is to forage for whatever they can find.

* * *

Despite the DPRK and the US being sworn enemies, the DPRK is the biggest recipient of US aid in East Asia. However, the DPRK 'newspaper' *Nodung Sinmun* declared in 1998 that:

There has never been any foreign capital that contributed to national economy development never before and no such incident should occur. Foreign capital is like opium.

* * *

I went to Mass in Pyongyang yesterday. It wasn't really Mass though; it was a prayer meeting of some sort, all in Korean, and I couldn't understand a word of it. Our young former translator, Miss Chae, who left our office to return to the Ministry of Foreign Affairs, was translating for a group of Italian delegates visiting Pyongyang. She told me that they would be going to Mass in the Catholic Church on Sunday, so I had to go and check it out. Miss Chae asked me to explain Mass, a prayer meeting, and a priest.

The Church was full. Initially I thought it looked too perfectly full, with exactly three people in each row, but in fact there were

Summertime And The Living Is Not Easy

a few rows with only two people. Most of the women there were middle-aged, wearing traditional Korean dress, with white gossamer scarves on their heads. The men were similarly aged, in regular Korean clothes. There were no young people. There were three Italian delegates, and the Italian representative in Pyongyang, who blanked me on his way out after the Mass, as he did later that day at a reception in the German Embassy marking five years of diplomatic relations with the DPRK.

Before that reception, I went to an Italian operatic performance. I wouldn't normally consider myself an opera lover, or in any way cultured. The singing, though operatic, was okay. The faces the female singer made while singing were frightening, reminiscent of *The Scream* by Edvard Munch. The theatre hall was too warm. I was in a shirt and trousers, and not comfortable in them, especially in this humid weather. I was sweating profusely, and was delighted when the air conditioning finally came on about halfway through.

* * *

Today I went to the *Friendship* to help one of the waitresses. She is tasked with getting the newly built cafe up and running, looking and acting like an Italian coffee shop. She is learning all about this from a book. She has to learn how to make a number of different types of coffee. She gave me a very brief history lesson on coffee and tea. I learned about the Boston Tea Party, and coupons, and India and Sri Lanka. She has never seen any of the coffees she is trying to make. I don't know how she will master a café-macchiato-latte or a skinny-decaf-flat-white.

* * *

I was in Songchon, comparing the actual town to the extensive survey we have carried out. I have put together a map that I can only print out on A4 paper. To get the requisite detail, I have to print out about thirty sheets and stick them together with *sellotape*, then carry them to the county official's office. The survey was done with an old theodolite, measuring thousands of

Chapter 23

distances and angles. These were then inputted into an excel spreadsheet and the relative locations of each worked out, generating local coordinates. These coordinates were then put into a basic Geographic Information System (GIS) program, which produces a map of numbers. I then had to sketch in details around the thousands of points we had downloaded. The output of all of this is a slightly cartoonish map.

Today we went to a place with a birds-eye view of most of the town. The town is situated within about five interconnecting valleys, which spread out like fingers, with the centre the palm of the hand. There is only one place where you can really see the shape these make. We were not allowed to climb up to that vantage point until today. After much discussion and cajoling, we got permission to go and look at the springs in that area – springs in places we never knew existed. I can assume we were the first foreigners up that road and in that area in at least sixty years.

Looking at the town from that height made it much easier to visualise the potential water system, and much easier to relate our plans to the County Manager and his technicians. It was disappointing to find out that there are 55,000 people, and not 32,000 as previously estimated, in the town. The populations of the previously inaccessible-to-foreigners areas have been included. I think this indicates a certain increasing level of trust.

The view was fantastic. We were at a nice height above the town, looking straight down a valley. The new springs were a reasonable size – enough water to serve three hundred families at fifty litres per person per day. Fifty litres is a reasonable amount, for drinking and cooking – much less than I would use in my daily life in Ireland, but more than I would use in the desert in Darfur. There is also a large stream, which seems clean, and is presently supplying the existing tank with water for nine hundred houses. At present this water flows out through open pipes in the street. The question we have to ask ourselves is, whether to

Summertime And The Living Is Not Easy

rehabilitate the tank and provide lots of water – which may not be perfectly safe to drink, as it is coming from an open, though isolated stream – or to supply only three hundred houses with adequate, safe drinking water from the springs. There are other options, but those aren't feasible here for various reasons. This isn't an easy decision, but I guess you have to go for the clean water for a smaller population. The first principle is to do no harm.

* * *

Last night I had a very strange experience. I was driving home from bowling – did I mention I broke the unofficial expat record a few weeks ago? I was in the zone. Anyway, on the way toward the Koryo hotel, a soldier flagged me down. I assumed it was a traffic cop, but it wasn't. He opened the passenger door … and sat in. I froze. What to do? I looked at him and he looked at me. He reeked of beer. He told me – in his best, slurred Korean – to drive him: 'Kap-su-da.' I wasn't sure what to do. I drove. He took out his army-issue knife and started to clean it, while I drove aimlessly around the city. I tried to ascertain where he wanted to go, but it wasn't working. Eventually I just drove back to where we started, and he got panicky. He became even more flustered when he saw other soldiers. Then out of nowhere, fifty metres from where we started, he saw his high-rise home. He begged me to pull around the corner, away from the other soldiers. Even in his drunkenness, he knew he had crossed the Rubicon. I drove around the corner and he hopped out and meandered home.

* * *

A woman from the BBC website called the office, wanting to talk about food shortages in the DPRK. I had nothing to say.

* * *

I have just found out that someone has been reading this diary, which I have left open on my computer. This is a little

Chapter 23

disconcerting. Stupid of me to leave it open here. I wonder how much trouble I could get into for writing this? Would anyone care? I hope I haven't written anything that could get anyone else into trouble. It is very difficult to know. Someone could have made a copy of it any time I was out of the office. More care is required.

* * *

When Kim Jong Il was a kid, he had the nickname *Yura*. He saw his young brother, *Shura*, die when he was five. When he was being lined up to succeed his father, there was much debate as to whether hereditary succession was suited to a socialist state. The Korean Academy of Social Sciences, in its *Dictionary of Political Terminology*, denounced hereditary succession as 'originally a product of slave societies'. This was deleted in 1972, no doubt to suit the succession that was being planned at that stage. The young lad was often referred to, not by name, but as the *party centre* during his early days in the politburo. When he was young he had a short hairstyle, which he maintained for most of his life, but it has become increasingly *bouffant,* a style known as *speed-battle hair*. This style was much encouraged, and is adopted by all Korean athletes.

* * *

I have been going to the church fairly regularly now, and was enjoying being able to dedicate some time to God, even if I had my doubts as to the sincerity of the service in Pyongyang. Despite everything being in the Korean language, I was able to follow the service, which included many aspects of the Mass – a homily and most of the prayers, but rightly, no Gospel. If it wasn't real, they had done their homework. I was enjoying it until last Sunday, when I arrived ten minutes late. I walked in unannounced, and there was a panic of people rushing to get into place, including the speaker, to carry on as if they were in the middle of the usual prayer meeting. I was surprised to discover that it was really a show, put on for the very few

Summertime And The Living Is Not Easy

foreigners who would go there: namely me and the Italian. Any Sunday that neither of us turned up, the *congregation* must just sit there and chat for the duration, and then wander off home.

* * *

The succession of the young lad meant that the sort of trouble that occurred in China in appointing a successor to Chairman Mao was avoided. It also means that the legacy of Kim Il Sung will not be denigrated, as happened to Stalin under the reformers. The Propaganda and Agitation Department created a history for the young lad such that he was considered deserving of the title of General. He has made very few public appearances since his appointment, and has spoken even less, but has been a prolific writer on almost every subject under the sun. His visits to farms and factories are reported every two weeks in the *Pyongyang Times*. He and his image are carefully managed to maintain the charade of the dynasty. If ever anyone else lays claim to leadership of the country, the legend and the myth of the Kims will have to be torn to shreds.

There are contrasting descriptions of the young lad in circulation. Some have said he is bold, reckless and arrogant, and has a lack of respect for seniors (or rather, he had a lack of respect when he was a young lad). Others say he is cold and haughty, quick-tempered and even violent. A rare few say he is caring, compassionate, and thoughtful. Who do you believe? He does not have the charisma that the big guy had. He never needed it, as power was simply handed on to him. The old man had the look of a statesman – the swagger of someone who believed he deserved the pedestal he had built for himself. The young lad does not carry himself in the same way.

* * *

There have been a few positive sightings of Kiki with Korean kids outside the Diplomatic Compound. I haven't seen him, but it is good to hear that he is not soup just yet.

Chapter 23

* * *

A landmark day. The first colour edition of the *Pyongyang Times* was released today. What was in it? The same as every week, but this time brighter and better. Kim Jong Il inspected another army unit. Lots of colourful, smiley, happy faces. Apparently, events are taking place around the world to mark the fifth anniversary of the North-South Declaration of 2000 – in countries such as Romania, Finland, Sweden, Egypt and Poland. There are rallies, round-table talks, reading sessions, book and photo exhibitions and handicrafts displays. There was a Korean book and photo exhibition in the University of Newcastle. There is a colour photograph of Kim Jong Il and Kim Dae Jung, the South Korean President from 2000. They are pictured in front of a colourful mural, standing on an equally colourful mosaic, so that the actual photo looks like a mosaic. There is also apparently a metaphorical Kim Jong Il hurricane sweeping across South Korea, where he is described as 'a man of clever judgment and decision', 'a man of humour and artistic sense' and 'a great man who is moral, broad minded and informal'.

* * *

I am finding myself getting annoyed with people of late. I think it is a sign of stress, as is working too many hours and not getting a whole lot done. I know I should be planning to take a short holiday, but I don't know if I am able to now, as there is so much to do. I have to manage the stress levels somehow. All the other expats that work in my office have left, and I am waiting for reinforcements. Even some of our Korean colleagues have been re-taken by their respective ministries. One lady, who diligently manages all our finances and general office administration, has been returned to the tourism office, because of the impending Mass Games. That means I now have to face the drudgery of accounting as well.

* * *

Summertime And The Living Is Not Easy

There was a full-page advertisement in the *New York Times* when Kim Jong Il became general secretary of the KWP in 1997. It read (this was in the *New York Times*, remember!):

The Lodestar of the 21st Century

The North Korean leader Kim Jong Il is a man of great leadership, remarkable wisdom and noble virtues. He is always with the popular masses sharing the ups and downs of life with them. Indeed, he is equipped with all the qualities a great leader needs. Kim Jong Il, a new leader in the 21st Century, will surely break new ground in the political, economic, military and diplomatic fields of Korea, succeeding excellently to the cause of the late President Kim Il Sung.

Kim Jong Il has been endowed with a legacy of heroic victories and endeavours that is simply untrue. He is said to be 'the most distinguished of all military geniuses heaven has ever produced', and 'a great general who has won 100 victories in 100 battles'. One story tells of how he was aboard a torpedo boat and guided the crewmen and trained them in torpedo tactics. There is no end to his abilities. He is also credited with the 1968 capture of the US spy ship the *Peublo*, long before he was ever on the military scene.

In recent years, the rallying call to the people has been to protect Kim Jong Il:

To become lifeguards of the supreme commander is the first mission and great honour of our army ... The revolutionary spirit of suicidal explosion is the spirit of dedicating one's life for the party and the leader by becoming a self detonating bomb.

Kim Jong Il has said that the Korean People's Army is 'the pillar and main force of the revolution', placing the army in an elevated position in Korean life. The Spartan lifestyle that the Army is supposed to lead is promoted as desirable for any loyal Korean. For many peasants, life in the Army looks more comfortable than drudgery in the fields. I cannot comment very much on conditions in Army barracks. The closest I get is when I run past

Chapter 23

a small compound near the *MayDay* stadium. It does not look too luxurious.

* * *

You often hear things like, 'Pyongyang is like a huge stage set,' or, 'It is the closest thing to Germania, Hitler's grandiose visions of Berlin.' From what I can see, this view is exaggerated and unfair. It ignores that people here live a regular, everyday human struggle, albeit very different to the lifestyle that a European might be used to. It is true that from a distance Pyongyang is like a picture postcard, and that up close it is not idyllic at all. There are some redeeming features: wide, tree-lined streets, a lack of noise pollution and traffic, and some green spaces. The slow pace of life is somewhat unreal, however, and is a by-product of the system. People are no longer in a position to work for themselves; their autonomy has been severely curtailed and the space for growth and innovation limited. This has eliminated the normal buzz that exists in other big cities.

The widely circulated story is that when foreign dignitaries visit Pyongyang there is a *Potemkin* street-show put on, where people are mobilised to act as pedestrians, shoppers and drivers. This seems to me to stretch credulity, but apparently a former North Korean official tells the same story. I am pretty sure that I am not subject to a constant street show, but I know that people who pay top dollar to come to the DPRK on organised and stage-managed tours do get this special treatment. Foreigners working in the DPRK now have fairly good access to all areas of Pyongyang, except of course the Forbidden City.

There is an extremely thorough system of classifying Korean society. There are three loyalty groups: the Core Class, the Wavering Class and the Hostile Class. The names are fairly self-evident. The Core Class makes up approximately 28% of the population. The Wavering Class is 45–50%, and the rest are in the Hostile Class. The Hostile Class is made up of those whose genealogy positions them as people who may feel resentment

Summertime And The Living Is Not Easy

towards the system, such as families and ancestors of the former upper-class, who have been reduced to the bottom rung of the ladder. The Core Class is made up of farmers and workers, and represents those who were and are most loyal to the system. The Wavering Class consists of merchants and people whose families have upset the system. The Hostile Class have little hope for advancement, and are closely scrutinised by the Ministry of People's Security (MPS). The Hostile Class is divided into fifty-one subgroups, including, for example, people or relatives of people who are or were members of religious organisations. The Hostile Class get the least desirable jobs, often get sent to remote rural areas, and receive limited Government rations.

24
A Bit More Of The Countryside

State interference in social relations becomes, in one domain after another, superfluous, and then dies out of itself; the government of persons is replaced by the administration of things, and by the conduct of processes of production.

Frederich Engels

Last Monday, I went to Anju, a large town that the Government has asked us to consider working in, to carry out an initial assessment. They seem to like the work we are doing in Songchon and Namchong (which is worrying in itself), but Anju is a much more substantial city. We will probably set up some initial programmes, such as rehabilitating some of the urban water supply, to see how it is to work in a town of this size, and how relations with the city management progress. We seem to be getting into bigger and bigger towns, which is a little intimidating

Chapter 24

because no one in our office has experience in the design and construction of large water systems. It could be seen as a little irresponsible too, to move away from what our strength is: small, sustainable, easily maintained, village-level projects.

As an example, in Namchong, we replaced a kilometre of rising main to the water storage tank on the hill. We removed the original eighteen-inch iron pipe, and replaced it with 400mm PVC pipe. It was all installed and buried. When we started up the pump to fill the tank after installation, the rising main want 'pop' after about fifteen minutes. To this day, I don't know why, and I have asked a range of experts. I thought it may have been one dodgy length of pipe, so we replaced it, but it exploded in exactly the same place. Right now we are using the old rusting iron pipe – with leaks patched up – while the new, expensive pipe is unused. Bad decisions cost money.

However, it is interesting to be working somewhere new. Anju is only about forty-five minutes north of Pyongyang, a fairly built-up area, and, ironically, home of the main pump-building factory in the DPRK – a town whose own pumps are falling apart. Inside a pump station with five monster-sized pumps, we saw that only two are actually working. The problem is that the factory cannot access resources to carry out any work. Also, the factory's priorities are decided by the authorities in Pyongyang.

It is strange to stay overnight in Anju, after all the nights in Namchong, Songchon and Rongchon, in makeshift hotels or rundown guesthouses. In Anju, there is a real hotel. I nearly collapsed from shock when I realised I could sit at a bar and order a beer or a coffee, without it having to be organised in advance. There were even a few old cans of Carlsberg sitting on a shelf. There was a decent pool table to play on. (When I say decent, remember that all things are relative, and I have been here for a while now.) The hotel has an electric towel warmer, though it isn't plugged in. I guess, if they are to house foreigners

A Bit More Of The Countryside

at extortionate prices, then they have to attract them with investment in things like that.

We had lunches and dinners in the hotel, with the chairpersons of the FDRC and Ministry of City Management from the county. They see us as money people, and are being diplomatic at the moment to attract our investment in their town. We can make no promises without donor funding and, personally, I think that we should think this one through carefully. Are we moving away from focusing on the more marginalised areas?

We spent a day walking around Anju, getting an idea of the lay of the land. We looked at various schools and pump stations, as well as some springs at the edge of the city. Doing this, I immediately started to design the water system in my head. It happened almost automatically. It sounds nerdy, but it can be exciting. The manager of a nursery we visited wanted to build a swimming pool and have flush toilets. I told her I didn't think it would be possible for us to build flush toilets. She said she had no interest in regular pit latrines – the ones where you squat over a drop-hole!

We went to a kindergarten, where the kids were out on a morning break. The teachers were singing songs with them, in a nice and orderly manner. The teachers appeared happy at their work. We weren't expected, so I don't suspect this was a *show* for our benefit. We checked out a few other large schools, which look like the intimidating institutions that existed in old-style Ireland. They weren't built from granite, as they would have been in Ireland, but rather from mass concrete. They are situated in commanding locations around the town, slightly elevated, with high walls, overlooking the communities around.

* * *

When I get back to Ireland, I will be a danger to society. Habits here do not make one a good driver. As there are so few cars, it is easy to get lazy when approaching intersections – slowing instead of stopping, and giving only cursory glances left and

Chapter 24

right. On Sunday the streets can be very, very empty in Pyongyang. In the countryside, the main transport is on old trucks, many of them converted from diesel or petrol engines to some form of coal-burning engine. They spew out black smoke and move very slowly. When I approach a junction nowadays, I tend to just glance to the right as I make half an effort to slow down. By the time I look left I am halfway across the road. Instead of erring on the side of caution, it is the opposite.

* * *

Having spent a small bit of time with the Irish First Secretary to South Korea on his visit to the North, maintaining diplomatic relations between Ireland South and Korea North, I am not sure how much of the situation in the DPRK he really understands. Don't get me wrong, he is a really nice man, and very diplomatic. At dinner with Mr Su, the DPRK MFA Desk Officer to Northern Europe, I was getting annoyed by the number of times he tried to compare the situation and the history of Korea with that of Northern and Southern Ireland. The comparisons are very thin, and not really relevant. He was trying to be empathetic to the North Koreans: 'Oh, we know only too well ourselves ...' I suppose, being a diplomat, he is more attuned to the needs of the role than I am.

He and the Belgian First Secretary came on a whistle stop tour, to see some of our work in Songchon. Miss Chae, our former translator, was translating for the Belgian delegate, and it was good to have her around. She remains slightly cutting, but very engaging. Mr Cho in Songchon was very impressive. He should be a diplomat himself. He talked up our work far better than I could have. Then the two diplomats had to squirm a little as we pushed them for further investment in rural DPRK. I am not sure how impressed they were with me putting them on the spot, but I enjoyed watching them blustering their way out of actually committing to anything. Very diplomatic.

* * *

A Bit More Of The Countryside

In less than a week, I will have the pleasure of being in charge of our office for the foreseeable. A heavy load on narrow shoulders. Much of it will be a big distraction from getting on with my job. I will have lots of other things to think about as a country director. It could be a major headache, but still, it will look good on my CV. I am much less interested in fast-tracking up the ranks than I was when I arrived. Really, I would prefer to be able to focus on doing the practical things well. Administration and management can take up a lot of time.

* * *

I am working away on the design for the water-supply system for Songchon. It is a bit of a disaster at the moment. The town has 60,000 inhabitants, apparently. I had, until recently, thought it had 32,000. The new population has upped the cost of the project. The potential funding for the programme will not stretch that far. The town has three main pump stations. Big pumps push water way up to tanks on various hills, and these feed part of the town. However, the town stretches out and up, with numerous valleys, like fingers, reaching away into the distance, and there are some areas that the tanks just cannot reach. It is impossible without building new, higher tanks and installing pumps and motors to get water to those heights. We have tried to find springs up in the mountains that could cover these outlying areas, but the water-management teams in the county don't really like springs. They want big, powerful pumps. They don't understand that gravity could do all the pumping for them, with none of the cost and none of the hassle.

They also like to connect houses directly to the rising main from the pump. This means if there is a power surge of some sort, creating a sudden increase in pressure, people could have the pleasure of seeing their taps pop out of their sockets. Often, connecting like this is probably out of necessity. The old pumps do not have the power to reach the tanks, and managing water systems like this has become standard practice. It will have to

Chapter 24

change with the installation of new, powerful pumps. The system is a big challenge, but I am getting into a routine and have much of the design complete. I know some of it will have to be sacrificed if we can't get the funding, which will be a shame. It would be nice to do a complete job, but I don't want to be overly optimistic. I have it in my head that everything will run smoothly, but something always goes wrong.

* * *

I was kicked out of the *MayDay* Stadium island when I was running this evening. I knew I was pushing it, but I didn't expect to get a police escort off the island. It was a nice, if somewhat irritating, surprise. Now, do I dare go back and try again? A month or two ago, I was able to go to the stadium, park beside it, and then run around it; or run down to the walkway and then run the seven-and-a-half kilometre circumference of the island, get back in my car and drive home. I also enjoyed having thousands of teenagers, busily practising for the Mass Games, laugh at me. Then, a few weeks back, they stopped people (me) parking at the stadium. I was still able to cross a different bridge, park on the island, run around the track and the stadium, and then get back to my car. Then, checkpoints were set up to stop people (me) running in and around the stadium. I would get halfway and then have to turn and run back again, which was fine, as the distance was pretty similar.

A Bit More Of The Countryside

Then, yesterday, they moved the checkpoints so that I couldn't park on the island at all. So I parked at the *Gold Lane Bowling Alley*, about a kilometre away, and ran down to the island. Today, I had run to the island and done the first stretch, when a guard started blowing his whistle at me. He directed me to go back toward the slip road I had run down initially. I did so, but repeated the circuit, knowing that he really meant for me to leave the island. When I came around to him again, he stopped me and, very seriously, escorted me over to whoever had told him to stop me. A guy in a black suit was talking to other guards (about a strategy for stopping me running onto the island I figure). He told my escort to bring me up the steps. By now, I had changed from being a little peeved to being amused. A few curious bystanders, pretending to walk by very slowly, were watching the drama unfold. I have to admit, it is satisfying – though juvenile – to disrupt the elements of control that exist here, even in a small way.

* * *

Chapter 24

A Korean colleague who was in Germany recently was extolling the virtues of the public transport system there. She refers to buses, trains and trams as 'mass transport', which I initially thought was very cold, like a cattle transporter or something. But when you put it in the context of communism, and centrally planned mass labour, it is a very good way of describing it. 'Public transport' wouldn't be quite right, as there isn't supposed to be a private sector here. With the group mentality, all things communal are described as for the masses. People are part of the system, and they exist for the system, rather than the system for the people. Mass transport gets as many people as possible from A to B, in an efficient and economical manner. All the people go in the one direction, which avoids the chaos of cars in the streets, individually choosing their own direction. The masses, packed together, travel down predetermined routes. There is no buzz of rush hour; there is no road rage. And there is no efficiency.

* * *

It is almost the height of summer here now, and weather conditions are getting miserable. It is hot and uncomfortable, and humidity is almost constantly at one hundred percent. Going for a run is a challenge, and it is difficult to sleep. I feel like I am constantly wearing a layer of sweat. Even the Koreans are complaining. Around this time of year, Korea is inundated with floods, which affect people's lives and livelihoods. Already, in Namchong, where we work, there was a severe flood and landslide, which came unannounced one evening. Huge swathes of crops were washed away, which must be soul-destroying, considering the amount of backbreaking work that has been put into them over the last few months. I haven't been there to see what happened, but I am told it won't be the last of the summer.

A Bit More Of The Countryside

* * *

I have just been told again that my diary has been seen, and that I should be a little more careful about leaving it open and readable in the office. Noted.

* * *

One of the waitresses from the *Friendship* has been away for a week, and returned today. She told me she was in Wonsan, on the coast, visiting her sister and spending time at the beach. We have some really interesting chats, about life in general. I worry about spending too much time talking to her, or sharing too much with her, or vice versa, for fear that it could somehow compromise her. What if she had to go to a re-education camp because of spending so much time talking to foreigners, especially me? She is back, and seems happy and I am glad.

* * *

Chapter 24

We are having problems with one of our Chinese suppliers, who thinks another Chinese supplier is sabotaging the supplies that we buy from her. She thinks someone in our office is colluding in this. I would not be surprised, but I cannot be sure. What can I say? What can I do? The nature of the work here precludes me from doing much about it. Chinese suppliers working here know how the systems work.

* * *

Today, 8 July, is the anniversary of the death of Kim Il Sung. I wondered what was going on last night, when kids were putting flowers in front of the mosaic near the office. It didn't register with me there and then, mainly because I was out running and I was knackered. Running is difficult on the cobbled footpaths. I cannot really make eye contact with people – I am too busy watching my feet.

I went with my Korean colleagues to Mansu Hill, where the statue of the Great Leader stands, towering over Pyongyang. There were quite a few people there, mainly school kids, queuing up to leave flowers at the statue. Usually the place is quiet, and you can walk straight up to the statue, but today everyone had to queue. I saw one old woman carrying a flower; she held it in her hand as if it was the most precious and delicate thing in the world. For her, maybe it was.

Our Liaison Officer wanted me to lay flowers at the statue. I couldn't. I had already asked him not to ask me, especially in front of the other Koreans. I tried to say, 'Ah, no' in a humorous way, laughingly declining and getting someone else to do it. I wasn't trying to be a rebel. I wasn't. I desperately did not want to cause offence to any of the Koreans there, or disappoint them, and that was why I asked our Liaison Officer not to ask me to lay flowers. He did anyway. I had to say no. It was galling enough having to bow three times. Kim Il Sung and the Korean regime have told his people that there is no God. He withdrew the choice of believing, or not, and has taken away the opportunity

A Bit More Of The Countryside

for the population to get to know God. Though I can't verify it, it is pretty much accepted that religious persecution (as well as every other kind) has been going on here for decades, at the instigation of Kim Il Sung.

* * *

Since the flooding about a week ago, there has been even more devastating flooding in Namchong. About a hundred people have died and another hundred are missing at the moment. About six inches of rain fell every hour in the area, for a period of six or seven hours, which is massive. The land was already saturated from the rain a week before. The National Society of the Red Cross have started dealing with the emergency, mainly providing basic medicines and materials for shelter and cooking to the 17,500 that have been left homeless. We are heading out to Namchong in the morning, to see the damage and see if there is any way we can assist from our office. The FDRC have said very little to us – information is, as usual, difficult to get. Hopefully there is some way we can help those who have lost their homes. We are already working in the area, and some of the people we work with there have family who are still missing.

The flooding hit hard and quick. There was no early warning system in place. The houses that were destroyed were at the bottom of a long, narrow valley beneath denuded slopes where the forestry has been stripped away. Most people were in their houses when the floods came. Some were lucky. People who awoke with the first waters had a few minutes to get up, and get their families and neighbours, before the deluge really hit. I walked around the area. For one half of the village, you can walk over the land where the houses were. There is hardly a trace. Some houses were simply cut in half.

We are asking for some funds to support rebuilding houses for people who have lost theirs. City Management is suggesting building a new housing estate, away from the flood area. They say they have some materials, but need support to buy cement

Chapter 24

and steel. They want to know if we can buy the materials for a piped-water system for the houses. I want to say yes, but I don't have the final say. If we can get the money from somewhere, then sure.

25
At Breaking Point

The very concept of objective truth is fading out of the world.
Lies will pass into history.

George Orwell

It looks like we will be getting a small bit of funding to help with rebuilding houses in Namchong, and possibly for a water system. Our head office seems keen enough on the proposal. It looks like they will free up some money that they get from the public. We can't afford the wish-list that the FDRC in Namchong has requested, but we will do something. It is the responsibility of the Government. The people have lost everything, and the money we have will not do much. We have to stretch it as far as it will go.

* * *

One of the Koreans, looking at the sole of his shoe falling off, said quietly to himself, 'Jesus Christ.' Normally I would not smile

Chapter 25

at hearing someone taking the Lord's name in vain, but this time I did. I asked him where had he heard that, but he avoided answering.

* * *

I have finished reading *A Suitable Boy* by Vikram Seth, a tome that has preoccupied me for the last few months. I was sad when I turned the last page. It feels like the end of an era. It is not the most exciting book I have read, a bit like a very slow-moving soap opera, but bit by bit, the characters are developed, and become almost real. Now it is gone from me, and there is a gap in my life. I had kept one of the waitresses in the *Friendship* updated on the story as I was reading it, and she was as disappointed as I was, that it was finally over. It had become part of our routine. In the evening, I would come in, chat about the latest chapter, then go to the *diplomatic* restaurant for some food and coffee.

This restaurant caters for some western tastes. My usual choice is *oi salad* – pickled cucumber, very nice – and then a sandwich – usually cheese with cucumber. It is impossible to find a sandwich outside the *diplomatic* restaurant. Sometimes I would have the *tofu*, or *mo-du-bu* with a chili sauce, but it makes my face sweat.

The waitress asked me what other books I read – the usual: novels, a bit of history and some politics. I told her sometimes I read the Bible. She had never heard of it. I explained that it was a book for Christians, and she said, 'Ooh, about God,' and laughed a little nervously. 'We don't believe in a God in Korea.' This waitress regularly talks about the importance of having a good heart. She asked me whether, when I was young, my mother said to me, 'You must believe this,' all the time. She didn't. Nobody did, but I was taught the fundamentals in school, and I was brought to Mass. When I was a teenager, I temporarily forgot all that I had learned, but it was easily remembered when I made the effort to go looking. I don't know whether my explanation made

At Breaking Point

any sense to her, but she seemed to understand that it was something important to me.

*　*　*

I was teaching English to one of the other women in the *Friendship* yesterday, in return for some instruction in rudimentary Korean. In reality, it is just an excuse to spend some time with Korean people in an unthreatening manner. For this lesson, we decided to focus on the letter *r*, as the girl could not say the word 'stir'. The sentence for the day was, 'The girl walked for four hours before she met her at the tower.' The letter *r* is difficult. I am not mocking, but it *was* funny, and the other Korean girls got a kick out of teasing her.

*　*　*

I thought I was going to the British Embassy for a buffet with a delegation from the European Commission today, but it turned out that it wasn't a crowd from the Commission, only a few MEPs. Only one or two of them seemed to have any idea about the country; the rest, it appeared, were sightseeing. The word 'junket' springs to mind. There was a Hungarian woman who complained about having to visit a place where one of the NGOs works on occupational therapy for amputees. Another was complaining about the hotel, while one woman was not happy with the level of diplomatic interaction from the Koreans.

I was talking to an Ulster Unionist Party MEP for the UK. He made a point of telling me he was from Northern Ireland, not Ireland, when we were introduced. I told him I don't really care for making a distinction. He mellowed a little bit over some wine, and was almost cordial. We talked about where my Da is from, a small Catholic enclave in Belfast. He knows it well – well, he knows some places right beside there.

The MEPs were supposed to use the dinner as an opportunity to talk to the NGOs, the UN and some Eastern European diplomats, to get another view of the DPRK. Once the buffet

Chapter 25

was finished and they had had their dessert, they were very keen to leave. I really wonder about European politicians. Do they do anything? It seems that the unelected body – the Commission, with its administration and civil servants – makes all the decisions. MEPs, elected on five-year terms, have to rely on the civil servants to navigate the labyrinthine bureaucracy, without ever getting to influence policy or the direction of the *project*.

* * *

We have final approval from our headquarters to do some emergency work in response to the flooding in Namchong. There is not much money, but at least we can do something for the people whose houses have been wiped out. It is hard to know what we can do yet, especially as the Government here are not sharing what their plans are. Given what we already do, a water system to the new housing 'estate' could be a possibility. There is a spring not too far away with a lot of water, but it is too low to bring water to the second storeys of the proposed houses. A pump will be needed, and a reinforced concrete storage tank; and a lot of pipes, valves and taps.

* * *

Seriously, work is definitely taking its toll on me. I am worn out. I have only been acting as Country Director for a few weeks, and I am shattered. I am constantly on the go. There are too many things to do, considering I have to keep all the water programmes on track as well. It is good for me, personally, as I am learning about all aspects of the organisation. Many issues can be put on the long finger, but so far there is no sign of anyone on the way to take over any of the roles. I imagine there will be a month's lead-in time for someone taking on any of the positions, and so far no one has taken a single one. Will anyone take a job, given the possibility that the DPRK Government could ask us to leave at any time? I have my doubts.

I am getting lines under my eyes. I feel burnt out and I am sweating constantly in the humidity. I got a dose of bronchitis

At Breaking Point

from sleeping with a window open a few nights ago, when the temperature suddenly dropped. I have a sore throat, and it has got worse and worse. I think my defences are running low at present. I don't sleep enough and I don't eat well. I am drinking and smoking too much. Though I quit smoking two days ago, I hope I can maintain it for the next few days, as I will be in Namchong with Miss Chae. It is never easy, as my will is weak, and cigarettes are constantly on offer from the local FDRC people. It is nice to accept, to stand around and have a smoke together, even if neither speaks the other's language. Smoking, like football, is a universal language.

* * *

One of the waitresses in the *Friendship* seems upset with me at the moment, and I have no idea why. It is bugging me, because she is someone who usually cheers me up. When I am down, she is great, happy to talk away about *normal* things and about the world outside of here. She doesn't judge, except when she criticises my eating and drinking habits. She doesn't like how I hold my fork. It can get a little claustrophobic here in the expat bubble, and it is nice to have an outlet for conversation outside the intrigues of the small community inside the walls of the Diplomatic Compound.

* * *

After reading all my griping yesterday, it seems that putting thoughts into words has been cathartic. Today was a social day. I went to a wedding. Not a Korean wedding, but the wedding of a couple from New Zealand. It was in *Chilbo* Church, a Presbyterian or Methodist church just off Kwangbok Street, the ten-lane road that leads to Nampo. One of the hymns was one I know in English, so I even got to participate a little. After we left the church, a group of South Koreans arrived to meet the congregation. We had a meal on a boat, and a short cruise on the Taedong River. It was pleasant, even though the boat got stuck in the silt for a bit.

Chapter 25

I managed to find a super present for the wedding: a stuffed rat and a stuffed squirrel, fighting taekwondo style, from the top floor of Department Store Number One, just off Kim Il Sung Square. I found out that there is a Department Store Number Two as well. It is not possible to spend euro in it though, only won. I still have not changed any euro to won, which is limiting. [Postscript: Incidentally, the super present described above got redistributed by the happy couple as a going-away present to another couple. They were equally unimpressed by it, and it was finally given to me as a present some months later, on my departure from Pyongyang. The giver was completely unaware of its origins. I was delighted to receive such an unusual item.]

* * *

There was a pool party today, hosted by the Swiss and the Germans. It featured a performance of *Aquarius*, and about ten brave souls risked the ire of the rest of the expat community by taking part. I didn't. I am not a performance person. It wasn't nearly as embarrassing as I thought it might be. I am not sure everyone will appreciate their photos popping up in the future though. The costumes were ... interesting.

* * *

This is my fourth day not smoking, and I think I am through the worst of it. The first two days were tough, as I had bronchitis and felt really poorly. A number of issues were annoying me, and not smoking did not help me deal with these either. I think I could make it this time. I could be smoke-free forever. Even if it is just for a few weeks, it will help the body recover. I would like a cigarette right now, though. I can feel that thin line – that is so easy to cross, but so easy to remain stuck behind – right there in front of me.

* * *

The Korean War by Max Hastings comments frequently, through the recollections of those involved in the fighting, on the Korean

At Breaking Point

weather, both the extreme cold and the oppressive heat. As I was reading it, I was thinking, they're right about the winter, but surely the summer cannot be that bad. It is only about thirty-five degrees Celsius; that should be manageable. It was about forty-five degrees in Afghanistan, and it was hot, but bearable. Now I understand. It is tough. It is very warm and sticky. I sweat no matter what I do, and constantly feel ready to faint. It is difficult to sleep, so I am exhausted all the time. There is nothing worse than going to bed and not being able to sleep. Everyone here is in the same state at the moment, and it is affecting everyone's mood. I have no energy, and I have big ugly bags under my eyes. When I am sitting in my office, I wish for air conditioning. I have only a little fan that rotates around the room. It is like a piece of heaven when it passes by, and when it is gone the sweating starts anew.

I am told the summer is nearly over. I really hope so. The swimming pool on Saturdays is about the only relief from it, and then, for some reason, I put myself in the sauna after my swim. Why?

26
Six-Party Talking Shops

Man is born free, and everywhere he is in chains.
Jean Jacques Rousseau

Problems the world is having with the DPRK at the moment: nuclear weapons; chemical and biological threats; missile proliferation; conventional weaponry; drug smuggling; counterfeiting; refugees; and human rights abuses. Where do the representatives at the Six-Party Talks start in dealing with all of those problems? To make it even more complicated, there is no clarity on who to talk to. Is there ever really a decision-maker at these meetings? Is it clear who the decision-makers really are? The jury is out on whether Kim Jong Il is a decision-maker or a puppet.

Prime Minister Pak Pong Ju, whose star is apparently in the ascendency inside the system, is a technocrat who is driving the slow economic reform. It is hard to know how long he will last if

Chapter 26

the economic reforms backfire either by creating further poverty or providing the chink that lets the light of progress in. Two other names bandied about as possible power wielders are Kim Yong Nam, President of the Supreme People's Assembly Presidium, and Jo Myong Rok, the political representative of the Korean People's Army. Kim Yong Nam is the *de facto* leader of the State. He does a significant amount of representation for the country, going on foreign visits and leading most of the high-level meet-and-greet sessions. Jo Myong Rok is a military heavyweight and acts as a face for the Army, both inside and outside Korea. Both of these individuals are theoretically subservient to Kim Jong Il, but whether that is the reality is unclear.

* * *

George W Bush recently called Kim Jong Il:

... a dangerous person, a tyrant who starves his people and has huge concentration camps.

Kim Jong Il responded by saying George W Bush was:

... a hooligan bereft of personality, a half-baked man in terms of morality, a philistine, a cowboy at a ranch whose remarks often stun audiences as they reveal his utter ignorance.

* * *

Malnutrition here is a problem. United Nations figures for many areas are very bleak. In the northeast of the country, where the situation is worst, people eat meat, fish or eggs only once every three weeks. That amounts to serious protein deficiency. At the same time, the South Korean government has announced that it has its own nutritional problems to contend with: one in ten school-going children is suffering from obesity. If reunification ever takes place, the two halves of the one race will look at each other as strangers. Both sides will be instantly recognisable: the Northerners stunted and undernourished, and the Southerners taller and fat.

Six-Party Talking Shops

* * *

The Six-Party Talks are underway at the moment, and have lasted an unprecedented six days. Christopher Hill, the US representative at the talks, continually extols his own patience. There are rumours of difficulties in the talks, however, and it seems that after six days, even Hill's patience is wearing thin, as is that of the Koreans. The Japanese, though seemingly on the sidelines, are, according to our Liaison Officer, kicking up a fuss about abductions of its citizens many years ago. This seems fair enough. If the US wishes to discuss its issues, every other country should also be able to state their grievances.

The talks definitely have a feeling of the DPRK against the rest. Though the Chinese, the South Koreans and the Russians are saying very little, the whole point of the talks is to deal with the *North Korean Problem*. This attitude in itself is problematic.

The talks are reaching a stalemate, as there are a number of things that the parties cannot agree on, though they all say they are very close. One major stumbling block seems to be the DPRK's refusal to admit that it has a uranium enrichment plant in the country, as well as the plutonium one at Yongbyong. It seems a strange thing for the US to get hung up about – the DPRK probably does not have such a plant, and the US seems to be insisting that they admit this. Maybe it is a bluff. I think the US will yield and take a step back, and then agree to a step-by-step cajoling approach to the denuclearisation of the Korean peninsula.

* * *

I spent the whole weekend in the office, trying to figure out budget revisions that I don't really understand. I have no idea where some of the previous figures have come from. There is still no confirmed date for new staff to arrive, but a *WatSan* programme manager and a country director have been identified, both of whom have agreed verbally to take the respective posts.

Chapter 26

* * *

Yesterday I saw a child begging on the streets. That was a first for me in the country, and especially surprising in Pyongyang. The street urchin was in no way abashed at approaching me and asking for money. No one else on the streets even looks at me, yet this young guy came straight up and followed me across the Taedong iron bridge, before giving up and turning around. I couldn't give him anything. I have no idea what the consequences would be for him if I did. I also had no Korean currency to give him, only dollars. I don't think he could use them.

* * *

Last night there was an *evening* at the Swiss and German compound, to celebrate Swiss national day. It was good, though very warm for wearing a shirt and tie. I thought I was going to melt when I arrived, but I seemed to acclimatise (maybe it just got cooler) after a while. Five of the waitresses from the *Friendship* were there, doing the catering for about 150 people. It was too warm, yet they ploughed on, looking very hot and flustered but always nice, polite and friendly. In a way, this attitude is unfortunate – perhaps people would respect them more if they didn't have to be so pleasant to the foreigners all the time.

At the end of the evening, they were tidying up and washing, carrying heavy boxes of plates and food. Almost none of the people still sitting around drinking thought it appropriate to get up and at least offer to help. Plenty of those people go to the *Friendship*, and are all smiles and hugs for the girls when they see them, but they had no interest in showing the slightest bit of solidarity. Some were even a little snide.

In any other walk of life, in Ireland or America or Afghanistan, you would not treat people like that. Sometimes I think the foreigners here, working for the UN and the NGOs, and even the diplomats, do not see Koreans as people. I am not sure why this is, but I guess it is partly because there is a barrier here that makes it difficult to get to know North Koreans as individuals.

* * *

I have done something to my shoulder. I asked a physiotherapist, and she believes it may be a swollen tendon. Ouch.

* * *

I am in Namchong today, back in one of my usual haunts. It started raining heavily yesterday evening while I was in Pyongyang. I decided it was perfect weather for a run, with the rain breaking the humidity and the evening being cool. I figured it is better to be wet from the rain than wet from sweating. I think I was helping to perpetuate the belief among the locals here that the foreigners in Pyongyang are slightly mad. I was running past a tram as it was starting to move off after picking up passengers. I tried to keep pace with it so that we were moving at the same speed. I don't know what the masses inside the tram, seeing a foreigner in shorts and a stringy vest in the teeming rain outside, thought.

It is still raining in Namchong. The street in front of the hotel is flooded, almost up to waist height — depending how tall you are — and the street is full of legless torsos. People are dragging carts through the floods, and water seems to be coming from everywhere. I went down to the river to see what level the flow was at. It was disappointingly low, because there is a dam just upstream of the town that the local officials are getting worried about.

* * *

It looks like I am finally getting some concrete answers regarding replacement people in the office. I will soon have two new bosses. After ascending the ladder by default, I am on my way back down again. What a fall from grace, but at least I will be able to take that long, long overdue holiday.

Chapter 26

* * *

The Six-Party Talks are nearing their conclusion, and it seems that all parties are at make-or-break point. Either they will sign an agreement or they won't, in the next twenty four hours. All of the non-DPRK countries keep saying it is for the DPRK to make the next move. I don't think it is; I think the US will agree to something in order to keep the ball rolling. They do not want to encounter the situation that occurred eighteen months ago again, during which the DPRK gained the perceived moral high ground.

* * *

I am just back from a few pleasant days in Wonsan, a coastal town in the east. I went with all the Koreans from our office for two nights. Some of them had not been to the sea before, and spent hours just paddling and having a laugh. Mr Ko brought his wife along, and I could tell he was very uncomfortable with it all. I don't think he really knows how to deal with mixing his private and work life. He is a bit childish in many ways, but very good fun. He seemed happy when it was just the two of them in the sea, having a laugh and splashing each other with water. She seemed nice, though I never got a formal introduction.

It was different being away with the team on a relaxing weekend. Mrs Chae, who can be very uptight, was at ease. She is our very dedicated and serious, though slightly nervous, administrator. She was reluctant to go on our *team-building* weekend. We visited Wonsan Hospital, asking a few questions and comparing it to the clinics we are rehabilitating further north. Then everyone was keen to get down to the business of swimming. (I went swimsuit shopping with Mrs Chang on Thursday before we left. I don't think there is another Korean woman who would do that. The few shops here tend to be multifunctional, with groceries and swimsuits all in the one room.)

The hotel in Wonsan was a step up from what I am used to in Namchong or Rongchon. Quite expensive at €50 for bed and breakfast. There was a working elevator, and the décor was reasonably clean and newish. The hotel has aimed to replicate regular hotels outside Korea. It goes close but doesn't quite hit it. The towels are laid out as in a real hotel, and the toilet roll in the holder is nicely folded. There is a fridge. There is a TV, though the same station is on each channel. There is also a nice view of the sea.

Breakfast was interesting. I was the only person sitting in a big dining room for about fifty people, with a place already prepared for me at a big table. There were many Koreans staying in the hotel, but they must have had breakfast before me, or somewhere else. I drank what I believe to be a bad can of Chinese Guinness in the RAC the night before we left. When we were driving from Pyongyang, I thought I was going to pass out from the pain in my stomach. Four days later, I am still feeling under the weather.

The beaches here are restricted to wealthy, connected Koreans and foreigners. It is hard to figure out exactly what the situation is. The areas I was in were much quieter than the surrounding beaches, separated merely by a sign saying 'STOP'. I managed to have a conversation in Korean with a Korean woman, someone I don't work with and who wasn't serving me food or drink or something across a counter. She told me she was thirty-four years old. She asked how old I was, and then told me there were seven years between us. I don't understand the significance of this, but regardless, I held a full – albeit limited – conversation in the Korean language with no props and no translator. There was a group of four beautiful Korean women in their early twenties on the beach. They didn't pay me the slightest attention.

On the first evening, our fun deteriorated into a night of Karaoke. Mrs Chang took centre stage, much to the annoyance of Mr Kang, who fancies himself as a singer. They all think they are Sinatras. No one is shy about singing a few bars. Mr Chol is the best of them – for a skinny guy, he has a great pair of lungs.

Chapter 26

On the second day, we went for a picnic on a quiet beach. Our Liaison Officer had borrowed a chef and a waitress from the hotel to prepare some *bulgoggi* on the beach. The waitress was a nice girl, with a little English, who seemed nervous around me, a foreigner. She was delighted when I insisted on helping her carry the heavy box of plates. None of the Koreans offered. The next morning in the coffee shop, she was chatty, as much as she could be. Conversation did not move beyond ages and countries. Neither my Korean nor her English were capable of much else.

It was a nice change to spend a little time outside of Pyongyang with my Korean colleagues, watching them having a good time, playing and relaxing. They seem to be used to me now, and more at ease in my company. Everything will change when the new foreigners arrive.

All in all, it was a nice weekend, except for half of us having a dose of the runs. Mr Ho was in hospital getting rehydrated all day Saturday.

* * *

Today or tomorrow, I will get to go to the Mass Games. I think. It isn't confirmed as of yet. The games were supposed to be on this evening in the *MayDay* Stadium, but seem to have been postponed until tomorrow. No one is really sure. How they can leave something so big – if they fill the stadium there will be 150,000 people there – to be organised at the very last minute really baffles me. It will be fascinating to watch the spectacle. It is a real treat, as very few people from outside Korea ever get to see it.

* * *

I am getting annoyed with our head office. I don't think I am getting as much help as I should be, given the situation I am in – doing all these different jobs, with my general youthfulness and inexperience. I am not getting feedback when I ask questions, and generally not even getting a response to acknowledge that I

Six-Party Talking Shops

have asked a question. I was hoping to get home for Mam's fiftieth in September, and now I can't, because the Regional Director is coming for her annual visit to the DPRK. I have to be here, as there is nobody else to organise everything. On top of that, I have organised, or am attempting to coordinate, a study tour to Ethiopia for some of the county agriculture teams, to learn about integrated slope management. The Korean hierarchy is not happy about learning from Africans, so it has taken a lot of persuasion for our Liaison Officer to get approval from the bosses in the big buildings. He has received the necessary permissions for the people to go, and now our HQ has turned around and tried to cancel the trip. I told them there is no way this trip is being cancelled. We have too much to lose, as does our Liaison Officer. He told me he has had to call in a few favours to get this passed, and it would not be looked on too kindly if it were to be cancelled now.

* * *

On the engineering front, materials for the Namchong and Songchon urban water systems are arriving bit by bit. These are made-to-measure pieces, based on reasonably intricate designs and there is very little contingency stock available, or contingency funding. The local water board are already trying to change the plans. They want to move a water storage tank or two. Some of them want to connect directly to people's taps from huge pumps. I have a feeling that they agreed with me previously just to ensure that I bought the materials. Now that the pipes are on their way, the local water managers want to change everything. I feel used, but I can give as good as I get. There is much more to be done next year, and much bigger orders for materials to be placed, so they really aren't in a position to mess around.

The reality is that resources like these are scarce, and optimum use must be made of what is available now. There is no guarantee that anything will arrive next year. Some of the things the local managers want to do are infuriating. They want

Chapter 26

everything done as it was thirty years ago, regardless of design or efficiency.

Given intimations from the North Korean Government, the county officials may be well advised not to wait for further investment next year. There are rumours that there may be announcements regarding our presence here sometime soon.

27

Group Think. Tank

The Catholic Church has rejected the totalitarian and atheistic ideologies associated in modern times with 'communism' or 'socialism'.

The Catechism of the Catholic Church

The Six-Party Talks have gone into recess for three weeks. The representatives have all headed home, to reassess and get further instruction from those above. The South has told the US that they believe the North has a right to peaceful nuclear power. The North has apparently said that they will allow very intrusive nuclear inspections. We will see.

The last few days saw the run up to the sixtieth anniversary of the liberation of Korea from the Japanese. There were parties, and big parties, Korean style. There was an evening of dancing at Kim Il Sung Square, involving big crowds of teenagers and young adults, the men in white shirts and the ladies in brightly

Chapter 27

coloured traditional dresses. The dances are standard set-dances, quite similar to 'The Walls of Limerick' and 'The Siege of Ennis' for Irish dancing.

The dancing was enjoyable. All foreigners had been issued with invitations. This was a big event, so most of the expatriate community was there, NGOs, UN, and diplomats alike, though the diplomats were in the VIP area. I went with Mrs Chae Yong Nam, and you couldn't find better company.

On arrival at the rear of the square, we were shepherded to the seating area as if entering a stadium, though the square is open air and you can usually drive through it. Twelve thousand (my estimate) Koreans, mainly women, brightly attired in Korean traditional dress and forming a series of human squares, were ready and waiting to start dancing. The dancing started at eight o'clock, to the accompaniment of fireworks. The 12,000 danced for about half an hour in set-dances, and then the crowd was allowed to join in for the *free* dancing stage, where the set of dances were pretty much repeated.

It is novel to see all the foreigners being led around the square, participating in this mass exhibition, a symbol of what most of them sneer at – the rigid, controlled, centralised system here. Each foreigner had a Korean partner to lead them through the dances and ensure they followed the moves as best they could. I had Mrs Chae, who used to participate in these dances way back in her youth with Mr Kang, another translator in our office. From what I can gather, they fell out after *courting* for a short while. Mrs Chae is very entertaining most days. She can be a witch when she is in a bad mood, but generally she is the liveliest person in our office, the polar opposite of the popular caricature of the dour Korean.

I was soon accosted by a young Korean lady in a luminous yellow traditional dress, who showed me the ropes for the next twenty minutes. Unfortunately, the one dance I know – the one about the farmers in the fields, wiping the sweat from their

Group Think. Tank

brows – was not on the menu, so I was uncoordinated for the duration.

It ended at exactly nine o'clock. Myself and Mrs Chae had to go looking for our car, which took a long time. She seemed to be getting nervous. Whereas I would happily have walked the three kilometres home, she had no intention of doing that. She told me there are usually lots of courting couples hanging around the streets after these dances, and in bushes and dark corners. I didn't investigate.

I don't endorse the regimented mentality that the dances represent, but it was fun. Everybody seemed to enjoy it. The fact that it may be used as part of the propaganda machine is not a good thing, but many things that happen here are created and used for that purpose. Even road construction and land re-zoning are used as symbols of the power of the masses.

The day after the dance, there was the spectacular of spectaculars, the Arirang Mass Gymnastics Exhibition, or the Mass Games to the layperson. Every foreigner wants to see the Games, and it is the biggest tourism boon in the DPRK. It is the only one. I had never seen so many foreigners here before, including a troupe of about fifty blonde teenage Russian dancers. I don't know what kind of dancing they were here for, but they stole the show on entering the foreigners' section of the *MayDay* Stadium before the exhibition started. Fifty blonde heads and one hundred blue eyes did not fit in.

Before the evening, there was speculation that the young lad would turn up, and that this was the reason for the cancellation yesterday. I was a little apprehensive at the prospect of being in the same place as him. He did turn up, and was seated not far from me. He arrived at 8:37pm, after the beginnings of the ceremony, which involved a display of synchronisation movements and co-ordination from child placard bearers, forming a giant human mural along one side of the stadium. In my estimation, there were about 40,000 children, each holding a

Chapter 27

sort of book of coloured pages. On instruction, from a variety of little men standing on the ground below, they change the colour of the page, to reveal a huge jigsaw-type mural.

It is not as simple as it sounds. Sometimes it is a static, uniform image, and then a single, simultaneous change. Twenty thousand children all change the open page of their book from the yellow to the red page. Sometimes the change has to be done with a particular timing to create movement, like a Mexican wave, but not so simply. The children would change the pages consecutively, flowing from left to right and then right to left. There were multiple complex combinations, of colours and patterns. There was one movement through the 40,000 that was like playing *snake* on a mobile phone, the cards momentarily changing colour, at lightning speed, to give the impression of two snakes moving across the mural. It must take an enormous amount of practice.

Throughout the show, for an hour-and-a-half, the mural changed, forming a huge variety of pictures, depicting different aspects of Korean life, usually in tandem with the theme on the gymnastics floor. There were scenes of country life, of war, of Kim Jong Il, of Kim Il Sung, of technology, of industry, of hydropower, of children, of art, of space exploration. The timing of the page turning had to be accurate to the millisecond, each and every time, and there were hundreds of changes.

This element of the Games was probably the most impressive, given the harmonisation required, and the sheer number of participants. These page-turners were only primary school children – impressive, but also unnerving. How can you instil that sort of discipline in so many school children? When I was in primary school, it was a struggle to get three of us to play a tune in time on tin whistles.

To give an idea of the scale of the performance, I estimate that there were 100,000 spectators, and 40,000 children making up the human wall. There were at least 8,000 performers on the floor at the start, and there must have been double this number, at least, as huge numbers of performers were going off and coming on. There was a performance by children alone, which was another 4,000, and added to this was the military performance/show of strength, which was another 6,000, minimum. I think we are talking about 66,000 performers in the Games. I could be way off – possibly by 30,000, up or down – but this is a ballpark figure.

This was a unique experience. Not many people get to experience such an event, under these circumstances. It is hard to know how to react to it, because it is such a strange event, with an insidious purpose. It is designed to show the might of central planning, and it does show what can be achieved by the subordination of the unit to the mass. I don't think there is anywhere else in the world where 40,000 high-school children could be trained to create a human billboard with such coordination. You would never get them in place to rehearse together, never mind perform.

One of the best bits was when they made a blinking eye on the human billboard. About a hundred cards changed, to display an image of an eye blinking, while the others stayed the same, then another hundred in another place, then another hundred in another place, and so on. Another impressive image was the land reclamation scene, in which a bulldozer moved back and forth. Only the bulldozers move, by the swaying of perhaps 10,000 of the participants in time with each other, while the others remained static.

Some of the other foreigners here commented on the lack of euphoria displayed when Kim Jong Il appeared. It's a fair point. The people accompanying the foreigners, mostly from the Ministry of Foreign Affairs, clapped very sedately. Nobody was chanting his name. The army section was definitely adding voice to the crowd, though, of course, this is their duty. I could not judge the reaction of the common folk in the far corners of the

Chapter 27

stadium, where the old women in traditional Korean dresses were. A lot of sound was amplified through loudspeakers, creating a wall of noise across the stadium. It was unnerving. There were thousands of fists being punched in the air. He eventually sat down without speaking.

I still haven't made up my mind what to make of the whole spectacle. It was very impressive, but clearly representative of the control the State has. It seems that the participants take part willingly – they all want to be a part of it, despite the demands of the training. But surely it is the relentless propaganda and the information control that makes them want to? If more information, and different perspectives, were available to them, would they be so keen?

* * *

It is a few days since the Games, and the humidity has almost disappeared, at least for a while. Summer is officially over, and the oppressive heat has gone. Thank God. I don't think I could have hacked it much longer. I am heading off on holidays on 17 September, two days late for my mother's fiftieth birthday. Bad form.

* * *

The DPRK did not create its modern Hermit Kingdom overnight. The cult of the leader had to be built up over time; the flow of information had to be stifled bit by bit; the elimination of a communal memory, and the creation of a new discourse, had to be put in place slowly. The communalisation of the State did not occur in one fell swoop – Kim Il Sung had to eliminate opponents and competition for demagoguery through a series of purges, while carefully building and maintaining alliances.

While Korea has been gradually changing, so too has the world outside. The world that North Korea gradually lost contact with has gone through radical changes since the sixties and seventies, and the two different worlds have diverged hugely. I wonder what the Koreans would think of the moral relativism of the western world. What would they think of the lack of respect shown toward old people in modern society? In Korea, and in Confucian thought, the elder is deserving of respect and appreciation, and occupies a central role in society. In the developed world, the aged are gradually becoming isolated, and are increasingly viewed as a burden as society increasingly emphasises individualism.

The gradual decline of marriage and the family as the fundamental unit of society would be viewed with shock in Korea. Despite the socialist system socially reconstructing community as the fundamental unit, and eroding the foundation of the family, in Korea, marriage and family continue to be the basis of everything. The traditional family, including grandparents, forms the basic unit in Korea. The State has tried to erode this, for example by forcing children into kindergartens, and pushing mothers to return to work as soon as possible after giving birth. The regime tries to prioritise loyalty and love of the country and leader over that of the family. This has largely failed, perhaps partly because the family has become a refuge from the State and the system.

The approach of the Korean State in blinkering and moulding society, from an outsider's perspective, seems guileless. It all looks very crude and blatant. It is difficult to comprehend how it looks from the inside. The attempted undermining of the family has been quite open in Korea, while in the developed world, society itself has contrived to erode the primacy of the family. The family in Korea remains the last remaining bulwark against the State, while the family is almost perceived as an obstacle in societies outside Korea. I can see our own systems, our own way of life, becoming more and more controlled by a different type of totalitarianism, one which threatens speech that challenges positivism or liberalism. The new absolutism is one that *de facto* rules out any other absolutism. There are foreigners here who think they have it sorted – they know how life should be lived

Chapter 27

and how the world should function, and they want to import this into Korea as well, without contemplating for a moment that they may not be right. The absolutism of the Korean system is utterly wrong. It represents an end-point that I don't think was ever envisaged by the founding fathers of communist theory, though, in hindsight, it seems absolutely inevitable.

28

Last Orders?

The future belongs to socialism.
Erich Hoenecker

The DPRK Humanitarian Coordinator has outlined what is now happening in Korea in a letter sent to all of the organisations providing humanitarian assistance and working on development programmes here. The UN website outlines the general substance of the communication to us. It is very disturbing – personally and for the aid organisations.

UN talking points on DPRK Government's position on humanitarian assistance

On Friday 26 August, the vice-minister for Foreign Affairs, Mr Choe Su Han, called a meeting to brief UN Resident and Humanitarian Coordinator and WFP Country Director on the DPRK Government's position on humanitarian assistance.

Chapter 28

The message was that after 10 years of humanitarian assistance, the humanitarian situation in DPRK had improved.

He expressed gratitude for the support provided to DPRK but noted that 10 years of humanitarian aid is an abnormally long time, and the Government is concerned that this could ultimately lead to a culture of dependency.

The vice-minister went on to explain that while it was time to stop humanitarian aid, development oriented programmes both bilateral and multilateral would be welcome. Only in cases such as the train explosion in Ryongchon in 2004, will the Government request humanitarian assistance from the international community ...

This letter, and various official statements, triggered all sorts of meetings between all sorts of people, attempting to find a resolution. The NGOs and the European Commission's Humanitarian Office (ECHO) had a meeting with the Vice-Director for the Ministry of Foreign Affairs (European Department). We were effectively told that all humanitarian assistance is to cease by the end of the year. All NGO offices are to be run by Koreans. Foreigners may have access for monitoring from time to time, but will not be resident in the country. When asked what other options there were for the organisations who felt that they could not comply with these demands, we were told there were no other options. Effectively that means we – myself in our case, as I am the only expatriate in our office at present – will have to leave the country, as will ECHO, who fund most other NGOs here. Even if ECHO doesn't leave, it will not fund partners without a physical expatriate presence here, so it is doomsday for NGOs. It looks like I will be leaving the country.

Inter-agency meetings have been more interesting of late though. The WFP want a more dogmatic, pro-active approach, to try to force the hand of the Koreans, while most other actors want to take a softer approach for now, just sitting and waiting to see what will happen. The British Ambassador says the United Kingdom will demand a full reversal of the statement. Each

Last Orders?

NGO is being told that they will be contacted individually for further details, indicating that the situation may not be the same for everybody.

Most NGOs are dependent on ECHO, and ECHO knows this. The ECHO representative has asked that NGOs inform ECHO when they are contacted or have meetings on the situation. I quietly pointed out that we are not dependant on ECHO – we are, after all, supposedly impartial humanitarian organisations, many with substantial funding from public donations and other donors. It is good for them to bear this in mind. It must be recognised that the EC decision to provide only ECHO funding at the current time is politically embarrassing for the regime internally – they would rather see the EC commit to longer-term development funding. This would give substance to the claim that the regime has brought its people through the crisis and into the sunlight of progress again. Externally, I don't think this is politically desirable.

Personally, if we have to leave the country, I will be sad – sad for me, though I will be leaving anyway at some stage; and sad for a few people here that I have got to know and consider to be friends, both Korean and non-Korean. Most of all, I will be sad for the general populace. It looks like the Government really wants to shut up shop, close the doors, lock the peasants in, and bolt the doors on intrusive foreigners. I suppose it doesn't help our cause when I go running to Kim Il Sung Square, stop for half an hour, all sweaty, and just hang around right outside the Ministry of Foreign Affairs, gawking at all the curious youngsters preparing for the midnight torchlight march.

Before it all ends though, I'd better get that marathon I had planned out of the way.

* * *

Yesterday, I got up at seven in the morning, drank a litre of water and a few spoons of sugar, put on my shorts and my nice runners and waited for my two volunteers to pick me up. They

Chapter 28

dropped me at the big mural of Kim Il Sung near the six-lane highway to Nampo. Last time I was in Nampo, I clocked the distance to Pyongyang from the big orange mural at the edge of the town (which looks like a picture of Kim Il Sung and Kim Jong Il in hell, rather than a sunset). It measures just over twenty-six miles. Interestingly, that distance brings you very close to another mural of Kim Il Sung, on Kwangbok Street. This is where the solo marathon began.

I was dropped off just after eight in the morning. I had chosen the day carefully: low humidity, lower than usual temperature and the wind at my back. The road from Pyongyang to Nampo pretty much follows the Taedong River to the coast, so it is mostly very slightly downhill. Everything was set for a good marathon. My last one, in 1999, took me three hours and fifty minutes. I was sure I had myself set up for a new personal best. After ten kilometres, I was not feeling so confident. My prevailing wind was prevailing in the wrong direction, and I was feeling the pace. I was sure I would give up. I had to keep going though – my support team was not due to finish their breakfast for two hours, so if I stopped I would be stranded.

I hate to use the word surreal, but that's what it was – running along that huge highway, almost completely devoid of any form of motorised vehicle, for four hours. I was worried when I started that soldiers or police would stop me, either to ask what I was doing and disrupt my run, or to make me go back. There was no blueprint for this! I passed a few solitary soldiers at ease along the road, a few oxen and carts and a lot of farmers. No one paid me any attention.

I kept going, and got to the halfway mark in under an hour and a half. I was amazed. For a few miles I thought I would do a super time. Then it all went wrong. At about mile fifteen I hit the wall. I struggled on, thinking about the last three miles, downhill straight into Nampo, imagining this would spur me on. It didn't. By the time the town came into view, I was walking for a few

Last Orders?

hundred yards, and then running the same amount. I was getting worried I wouldn't even beat my previous best. I struggled, and just barely made it in three hours and forty-eight minutes. No small thanks to the constant supply of water from my support car.

* * *

I described the very strange event at Koppensang guesthouse last year, where the Ministry of Foreign Affairs invites the European embassies and NGOs along to an evening of singing, as a mutual 'thank you' for engagement with each other. Despite the fact that they are asking us all to leave, they went ahead with this again this year. We all had to go along with it. We were down on numbers this year, as most of my colleagues have now left, and it was up to me to find an Irish song for us to sing. Luckily, I acquired a Sinead O'Connor CD in Beijing a few months ago, on which she sings a lot of old Irish sings. This saved me having to teach by singing. I can't sing. I brought the CD to the office, and played a few of the songs I know. We selected 'Óró Sé do Bheatha Bhaile', because the beat is similar to some Korean nationalist tunes, and the Koreans seemed to like it. When I explained that it was an old Irish rebel song, about throwing off the yoke of the oppressors, they were even more delighted. It translates as:

Welcome oh woman who was so afflicted,
It was our ruin that you were in bondage,
Our fine land in the possession of thieves ...
And you sold to the foreigners!

I had to write out all the Irish words phonetically for everyone to read. This was then retranslated into *hangul*, the Korean script. It would not be possible for a Korean to read Irish words such as *bheatha* (and get the pronunciation *vah-ha*). We practised for a few lunchtimes and then decided to ratchet up the pace a little, to make it more forceful. By the time the big night came along, we were ready to pump it out. We were probably the best of the

Chapter 28

foreign performances that night, second only to the Korean MFA male voice choir, even though we were more like a rabble than a chorus.

The Guardian Newspaper, on 3 October 2005, my 27th birthday, captured the mood of sadness and strangeness that was facing the NGO community in the DPRK, in a melancholic article about the potential closure of the RAC:

Of all the bars in all the world, there is probably none as exclusive, surreal or intriguing as the Random Access Club in Pyongyang ... Open for business only on Friday nights, the RAC is a watering hole for North Korea's tiny expatriate community ... the club inside the compound of the United Nations World Food Programme could not look more mundane nor the clientele appear less exotic ... The few dozen customers seem so earnest and engaging that they too could be mistaken for a suburban congregation rather than the disaster and war hardened aid workers and diplomats they really are ... To find a place like the RAC in the midst of this is like seeing a tiny postcard of Brighton beach stuck on Picasso's Guernica ... By 1997, North Korea had become the biggest humanitarian operation on the planet ... The RAC emerged in response to the growing need among this group for a communal gathering point and a place to let off steam about the frustrations of working in such a difficult political and humanitarian environment ... There are no other foreigners, their local guides leave them at the weekends, and they are not allowed to socialise privately with Koreans ... at the RAC, it is time to drink up. The government may soon be calling last orders.

Epilogue

When tigers die, they leave behind leather.
When people die, they leave their names.
Korean Proverb

The decision by the North Korean Government to cease humanitarian assistance in the country was never reversed. The Government provided NGOs with alternative options after a substantial period for all of us in limbo. Over time, the government contacted a few agencies and explicitly told them they were persona non-grata in the DPRK. We were not one of them, but we were very close. By the end of the culling period, there were only six non-governmental agencies, very much reduced in size and scale, operating in the DPRK. The UN organisations were severely reduced, and increased restrictions on travel were introduced.

Epilogue

For the agencies that remained, the few months after the announcement were fraught. The uncertainty was hell. We watched on as other agencies were summoned to the Ministry for Foreign Affairs, and told that they were not welcome. Friends and people we had got to know had to pack their bags and close down projects that they had put their souls into. For ourselves, our headquarters didn't want to wait for the axe to fall, and decided to pre-empt the decision and leave voluntarily. Our Liaison Officer asked me to convince head office to hang in there. I was told to travel to Songchon and Namchong to say our goodbyes to the people we were working with. We had to tell them that this was the end of our office supporting water and agriculture programmes in their counties. The water system in Songchon would not be finished. The water systems in Namchong would not even be started.

My new bosses arrived and left again, not wishing to hang around. They had families to feed, and needed job security. It was back to just me in the office, keeping things ticking over. I was called, along with our Liaison Officer, to dinner with the Minister for Foreign Affairs. It was a diplomatic game. He officially thanked the organisation for supporting his country and people in their hour of need, but emphasised that we were no longer needed. I had to play along. I thanked him for his gratitude, and for giving us the opportunity to work in his country. I said that we were happy that the State felt it was in a position to fulfil its duties to its people, and hoped that that would indeed be the case. I could not say that I was happy with the decision. I let him know that we were still keen to link our emergency work with longer-term development. I let him know the plans we had in place.

While these meetings were taking place, the various agencies that had been advised not to act rashly were having meetings with each other and with ECHO. ECHO was in direct communication with the Ministry. The Minister said that there was to be no further dialogue between his office and individual

Epilogue

agencies. ECHO would pass on any communications regarding European aid and development assistance. The MoFA made it very clear to ECHO that there would be no compromising. They were instructed that relief agencies had to be seen to leave, and emergency aid had to be seen to cease. It was for ECHO, as the representative of the European Commission in the country, to figure out a way for European assistance to continue in a manner that would be agreeable to the Korean Government. At this stage, the few agencies that were left, mostly reduced to a single person, started to think about a plan.

Dialogue went back and forth on what could be done. It was clear ECHO could remain, but the individual agencies could not. The Government was not interested in the modalities of EC aid, or how agencies worked. NGOs had to disappear, and assistance had to be seen to be coming from the EC. It was clear what we, as a group of agencies, had to do. The question was whether we were willing to do it. There were question marks already about the efficacy of development assistance – and emergency assistance – to the DPRK. Some would advocate strongly for it; others view it from a geo-political perspective; and others feel that it helps to support and maintain an illegitimate regime. Relative to how agencies try to operate in other emergency and development contexts, in terms of transparency and accountability, participation and inclusiveness, impartiality and humanity, there was a view that much had already been compromised in working within the parameters set by the Korean government. Would it be a step too far to yield more?

Five of the six agencies relocated to one building in the Diplomatic Compound. Each became a generic part of a greater whole. Agreeing to become faceless agencies, to give up our individuality and our identity, we effectively submitted to the mindset of the system. No individual is more valuable than the functioning of the system itself. These decisions were not taken lightly, and they were essentially the decisions of individuals, rather than organisations. The individuals were those who had

Epilogue

been in the country for more than a short while, who had fallen under the thrall of the Korean people, adapted to the system and wanted to believe that what they were doing was making a difference, just some sort of difference. These individuals had made friends in Korea, had a life, however obscure, in the country, and did not want to leave.

I think there was a fear, also, that if we were to succumb to the demands of the State, we would be responsible for turning our backs and closing the door on the Korean people. The lights would be switched off again. For me, it meant that I would get to stay a little bit longer, and some of the work I had burnt the midnight oil for would come to fruition. I would get to spend a little bit more time walking the streets of Pyongyang, and learn a little more about life on the inside of the Hermit Kingdom.

Postscript: The View From 2013

I was able to stay a few more months in North Korea, once the Government had confirmed the parameters within which NGOs could continue to work in the country. It took time to physically move to the new office, and then we had to find some new funding to keep the water/sanitation and agriculture projects ticking over. I also had to wait until reinforcements arrived. They duly did, and I left for home.

The journey home began with a quick hop to Beijing, and then onwards to Seoul. I spent a few days sightseeing, and had dinner in a very nice restaurant with the Irish Ambassador, his wife and the first secretary. Seoul was an eye-opener. The contrasts between the capitals of the South and the North are stunning. South Korea is one of the leading technological lights of the modern world – especially in terms of mobile technology, computers and so on – and the North is very much at the other

Postscript

end of the spectrum. I struggled to adapt. It felt like a case of country mouse in the big city.

I enjoyed observing, albeit for a very short time, the idiosyncrasies that translate across the DMZ. The contrasts are stark – wealth, mobility, infrastructure, economic development – but similarities are evident also. Despite sixty years of separation, there are shared mannerisms that have not yet died away. The language is the same, though South Koreans speak less formally and, of course, are less wary of foreigners. It was strange to be able to engage with Koreans casually and without restrictions. I didn't know how to react initially. I found it particularly strange to be in a bar and see Korean women smoking. This is not done in the North at all, except for old women in the countryside with rolled tobacco wrapped in old newspaper.

After a few days catching up with friends in Busan, in the south of the South, I took the TranSiberian railway, from Beijing via Mongolia to Moscow, with a few stops on the way – Ulaanbaatar, Lake Baikal and Yekaterinburg. A couple of days in Moscow were followed by a few more in Munich, watching World Cup matches in a bar in a youth hostel. I woke up one morning, after drinking and smoking too much for too many consecutive days, and realised it was time to go home. I booked a flight for that very evening.

No sooner was I home in Ireland than I was asked to return to Korea, to start work on the water programmes we had submitted funding requests for just before I had left. It didn't take much persuasion for me to agree to go back for three more months – which turned into five. This time was spent redesigning two very large water systems, tendering for the materials, assessing the contracts and other very tedious administrative exercises. I was happy though that all the surveying, negotiating and data inputting, as well as the printing and sellotaping, was not in vain. When I left, a replacement engineer was installed in the office and the digging for those two systems was underway. There were

Postscript

warehouses full of valves, tees and couplings, and rolls and rolls of black plastic pipe.

I was back again, just for one week, a year and a half later, after twelve months spent in Sudan and four months travelling overland to Beijing. My final week in North Korea was filled with mixed emotions. I was happy to be back, and very grateful to get a one-week visa. It was great to see almost everyone still working away in the office, and it was comforting in a way that very little seemed to have changed. The old lady who was caretaker and cook for the office had left. She was told she had to retire. The water systems were essentially complete, with towns of about 60,000 and 30,000 people respectively serviced with running water from safe and protected sources. Apparently my designs were followed in the main – but not exactly. I never got to see the finished projects with my own eyes, as permits could not be arranged. I would have liked to meet the local officials involved, that I had developed a form of friendship with.

I was able to go back to the *Friendship* Health Service Centre, for a few beers and a dose of nostalgia. Most of the same people were there. There were a few that I missed – there seemed to have been a few marriages while I was away. I tried to arrange to cross paths with one waitress who had married, but this did not happen. It was not surprising, but disappointing. I had one more night in the RAC, but there were very few expats left that I knew. I felt like an outsider again. I left a week later, feeling sure that I would not be back. So far I have not.

My years since then have been spent working in a few different countries. After a challenging year in Darfur, looking for water in the desert, my next port of call was Liberia for a few months, building roads and bridges. A brief interlude back at university, and then a job in Ireland followed, broken up with time spent chasing emergencies. Food crises in Niger and Ethiopia took up a few months, as well as a cholera outbreak in Cameroon, and a

Postscript

huge typhoon in the Philippines. My life has become a little more organised in the last few years, living in Ireland and following the happenings of the DPRK from afar. Things are changing there, yet remaining the same.

Kim Jong Il died on 17 December 2011, focusing international attention on the country once again. International media considered the impact of the death of Kim on the geopolitical scene, on Asian economies and markets, and on the stability of the Korean peninsula. For the majority of the people of North Korea, the impact was more personal. External perspectives on Kim Jong Il are not very flattering. Inside North Korea, the view is often very different. When Kim Il Sung died in 1994, there was a public outpouring of grief on the streets of every town and village. This was replicated in 2011, but to a lesser extent. Cynics portrayed this as staged mourning; other analysts considered that each person felt socially obliged to enter into a state of public grief, in order to assure their neighbours of their loyalty to the system. The death of Kim Il Sung was a national tragedy. I don't feel that the death of Kim Jong Il had the same significance.

When Kim Il Sung died, the country was already long in decline. The Berlin Wall had fallen a few years previously; the Soviet Union and the eastern trading block had collapsed, with the Chinese communist party embracing market economics. Economically, Korea was isolated and in trouble. The years following the death of the Great Leader, the first years of Kim Jong Il's rule, saw the country enter a state of famine. It is estimated that ten percent of the population had died by 1997. This tragedy, in the minds of Koreans, was directly linked to the loss of the Great Leader. It meant that Kim Jong Il was never going to be held in the same esteem as his father.

However, on his death, the country announced twelve days of mourning. I found it ironic that those twelve days overlapped with the twelve days of Christmas, one final hurrah for the leader who had used Christian imagery regularly to reinforce his cult

Postscript

image. A new star is said to have appeared to identify the place where he was born, a small cottage on Mount Paektu on the Chinese border.

Without the luxury of real military exploits to fashion his image around – defeating Japanese aggressors, or fighting off the capitalist imperialists and their stooge South Korean allies – Kim Jong Il had to build a reputation based on fanciful stories of military genius, extreme intelligence and world-class golfing exploits. The State-sponsored media regularly followed his wise pronouncements at chicken farms, coal mines and bi-nylon manufacturing plants. He is supposed to have died on one of these inspection trips, from extreme exhaustion and over-work.

The average country peasant working on a State farm has been born, brought up and reached old age under the leadership of Kim Il Sung and Kim Jong Il. He will have lived in fear of imperial aggression, been educated on the wise words of the Great and Dear Leaders, and learned the Korean doctrine of *Juche*, 'socialism in our own style'. Every school lesson is flavoured with the exploits of the Leaders. He has learned Maths by subtracting the numbers of enemy soldiers killed by Kim Il Sung or Kim Jong Il. Contact with people outside his township or work farm is very limited, the only interaction with foreigners being brief glimpses of the very few aid-workers who traverse the country, so he knows of little except what he hears and sees on official State media. With mobile communication and Internet access limited to Pyongyang and strictly State-controlled, the death of Kim Jong Il probably feels like the death of a big brother, not the death of Big Brother.

Whether his successor will be able to fill that void is hard to tell. Kim Jong Il has been succeeded by Kim Jong Un, the third and youngest son of Kim Jong Il and his consort Ko Young Hee. For a country that is so difficult to penetrate, it was surprising that predictions in this regard were proven correct. He had been earmarked by external DPRK watchers as the likely candidate for

Postscript

a number of years – this being considered confirmed when he was pictured two seats away from his father in a 2010 official photoshoot.

Kim Jong Un comes with an impressive list of credentials. He has been First Secretary of the Workers' Party of Korea, Chairman of the Central Military Commission, Chairman of the National Defence Commission of North Korea, Supreme Commander of the Korean People's Army, and also a presidium member of the Politburo of the Workers' Party of Korea. After his father's funeral, he was anointed with another grandiose title, the 'Great Successor'. On 30 December 2011, he was formally appointed as the Supreme Commander of the Korean People's Army. It is, as it was with Kim Jong Il, difficult to know how meaningful these titles are. There is no way of knowing whether the Great Successor has any power, or is merely a puppet. Speculation abounds.

Inside Korea, prior to the death of Kim Jong Il, his third son had made very, very few public appearances. The average Korean knows almost nothing about him. There was no attempt to build a cult of personality around Kim Jong Un in the manner that Kim Jong Il achieved prior to succession, and only in recent years were there any news reports on him. I wonder what the peasant in the countryside thinks about the Great Successor. Does he/she accept the succession, and the greatness of this young man? Or does this raise questions, even little ones, about the regime they live under? Perhaps most individuals know they are being fed a cock-and-bull story, but can say or do nothing about it.

The little that is known about Kim Jong Un does not create the picture of a great leader. Born in 1983, he is thought to have spent some years in Switzerland, being educated under the guise of an employee of the Embassy in Berne. Kenji Fujimoto, a Japanese chef who was Kim Jong Il's cook, says Kim Jong Un is 'a chip off the old block, a spitting image of his father in terms of

Postscript

face, body shape, and personality'. His classmates say he was shy, awkward with girls, disinterested in politics but fascinated with basketball. His most notable and newsworthy story in his first few months was the visit of former basketball superstar Dennis Rodman to the DPRK. They hugged.

I follow news on the DPRK closely, but not with as much fascination as I did while I was there. Whatever news is reported is bound to be limited. It is generally either bombast from the Korean propaganda machine, often just to unsettle the neighbours, or speculation from outside. I hear that mobile technology is becoming more accessible. Foreigners can use mobile phones; more and more are appearing in Pyongyang and other major cities. Whether this will be an avenue for further control, or a chink in the armour of the regime, I am not sure.

North Korea qualified for the 2010 World Cup, for the first time since 1966. They were in the group of death, with Brazil, Portugal and the Ivory Coast. The Koreans were not given a chance by anybody. I thought that they would surprise people. In the first game they played well to lose by only one goal to one of the favourites, Brazil. In the next game, they were annihilated, losing by seven to Portugal before leaving the tournament with a whimper, losing three-nil to the Ivory Coast. The hammering by Portugal was unfortunate, but they did not embarrass themselves. Unfortunately, by cutting themselves off from the rest of the world, they are not able to compete at the highest level.

The Six-Party Talks ended in 2009. They did not achieve any meaningful agreement. The cessation stemmed from North Korea increasing its posturing, but also engaging in serious acts of provocation. The country launched a missile in April 2009, which many felt was a test of an intercontinental ballistic missile. The test failed, but both Japan and South Korea were shaken. The UN Security Council issued a resolution, and the North Koreans stamped their feet and kicked out the nuclear

Postscript

inspectors. They carried out an underground nuclear test in May 2009.

In November 2009, the North and South briefly engaged in combat, involving ships firing at each other, in the Battle of Daecheoung. In 2010, a South Korean military vessel with 104 people on board was sunk by a North Korean torpedo, and in 2011, North Korea shelled South Korea's Yeonpyeong Island, killing two soldiers but also burning sixty houses. Another failed missile test in 2012 has stalled any hope of further negotiation. In the last few years, the North seems to have ratcheted up the brinksmanship and posturing. One view is that the regime needs to create situations in which Kim Jong Un can be seen to stand up to perceived aggressors, in order to build his reputation. This also reminds the population that the country is continuously under threat. Vigilance is needed, and now is not the time to be questioning the succession of the Great Successor.

The fact that Kim Jong Un lived and was educated abroad had created some optimism that he could be the person to lead change in the North. Having engaged with modernity and experienced life in an open society, it was hoped that he could be encouraged to move Korea in that direction. At the same time, as leader of the DPRK, he will have to live in an ivory tower, a prisoner of the system that his ancestors have built. He has lived a life of privilege and, despite the poverty of the country, is able to have whatever he desires on demand. Would he want to give this up? Is he merely a spoiled child, a 'little emperor' who will throw his toys out of the pram if he is crossed? Does he have any choices at all?

In late 2013, Kim Jong Un had his uncle and close advisor, Jang Song Thaek, purged and then executed. According to some reports, he was eaten alive by more than one hundred half-starved dogs. The execution of his uncle, a perceived reformer, seems to indicate that Kim Jong Un will not be the person to liberalise the DPRK. Will the Hermit Kingdom remain as it is,

Postscript

locked up under the iron fist of a military dictatorship, a throwback to a long-gone communist era, for the next fifty years? Or is this brutal execution evidence of cracks appearing in the leadership of the country? I, for one, will be watching closely.

Other Books from Bennion Kearny

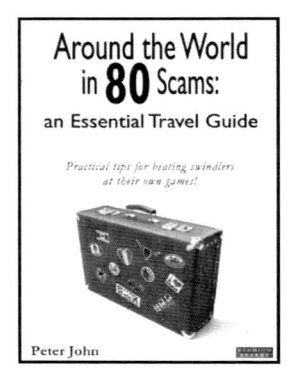

Around the World in 80 Scams: an Essential Travel Guide by Peter John

Every year, thousands of people fall victim to various travel scams, crimes and confidence tricks while they travel. Most people escape having simply lost a little money, but many lose much more, and some encounter real personal danger

This essential book is a practical, focused, and detailed guide to eighty of the most common scams and crimes travelers might encounter. It is packed with real-world examples drawn from resources across the globe and the author's own travels. Being aware of scammers' tricks is the best way of avoiding them altogether.

Small Time: A Life in the Football Wilderness by Justin Bryant

In 1988, 23-year-old American goalkeeper Justin Bryant thought a glorious career in professional football awaited him. He had just saved two penalties for his American club - the Orlando Lions - against Scotland's Dunfermline Athletic, to help claim the first piece of silverware in their history. He was young, strong, healthy, and confident.

Small Time is the story of a life spent mostly in the backwaters of the game. As Justin negotiated the Non-League pitches of the Vauxhall-Opel League, and the many failed professional leagues of the U.S. in the 1980s and 90s - Football, he learned, is 95% blood, sweat, and tears; but if you love it enough, the other 5% makes up for it.

Churchill versus Hitler: War of Words by Peter John

"A senile clown", "Bloodthirsty Guttersnipe", "Undisciplined Swine", "Gangster", "Drunkard".

Adolf Hitler and Winston Churchill clashed for years in public as their opinions of each other and feuding helped determine the course of the Second World War. As diplomatic and military episodes unfolded - both men analysed, commentated upon, and taunted each other with Churchill continuing to do so for many years after Hitler's death. Yet, until now, there has been no dedicated, detailed history of the men's rivalry.

Based on three years of research in archives across Britain, Germany and the United States, Churchill versus Hitler: War of Words shows how the opinions of the two leaders were more complicated and changeable than is often assumed.

Graduation: Life Lessons of a Professional Footballer by Richard Lee

The 2010/11 season will go down as a memorable one for Goalkeeper Richard Lee. Cup wins, penalty saves, hypnotherapy and injury would follow, but these things only tell a small part of the tale. Filled with anecdotes, insights, humour and honesty - Graduation uncovers Richard's campaign to take back the number one spot, save a lot of penalties, and overcome new challenges. What we see is a transformation - beautifully encapsulated in this extraordinary season.

Printed by BoD in Norderstedt, Germany